Winner of the 2012 *Award for Excellence* presented by the Greater Hudson Heritage Network

Praise for *Episodes from a Hudson River Town*

"...[the book] succeeds in portraying the nature and character of townspeople in New York State ... Bush's attention for the lives of common people can be explained by his academic background in public administration and urban studies, which shines through in this abundantly researched and well-written book about the people of New Baltimore throughout the centuries. Bush never loses himself in heavy scholarly details."

— *Hudson River Valley Review*

"...this is a book worth looking at ... Bush does a great job in tying local and national events together. He does a noteworthy job explaining the dynamics of settler and Indian interactions when the Town was the frontier, experiences of local soldiers in the Civil War, World War I and World War II, local agriculture, the businesses that developed from the Village of New Baltimore's location on the west bank of the Hudson River, and the arrival of the railroads and New York State Thruway."

— *Kaatskill Life*

"Thornton Wilder would smile on this detailed portrait of a small Greene County town."

— *Chronogram*

"During his fifteen years as town historian Bush kept meticulous notes ... [his] book provides a comprehensive perspective, beginning with a brief overview of prehistoric times, archaeological sites and the influence of the Mohican people."

— *Daily Mail*

Episodes from a
Hudson River Town

Episodes from a

Hudson River Town

New Baltimore, New York

Clesson S. Bush

excelsior editions
State University of New York Press
Albany, New York

Cover photo from the town of New Baltimore, New York, photograph collection. The cover map is an excerpt from Beers, Frederick W. *Atlas of Greene County, New York* (New York: Beers, Ellis, and Soule, 1867).

Published by State University of New York Press, Albany

Excelsior Editions is an imprint of State University of New York Press

For information, contact State University of New York Press, Albany, NY
www.sunypress.edu

Production by Ryan Morris
Marketing by Fran Keneston

Library of Congress Cataloging-in-Publication Data

Bush, Clesson S.
Episodes from a Hudson River town : New Baltimore, New York / Clesson S. Bush.
p. cm.
ISBN 978-1-4384-4033-0 (hardcover : alk. paper)
1. New Baltimore (N.Y.)—History. I. Title.

F129.N48B87 2011
974.7'37—dc22 2011014225

10 9 8 7 6 5 4 3 2 1

Contents

Introduction

New Baltimore is a small Hudson River town, not famous for anything in particular. No world-renowned people have lived here. No spectacular events occurred here. No magnificent skyscrapers have been built here. Nonetheless, townspeople have lived their lives, worked hard, endured tragedies, and celebrated triumphs. It is precisely the kind of place that needs to have its history documented, described, and preserved for the sake of remembering the common man and woman, their daily activities, and the impact that economic, military, and social circumstances have had on them. New Baltimore is typical of other river communities, but holds its own unique niche in history.

In constructing this narrative, I have attempted to place the episodes of town history within the context of significant national or state events: the innovations of steam-driven vessels and ice-harvesting on the river, the coming of the railroad, the building of roads from the earliest turnpikes to the New York State Thruway, the establishment and loss of the key community function of schooling, the terrors of war, and the demands of women's suffrage and prohibition.

If we look closely at the history of any small town on the Hudson, a picture of how it lived and, in certain senses, died is presented in clarity. The thread of routine life interweaves with the stories of a bigger picture. While the outside world was intruding, people were farming, rearing children, and socializing. They were making shoes and dresses; buying and selling meat, groceries, cigars, candy, and hardware; running boarding houses, hotels, and taverns; mining stone, gravel, and sand; shoeing horses; milling grains; constructing houses, barns, and stone walls marking out fields that filled with crops; building, loading, and piloting sloops, steamboats, and barges to carry people and products; and going to church, barn dances, and grange meetings. It could be a hard but spirited existence. A continuing theme is the community's dependence on agriculture. At its heart, New Baltimore was a farming town, at least until the costs outstripped the benefits and left a bare minimum of workers laboring in the fields.

We will look in a degree of depth at the time before the statutory town of New Baltimore came into being in 1811, starting with early geologic events that formed the land and the evidence of prehistoric life found within the town's borders to the days of the Mohican Indians' presence through the mixed blessing for the native populations of the coming of Europeans. The French and Indian Wars, the beginnings of the era of road building, the Revolution, the War of 1812, and the start of the influx of people of diverse backgrounds and religions will be covered generally in the topical chapters that follow.

The town founders completed a number of rudimentary tasks in setting up the government of their new municipality. Two measures had long-lasting effect on the residents and will be analyzed in detail in two chapters. When the newly elected officials came together for the first time at the beginning of April in 1811, one of their first actions was to create twenty-nine road districts and assign overseers to ensure their maintenance. Two years later, in the town's annual meeting, the men outlined a series of nine school districts. This was shortly after the State had passed a law promoting a system of common schools.

The coming of the railroad and the plotting of a more regional road network helped change the fundamental character of the town, opening up new, more convenient transportation outlets that could be used all year. These aspects of modern progress drew people away from the river industries that supported them for nearly two centuries. The accessibility provided by the New York State Thruway that slashed its way through New Baltimore may hold the keys to a commercial renaissance that is viewed with skepticism in some minds.

The town in the mid-1860s had seventeen school districts that were centers of community activities. Today, the only school in town is run by a local church. Otherwise the children ride the yellow buses to different towns for their education.

Regrettably, an all-too-significant part of New Baltimore's history is war, starting with the early settlers who were caught among dueling Europeans, Mohicans, and Mohawks. We will follow our valiant warriors from the colonial strife on their doorsteps to the Civil War horrors of Gettysburg, Petersburg, and southern prison camps to the European battlefields of two World Wars.

Home front events in and around the conflicts will be covered, looking at people's support behind the war efforts and the effects of contemporary social and political factors like women's suffrage, prohibition, and the 1929 and 1936 fires that virtually destroyed what was the remaining nerve center of nonagricultural commerce in town.

Throughout the narrative, we will introduce an array of characters who made town history, starting with the original landowners, the tavern-keepers Pieter and Hilletje Bronck; the miller Barent Coeymans; the land-speculating Marten Gerritsen Van Bergen; and the earliest settlers whose names resonate throughout town history, the Van Slykes, Vanderzees, and Houghtalings.

Paul Sherman traded goods as far away as the West Indies, sometimes even building vessels and selling them in distant locations. Charles Titus was a Quaker who parlayed a series of occupations into becoming the richest man in town in the 1830s. Samuel Van Slyke was an African American volunteer for the Union Army who spent his last days tending a garden near the banks of the Hannacroix Creek. Martinus Mulder made his living toiling in a handful of the mammoth ice houses that dotted the Hudson shoreline but also registered patents that greatly improved the storage and handling of ice harvests. William Baldwin supervised the building of about a hundred steamboats and barges and was renowned for his knowledge of vessel construction. Clifford Armstrong was a World War II hero who came back home to farm.

Outsiders also played important but less recognized roles. Daniel Drew and Cornelius Vanderbilt were the railroad barons who commanded the laying of track through land that had been in some families' hands for decades, dividing into separated parcels valued crop and grazing areas. The roaring steam engines could carry people and goods to far reaches of the country but the wary farmer now had to ensure that the stray cow did not wander into the speeding path of a stream of loaded freight cars. Colonel Frederick Stuart Greene pushed New York State toward modernizing its highway system between the World Wars, resulting in roads that could carry people further and faster. Governor Thomas E. Dewey spearheaded the building of the Thruway that now carries his name. These roads helped make New Baltimore a present-day commuter suburb of the state capital, Albany.

While the text may be of an episodic nature, there also is a chronologic coherence that provides a flavor of the whole history of New Baltimore. Looking at the larger picture, this also could be the story of any Hudson River town and how outside economic and social pressures and local hard work, biases, and personal interests can build a lasting community.

Despite New Baltimore's relatively small size, a wealth of resources is available to tell its story. J. B. Beers's *History of Greene County* and the New Baltimore Bicentennial Committee's 1976 *The Heritage of New Baltimore* are two fundamental resources. The original board minutes still are kept under lock and key at the Town Hall. Estate and land records are available through the Greene County offices in Catskill, New York. Trips to the New York State Library and State Archives at Albany brought access to vital federal and state census, land patent, and colonial documents. Military records at the National Archives and Records Administration are an invaluable source for recounting the war exploits of our heroic soldiers. Serving as official town historian for a decade and a half provided me with the gift of conversation with numerous longtime and knowledgeable town residents.

Finally, and perhaps most importantly, given the experiences of visiting numerous libraries and historical societies for genealogical and local history research, the Vedder Research Library of the Greene County Historical Society has to be among the best of its type for the bulk and range of its holdings from family papers through period newspapers. Tapping all these documentary treasures helps to bring alive the drama and the routine of a small town on the Hudson River.

1

Prehistoric Times

Our Landscape and First People

The countryside along the Hudson River and throughout Greene County always has been a lure for settlers and speculators. Newcomers and longtime residents find the waterway, its tributaries, the Catskills, and our hills and valleys a primary reason for living and enjoying life here. New Baltimore and its surroundings were formed and massaged by the dynamic forces of nature, the result of ongoing geologic events over millions of years.[1]

The most prominent geographic features in the region came into being during what geologists called the Paleozoic era, nearly 550 million years ago. It was a time when continents collided and parted, causing upheavals that pushed vast land masses into hills and mountains and complementing lowlands. The Kalkberg, the spiny ridge running through New Baltimore, is named for one of the rock layers formed in ancient times. Immense seas covered much of New York and served as collecting pools for sediments that consolidated into today's rock formations. The only animals around were simple forms of jellyfish, sponges, and arthropods with their characteristic jointed legs and exoskeletons, like grasshoppers and beetles.

The next integral formation event happened 1.6 million years ago during the Pleistocene epoch when the Laurentide ice mass developed in Canada. This continental glacier grew unyieldingly, expanding southward and retreating several times, radically altering the landscape time and again as it traveled. Greene County was buried. Only the highest peak of the Catskills, Ulster County's 4,200-foot Slide Mountain, may have poked up out of the frozen terrain. So much water was consumed by the glaciations that seas were a few hundred feet lower than today.

The latest significant geologic activity that defined today's landscape was during the Wisconsinan age with the last advance and retreat of the Laurentide ice formation. This icy accumulation covered all but a tiny sliver of New York about 22,000 years BP (i.e., before present, a common archaeological designation for time) and was gone from the state 10,000 years BP.

As the sheet melted, debris dammed outlets and led to the flooding of great glacial pools, including Lake Albany. This massive body of water existed between 15,000 and 10,000 BP, covering the Hudson River Valley area from near Lake George all the way down to around Staten Island.

As Lake Albany dried, it left hills and valleys and great deposits of silt, sand, and clay, which proved valuable for future residents in making pottery, ceramics, and bricks. This is the landscape much as we see it today after thousands of years of weathering and erosion. The remains of the sandy bottom of the lake still are very apparent in Albany's Pine Bush preserve. Some beach-like areas along the Hudson, particularly on the east side, also are remnants of Lake Albany.

One major by-product of the land shifting and upheavals and extensive glaciations was the creation of great stores of valuable chert and flint deposits that provided the earliest human arrivals with an important resource. Chert is a fine-grained, sedimentary rock related to quartz, with flint being a subcategory. The material is very hard yet susceptible to glass-like fracturing, making it well suited for crafting stone tools that were critical for survival in prehistoric times. The rock's hardness makes it very resistant to weathering and deterioration, which is why almost everyone seems to have either found or seen an old arrowhead.

Our First Human Residents

The cycle of long periods of icing and warming made the area rather uninviting, particularly when coupled with the large and hungry feral animals that roamed the wilderness. As early people gained basic tools, skins for warmth, and weapons for protection and food gathering, they were equipped to overcome such obstacles and move from their native Europe and Asia to exploit the abundant natural resources of the lands of North America.

Solid information about prehistoric times is sketchy and based broadly on examination of geologic features and fossil remains, the types of stone tools used by people at different times, and the use of more exotic scientific methods such as radiocarbon and radiometric dating. The evidence points to about 11,000 BP as the date for the first human habitation of the Greene County and New Baltimore areas, right as the ice and water finally left.

How people got here is subject to much ongoing guesswork. The initial feelings were that adventuresome travelers came across Beringia. This long-submerged strip of land linking Asia with Alaska had been created by the lowered sea levels caused by the ice ages. Some researchers now believe that people could have come in makeshift, seagoing water craft, landing at a range of possible locations along the west coast.

The newcomers then took hundreds of years to trek across North America, perhaps in search of viable food sources. The arrival of people to our area was rather late in the game. Discoveries in Africa date man's ancestors there to be six million or more years old. Our people do not even match up well with the earliest relics of human life in the rest of North America, which date anywhere from 12,500 to 20,000 BP.

As New York was recovering from the last ice age, the land became tundra-like with clumps of foliage and various grasses and ground cover. Pine, hardwood forests, and other woods and brush were becoming reestablished after the long period of icy cover. With the fresh vegetation came new sources of nuts, berries, and other nourishment that attracted foraging caribou, elk, deer, mastodonts, bears, giant beavers, wolves, and turkeys. Richer aquatic life also was appearing so fishing was increasingly possible. All these factors combined to provide incentive for human residence.

Who Were These Earliest People?

The Paleo-Indians were the first arrivals to America. These people are thought to have been hunters about 8,000 to 13,000 years BP who wandered the countryside in small groups to discover whatever adequate food supplies existed. [2]

As the people adopted more complex ways of life, researchers assigned other names to the groups to differentiate them. The last ancient settlers, the Woodland people, appeared about 3,000 BP in eastern North America and lasted nearly to the time of first European contact. They differed from older classification groups primarily through their more sophisticated development of pottery and agriculture (particularly growing of the three staple crops of corn, beans, and squash) and the use of funerary mounds, earthen works to entomb their dead. The Woodland people are the direct ancestors of the more familiar Mohicans who dominated much of the Hudson Valley for many years.

Archaeologists have found the mid- and upper-Hudson region, including Greene County, to hold many treasures documenting prehistoric man, starting with the Paleo-Indian culture and extending through to the arrival of the first Europeans. The most familiar and renowned sites may be Flint Mine Hill in the town of Coxsackie and West Athens Hill in the town of Athens. New Baltimore was part of Coxsackie until the State legalized it as a separate municipality in 1811. Another major finding was made at the Goldkrest site just north of New Baltimore across the Hudson River at Rensselaer County's East Greenbush.

Flint Mine Hill

For many years, amateur relic hunters had been digging on the ridge just south of the village of Coxsackie looking for arrowheads and other stony artifacts. In 1921, state archaeologist Arthur C. Parker started to investigate the plot of land that he had been eyeing for quite a while. Called Flint Mine Hill, this site was viewed as an Indian quarrying location for a considerable period, but no organized scientific investigation had been done.

What Parker discovered was "the most remarkable archeological monument in the state of New York. It was literally a mountain of arrowheads!"[3] Employing much hyperbole and poetic waxing, Parker wrote the first widespread documentation of the importance of the site. Flint Mine Hill still ranks as one of the largest chert quarries ever uncovered in the East.

In the mid-1990s, a team from the State University of New York at Albany found remains of tools used in the production process and tools that were end products themselves. The objects dated from about 3,400 to 5,000 BP back to the Paleo-Indians, suggesting that the site had been used as a quarrying workshop for thousands of years.[4]

West Athens Hill

In 1962, a local resident, R. Arthur Johnson, was poking around on a hill in Athens after hearing that a telecommunications tower was to be constructed on the site. Johnson began to notice significant deposits of flint and other evidence subsequently dated back to the Paleo-Indian culture. Professional archaeologists were called in, and research of the area has continued since that time.

Perched four hundred feet above its surroundings, West Athens Hill turned out to be the largest Paleo-Indian stone tool quarrying and manufacturing workshop and possible residential site found to date in New York State. The location is one of the most well-documented Paleo-Indian sites in the East. A key researcher throughout this period was longtime state archaeologist Robert E. Funk, whose work is summarized in *An Ice Age Quarry-Workshop: The West Athens Hill Site Revisited*, published by the New York State Education Department in 2004.

Goldkrest Site

Just a few miles north of New Baltimore on the opposite side of the Hudson, the Consolidated Natural Gas Transmission Corporation was planning in the early 1990s to set a natural gas pipeline across Kuyper Island in the town of East Greenbush. This formerly freestanding piece of land now is joined to Papscanee Island, which, in turn, has been linked to the mainland, mostly through deposits of dredging spoils.

As part of the required archaeological survey for such projects, investigators found numerous remnants of human life, including bone, wood, and stone artifacts, pottery pieces, and evidence of wood-fire hearths. The treasures dated from the middle of the Woodland period into the nineteenth and twentieth centuries.

Goldkrest is archaeologically and historically significant for two reasons. It was an undisturbed habitation site from the latter part of the Woodland and early European periods. This discovery was the first of its kind in this region and right near the center of the Mohican territory, solidifying the location's connection to that group of people. The area around Papscanee Island was the home base for the Mohicans for many decades. Perhaps most importantly, Goldkrest also contained distinct evidence of pole-frame living quarters, including a "long house," again a first for the upper Hudson Valley.[5]

New Baltimore

Important archeological discoveries in Athens and Coxsackie and nearby places like Bethlehem, Catskill, and Leeds have demonstrated the wide range of time for a human presence in Greene, Albany, and Rensselaer counties. What about New Baltimore itself? No sites quite as dramatic as

Flint Mine, Athens Hill, or Goldkrest have been found yet, but exciting discoveries continue to be made. While people may have been living in village-like communities during the latter part of prehistoric times, no compelling evidence has been found to link any of them to New Baltimore. More likely, the local findings relate to hunting camps and other temporary visitors.

In his influential 1920 work, *The Archeological History of New York*, Arthur C. Parker reported evidence of "Camp sites at New Baltimore village."[6] Regrettably, Parker often relied on anecdotal, ill-defined information as the basis for listing certain sites. In New Baltimore's case, there does not appear to be any additional details on the location of the "camp sites" beyond crediting prominent geologist George H. Chadwick and local residents Egbert Beardsley and Orin Q. Flint as sources of information on Greene County discoveries.[7]

Early populations were largely nomadic or semi-nomadic so the findings may be linked to those periods. The later Mohican inhabitants commonly had movable living shelters and other temporary quarters like lean-tos at locations used for hunting and fishing. Since they were prominent near the northern New Baltimore border, it is not hard to suggest that there was a relationship to the Parker "camp sites."

In 1977, Mary Ivey, Gary Berg, and Susan Halpern reported on an archaeological evaluation of the path a proposed sewer project was to take in the New Baltimore hamlet on the Hudson.[8] They had dug shovel test pits every fifty feet along the project's right of way except where bedrock was present. The only substantive artifacts found were in neighboring Coeymans, where the sewer system would have emptied into that town's waste treatment facility. As a result, they theorized that the Parker "camp sites" really were in that adjoining municipality.

Almost in New Baltimore, just a stone's throw to the north, lies what was once Barren Island. At the mouth of the Hannacroix Creek, in the town of Coeymans, this small plot of land is now part of the mainland. It has a long, interesting history and has been rumored to be the burial place of Barent Pieter Coeymans, an important European landowner who will come up again later in this narrative.

In 1959, and later in the 1960s, archaeologists excavated a number of places on the island and made some exciting discoveries.[9] Included were several hearths containing numerous remnants of native life such as charcoal, bone and shell fragments, and flint chips. Many stone and pottery artifacts also were uncovered.

The bulk of the materials dated from the early and middle parts of the Woodland period, although evidence of earlier times also was found. There even were human remains that could not be identified, nor could the writers offer an idea of a burial date. The researchers proposed that Barren Island was a long-term spring and summer hunting and fishing encampment.

At a site in the southern part of New Baltimore on the Coxsackie Creek, two amateur archaeologists digging by hand in the summer of 1967 found stone projectile points, spear points, knives, scrapers, drills, and other items.[10] These artifacts generally were discovered in plowed fields, near the surface of the ground, and were attributed to Archaic people who lived between the Paleo-Indian and Woodland eras, about three to four thousand years ago.

The location was conjectured to have been a fishing or hunting camp or winter quarters for wandering natives. However, no evidence of fishing was found beyond one possible net sinker, despite the site being only about half a mile from the Hudson. The men also dug up the remnants of what were considered two small hearths, which lends credence to the theory that the place was a temporary camp of some sort.

Over an extended period between 1982 and 1984, the same two individuals who unearthed the Coxsackie Creek site artifacts were exploring near the Hudson River again in the southeastern corner of town.[11] They found more projectile points from the Archaic period. This research has never been formally published so details are lacking, and dates have not been confirmed. Interestingly, at least one of the people responsible for this work subsequently gave up such explorations because of the damage untrained searchers could do to important historic sites.

As we entered the twenty-first century, the Greene County Industrial Development Agency (IDA) was busy attempting to entice businesses to locate in a spot along New York State Route 9W straddling the New Baltimore and Coxsackie town lines. The southern portion was developed first into the Greene Business and Technology Park, becoming home first to a Save-A-Lot grocery warehouse. The northern section of the property was named the Kalkberg Commerce Park, commemorating the spiny ridge running its way through both towns. In 2004, the National Bedding Company, makers of Serta mattresses, became the initial company committed to locating in the park on the New Baltimore side.

As part of the State's requirements for evaluating the environmental impact of such projects, intensive archaeological surveys were done across the proposed development area. To examine the section extending into New Baltimore, the IDA commissioned Edward V. Curtin, a consulting archaeologist, who identified sixteen previous reports about the locations of prehistoric archaeological artifacts within a two-mile radius of the site.

After examining the ground's surface and digging a series of test pits, Curtin and his associates uncovered a number of places with concentrations of artifacts. The materials at the Kalkberg site included a scattering of projectile points, flakes, and similar items, again indicating evidence of short-term camps.

Curtin suggested a wide spread of time for dating the bulk of the discovered objects, from the latter part of the Paleo-Indian period to the middle of the Archaic period. He also described more isolated examples of the late Archaic and middle Woodland periods. Given the site's location along a historically prominent roadway, Curtin also found artifacts from the nineteenth and twentieth centuries—glass, ceramics, and nails that would be associated routinely with more modern human settlement and buildings.[12]

The Mohicans

As the seventeenth century dawned, New Baltimore was part of the area controlled by the Algonquian-speaking Mohican people.[13] One of their primary living places for many decades was at Schodack, right near the modern northeastern New Baltimore border. Their exact history is fragmentary and confusing given the lack of a written record from ancient times. Later, the Europeans compounded issues with their imprecision in differentiating among various native groups.

Recent studies based primarily on similarities in historical language patterns suggest that an ancient home for Algonquian speakers was near the eastern Great Lakes. From there, they migrated to many places, including the Hudson River Valley, perhaps as early as 1,500 BP.[14] Earlier tradition had the Mohican ancestors come from a more ill-defined "west," perhaps as far away as the Pacific northwest coast. A centuries-long migration occurred until the travelers found the curious and spiritual river that flowed both ways, the tidal Hudson. Of course, neither of these cases would be mutually exclusive.

As the Mohicans began to predominate along the Hudson, their homeland extended from around Saugerties and northern Dutchess County up to the Lake Champlain region. On the east, the territory went into the edges of Connecticut and Massachusetts, and in the west, to near Schenectady and the foothills of the Catskills in Greene County. Keep in mind, though, that boundaries in those days were vague and prone to varying interpretation and change.

Despite having their council fires or headquarters in specific locations, the Mohicans were a relatively mobile people, establishing temporary camp sites as sustenance needs varied. The more permanent settlements were moved for various reasons. Exhaustion of fertile lands and firewood supplies, intolerably unclean living quarters, or pressure from other Indians and European settlers all took a toll. It also seems probable given the low terrain of some of their island and shoreline lands along the Hudson that occasional flooding would have forced them at times to seek higher ground. Seasonal relocations also likely occurred with shifts in available hunting and fishing stocks.

The Mohicans subsisted on foraging, fishing, and hunting, and the growing of maize, squash, beans, and other crops. The tribal members tended to be gentle, spiritual people with close-knit families and communities and a healthy respect for their children and elders. This strength of character appears often in the narratives of their meetings with white colonial administrators, even when faced with the strongly negative circumstances of their later history.

Mohican women had a prominent and honored place in society. The sachems or chiefs were selected based on heredity from a mother's side of the family. At least one woman leader was recorded, Pewasck, at Catskill in the 1640s. Women also could be involved in property transactions. In 1649, Pewasck, along with her son Supahoot, sold land at Catskill to the Van Rensselaers, early settlers in the Albany area.[15]

Hendrick Aupaumut

Little was written on the history of the Mohicans before the coming of the white man. The Mohicans did not read or write. They did hold regular meetings to exchange historical anecdotes, hoping to transfer knowledge of their proud and long heritage to willing listeners and future generations. It took foreign intervention, though, to ensure that the oral tradition was carried to modern times.

The arrival of European settlers brought eager missionaries who sought to convert the native populations to Christianity. One necessary vehicle for this movement was to teach the Indians how to read and write so they could understand Christian teachings. In 1734, John Sergeant, a Yale-educated missionary from Newark, New Jersey, came to the Mohican settlement that is today's Stockbridge, Massachusetts, and created a school to accomplish that goal.

One student, Hendrick Aupaumut, had committed to memory a good measure of the tribal history and gained sufficient literacy under Sergeant's tutelage to put some of his knowledge on paper. The Aupaumut narrative provides a brief but fascinating glimpse into the Mohicans' simple life among the natural treasures along the waters they called Muh-he-kun-ne-tuk, "the river that flows both ways."

Aupaumut says that the Mohican territory, encompassing land in New York, Massachusetts, and Vermont, was "in many places mountainous, supplied with excellent rivers, creeks and ponds; the side of these rivers, &c. was only known by natives capable of producing skommonun or Indian corn, tupohquaun or beans, and uhnunnekuthkoatkun or Indian squashes, until it fell into the hands of white people, who convert even many swamps and rocky hills into fruitful fields."

Using rudimentary bone and stone tools, the managing of the fields fell largely to women, elderly men, and young boys, burning the trees and shrubs to clear for planting. Aupaumut provides a view of the riches of the area:

> This extensive country abounded with almost every kind of wild game, such as moose, deer, bears, tigers, wolves, beavers, otters, minks, muskrats, martins, foxes, wild cats, fishes, ground hogs, back hogs. Of the feathered kind, turkies, wild geese, ducks, partridges, pigeons, quails, owls, &c. and the rivers, &c. abounded with variety of fish and turtles.
>
> The inhabitants chiefly dwelt in little towns and villages. Their chief seat was on Hudson's river, now it is called Albany, which was called Pempotowwuthut, Muhhecanneuw, or the fire place of the Muhheakunnuk nation, where their allies used to come on any business whether relative of the covenants of their friendship, or other matters. . . . But the employment of men consisted in hunting and fishing. They used bow and arrow to kill game, with which they were expert. They used to catch deer by insnaring them with strings. By hunting they supplied themselves with cloathing and diet; they seldom felt much want, and they were very well contented with their condition; having food and raiment was their only

aim. . . . In fall, they hunt for deer, bear, beaver, otter, rack-oon, fishes, martin for their cloathing, and drying meat for the ensuing season; and in the beginning of March, they used to go out to hunt for moose on the green mountains, where these animals keep for winter quarters. From thence they go again for beaver hunting as soon as the rivers, ponds, and creeks are opened . . .

In this discussion, the prominence of securing beaver pelts for trade is inferred. Also, despite the reference to Albany, the center of their homeland would have been on the east side of the Hudson, moving south over decades to the Schodack islands at New Baltimore's doorstep. Aupaumut's brief discourse ends with a comment on the Mohicans' bravery and competence in war, prefaced by a poignant statement of how European afflictions and influences helped them lose their valor and their communities. Those "disorders or sicknesses" also would have included the insidious demon rum, which had a primary role in the Mohicans' decline.[16]

European Gains and Mohican Losses

During the 1500s, European visitors began trading weapons and various goods for furs in eastern Canada. Aggressive entrepreneurship led to a long period of conflict as the Europeans and Indians often violently jockeyed for economic supremacy, seeking new grounds for hunting and control of trading routes. As the warring intensified, it became increasingly difficult for the Mohawks, the Mohicans, and other parties to get their furs north. Henry Hudson changed everything. His legendary voyage opened up a whole new avenue for commerce and also helped speed the destruction of the Mohicans as an independent group.

Sailing from Holland under the employ of the Dutch East India Company, the Englishman Hudson, his son John, and a small band of English and Dutch sailors set off for parts at least partially unknown. (There were some maps and narratives of ocean travel and far lands, including information sent to Hudson by John Smith of Jamestown and Pocahontas fame.) Their charge was to seek a northeast path around northern Russia to the rich spice resources of China and Japan.

Just one of four trips Hudson made for this purpose, the passage was not a pleasant adventure from the start. Just off the north coast of

Europe, there was treacherous weather with hard winds, ice, and fog. Topping it all off, the crew was in turmoil and near mutiny. Hudson, faced with a recalcitrant group of sailors and unyielding poor conditions, altered his plans and abandoned his masters' orders. He instead headed west to warmer climes and toward what may have been his preferred end, seeking an elusive northwest passage to Asia.

After exploring the territory around the modern Connecticut and Delaware rivers and floating down to Virginia, the men aboard the *Half Moon*, a relatively old and small craft, finally sailed into the bay at the future New York on September 11, 1609. Before the month was out, the band of intrepid mariners traveled north and ran afoul of the shallow and sometimes impassable waters just above New Baltimore that were to plague many other travelers in the centuries to come. One mate, the Dutchman Robert Juet, recorded that noteworthy grounding event in his journal of the expedition:

> The seventeenth, faire Sun-shining weather, and very hot. In the morning as soone as the Sun was up, we set sayle, and ran up sixe leagues higher, and found shoalds in the middle of the channell, and small Ilands, but seven fathoms water on both sides. Toward night we borrowed so neere the shoare, that we grounded: so we layed out our small anchor, and heaved off againe. Then we borrowed on the banke in the channell, and came aground againe; while the floud ran we heaved off againe, and anchored all night.

Continuing his account of the voyage, Juet writes that on September 22, "This night at ten of the clocke, our Boate returned in a showre of raine from soundng of the River; and found it to bee at an end for shipping to goe in. For they had beene up eight or nine leagues and found but seven foot water, and unconstant soundings." A small band of seamen had rowed "up the Rivere neere to fortie three degrees."[17] This may have been as far north as the present Waterford, a few miles above Albany.

The end result was that they could sail no further. This was not the route to the hoped-for riches, not at least for those they had planned to find. Hudson was impressed greatly throughout the trip by the friendly and hospitable Mohicans, by the area's abundant natural resources, and by the surplus of fur-bearing animals whose hides would be a premium catch to satisfy willing European buyers.

Upon the expedition's return to Europe, word of the prime location, fertile lands, and temperate climate of the river and its valley spread rapidly. Dutch merchants began to take serious interest in tapping those treasures.

The small fur supply Hudson carried off with him became a particular attraction. Logistically, the voyage proved that the Europeans now had a ready supply route away from the unhealthy and volatile Canadian avenue. In the next few years, a steady assortment of Dutch traders sailed upriver in the warmer seasons to deal with the Indian suppliers of precious pelts. The Mohicans, the dominant group in the area, became fast friends and business partners with the Europeans.

In October of 1614, the Dutch government officially licensed fur traders to conduct business with the native people. That same year, Fort Nassau was established on a small island a bit south of modern Albany. It was a ready spot for the newcomers to conduct business on a more year-round and permanent basis with the Indians. Not a particularly advantageous location, it flooded regularly. A strong freshet destroyed the structure a short four years later. The die, though, was cast for further action and more organized commerce.

The problem for the aggressive Mohawks, who lived inland, was their need to pass through Mohican territory to get to Hudson's river and its link to the outer world. The two tribes were not on the best of terms, warring frequently over decades. The Dutch soon persuaded the Mohicans to relent on their fur-trading monopoly at the river, allowing the Mohawks freer access to the marketplace. Both the Dutch and Mohawks and other Indians now were increasingly infringing on Mohican territory.

Dutch Settlers Predominate

The Dutch continued to expand their horizons. In 1621, the Netherlands government chartered the West India Company, granting that body exclusive trading rights for twenty-four years in Africa, the West Indies, and America. As part of their charter, the company built a small, stockaded outpost in 1624 near the wreckage of Fort Nassau. Named in honor of the Dutch royal family, Fort Orange was inhabited by traders and a small military force.

The early pioneers began to clear the land, planting sustenance crops and starting to build a rudimentary community. They also had to adhere closely to a fixed set of rules established by the company, which essentially meant that they were beholden to that body, including the requirement that all profits from exports went to the head office. The hard frontier life turned out to be neither a pleasant existence for the newcomers nor an attractive motivator for additional recruits. Why would someone travel from one of the world's most preeminent commercial and cultural centers, the golden-age Netherlands of Rembrandt and Vermeer, to a rough wilderness with an ephemeral lure of possible riches but a certainty of hard work?

By 1629, the West India Company directors had come to realize that the costs of underwriting the lives and labors of a dwindling number of settlers in the wild interior of New Netherland was outstripping any profits that may have been gained. There had to be an alternative arrangement to entice people to settle in the new land for the long haul, people who would put down roots and not just seek to get rich quick through the fur trade. The Dutch response was the patroon system.

In exchange for extensive plots of land, willing participants would agree to establish a settlement of fifty adult tenants (over fifteen years old). A patroon was granted broad powers, controlling all mineral rights, all fishing and hunting, and all legal matters. Although others tried, the only successful subscriber to the plan was Kiliaen Van Rensselaer, a pearl and diamond merchant from Amsterdam. Called Rensselaerswijck, his property included present-day Albany, Rensselaer, and Columbia counties, about 700,000 acres surrounding Fort Orange. The holding stretched south as far as the Hannacroix Creek, although borders were debatable. At one point, Barren Island, at the mouth of the creek just north of the New Baltimore–Coeymans border, was a site used to guard the Hudson River entrance to the patroonship.

The patroon system beyond Van Rensselaer's fiefdom was not a success. Meeting the criteria for a patroonship and maintaining the structure were difficult tasks. A majority of new arrivals ended up being independent agents who bought their own land. Van Rensselaer's representatives, however, continued to expand his holdings with numerous additional purchases throughout the region.

By the 1660s, fur supplies near Albany became markedly depleted, and demand in Europe began to decrease. Trade ground to a near halt. This meant that hunters had to look further afield, into Canada and New England and out along the Mohawk Valley and points west, to reinvigorate the market. As the fur trade petered out, the economy broadened, at least for the Europeans. Farmers, millers, and dealers of various goods took up the reins of business. Traffic was increasing greatly on the Hudson. Vessels sailing to and from New Amsterdam and later New York and as far away as the Netherlands and England were commonplace.

The Mohicans, though, had lost their main source of income. The need to travel further away to hunt was a great inhibitor, and there was no other lucrative vocation to take its place. The Indians were reduced to more menial tasks just to survive. Driven into rank poverty, their people often were unable to afford the basics of clothing, tools, and weapons. The men became hunting guides and cut and sold firewood. Women, children, and the elderly worked for white settlers and made and sold crafts.

By this time, European goods had become quite an attraction for the Mohicans, replacing many common items previously made by the nation's members, and increasing their dependence on the new neighbors. Metal tools and utensils became substitutes for stone tools and earthen pots, metal projectile points for bone or stone, and, subsequently, guns for bow and arrow. Cloth duffels or strouds (i.e., wool broadcloth), a very common medium of exchange, began to replace fur and leather in making blankets and clothing. Running out of trade resources, Mohican land quickly became a critical medium of exchange.

In 1664, an English naval force captured New Netherland in a surprise, nonviolent invasion during a time of relative peace. Except for a brief renewal as a Dutch colony in 1673–1674, the English were in charge for the next hundred years. The change did nothing to relieve the downward spiral of the Mohican nation.

A Sad End

As Albany and the river valley became more populated, living space was at a premium. The Europeans coveted readily accessible fertile acreage near the tributaries that flowed into the Hudson in the modern Albany, Rensselaer, Columbia, and Greene counties. This was prime Mohican territory, and the settlers were as interested in buying as the Indians were in selling the valuable land.

Starting with the efforts by the Van Rensselaer agent, Brant Van Slichtenhorst, to expand the patroon's real estate holdings in the 1640s, the river islands and other rich Mohican territories were sold off. The attraction of Dutch goods was a tolerable medium of exchange for the millstreams, prime forests, and fertile flatlands that were a fundamentally valuable commodity for both the Indians and the Europeans. The

Mohicans regrettably did not subscribe to the European concept of land transfer and ownership. To them, the transactions were more a matter of temporary loaning for farming and hunting, a sharing of resources with the newcomers for common gain. In reality, they were losing the land for good.

Credit became a predominant economic reality with the need to pay back debts increasingly difficult. Fervent missionary work intruded on traditional spiritual practices. General exposure to Europeans and their lifestyles and diseases broke down Indian culture, beliefs, and health, splintering communities. Alcohol was another increasingly frequent medium of exchange, becoming a debilitating contributor to social dissolution. This happened despite the opposition of the colonial authorities who regulated against and punished certain liquor transactions.

Illegal alcohol sales stretched even into the future Greene County. On June 10, 1653, Jacob Clomp was brought to task by the Fort Orange magistrates for selling spirits to the Indians at Catskill and Esopus, causing the authorities to attach his "yacht" until further investigation that led to an additional financial penalty. By the following May, the Fort Orange court had had enough of the alcohol situation down the Hudson:

> Whereas it is found by experience and brought to the attention of this court that some of the inhabitants of this jurisdiction venture to sail in canoes, rowboats, or other vessels from here to the Esopus and Kats[k]il plain to sell brandy or liquor to the Indians along the way, or at the aforesaid places, to the considerable detriment of the good inhabitants there, it is decided to have notices posted that no one residing within this jurisdiction and consequently belonging thereto shall be allowed to sail thither from here in any rowboats, canoes, or other vessels without having the same inspected here by the officer and without having obtained proper consent to go thither from and in the name of this court, on pain of forfeiture by those who shall be found to have acted contrary hereto of the sum of fifty guilders for each offense for the benefit of the officer here.[18]

All these events took their toll on Mohican society, forcing them to abandon the river valley for the most part to settle in more remote locations northeast of Albany and in New England, particularly in western Massachusetts at Stockbridge. Peaceful coexistence with the

Europeans ironically may have helped extend the Mohicans' survival in their longtime homeland. Taking such a pragmatic approach, they were able to stay on their native lands for a longer period than otherwise may have been possible.

Their numbers by this time were severely reduced from the thousands of their dominating years. In mid-summer of 1701, the Schaghticoke Indians' sachem, Soquans, spoke at an Indian conference, representing his own group and the Mohicans still on the river. His words, tinted with a futile sense of optimism, underscored the diminished size of the Mohicans' domain from Schaghticoke down to Catskill:

> Itt is by Gods permission wee meet here together and wee are heartily glad to see you, and since itt is requisite you should know our strength wee have made an exact calculation and wee are now two hundred fighting men belonging to this County of Albany from Katskill to Skachkook and hope to increase in a year's time to three hundred.[19]

In August of 1720, a group of Mohicans traveled upstream to Albany to meet with Peter Schuyler, substituting for the absent governor, and a committee of Indian affairs. Noting their position as "antient Inhabitants of those parts," they were seeking to renew the covenant binding them in peaceful and helpful coexistence with the whites and to reassure the administrators of their desire to accept Christianity.

Schuyler was worried about the continuing fever of war among the French, British, and Mohawks, and the potential for the Mohicans to join in the conflict. Adopting a scornful, paternalistic tone, he hoped that his visitors would "behave your selfe as Dutifull Childrin and keep your selves sober and eat Drink Hunt and Plant in Peace." In granting the covenant renewal, Schuyler also provided ammunition and clothing to the Indians but managed to scold that you "Complain of your Poverty and are so bare & nake which must be ascribed to your Drinking and Laziness hopes in that you will be for the future sober and active to hunting and Plant . . ."[20]

In late August 1722, William Burnet, Dutch-born colonial governor of both New York and New Jersey, convened a conference with the river Indians to discuss various concerns. The Indian liaison, Ampamit, had ascended to the sachem position and lived on Moesimus (Lower Schodack) Island in the Hudson. The whole of the recorded discussion illustrates the ongoing dignity and dire straits of the Mohicans and the paternalistic demeanor of the colony's European administrators. The crushing social problems faced by Ampamit and his small group of followers remain heartrending. Still, Governor Burnet hastened to chastise the Indians as to:

> how destructive your Intemperence has proved and how much your people are diminishd by your excessive drinking of Rum the Women as well as the men being guilty of being often drunck, let me advise you to be more sober for the future, and not to spend what you get by Hunting on strong drink, but lay it out on clothing and other necessaries for your support & above all not squander your Indian Corn for Rum which you ought to keep for your subsistence all the year . . .

Ampamit, seeking to defend his group, acknowledged that a problem no doubt existed, but it was perhaps not wholly of their own making. The Europeans had a good measure of blame that could be ameliorated:

> We are sensible that you are much in the right, that Rum does a great deal of Harm, we approve of all that you said on that Point, but the matter is this, When our people come from Hunting to the Town or Plantations and acquaint the Traders & People that we want Powder and Shot & Clothing, they first give us a large cup of Rum, and after we get the Taste of it crave for more so that in fine all the Beaver & Peltry we have hunted goes for drink, and we are left destitute either of Clothing or Ammunition, Therefore we desire our father to order the Tap or Crane to be shut & to prohibit ye selling of Rum, for as long as the Christians will sell Rum, our People will drink it . . .

Ampamit lamented graciously but firmly that:

> our Father is very much in the right to tell us that we squander away our Indian Corn which should subsist our Wives & Children but one great cause of it is yt [yet] many of our People are obliged to hire Land of the Christians at a very dear Rate, to give half the Corn for Rent & the other half they are tempted by Rum to sell, & so the Corn goes, yt

> [yet] ye Poor Women & children are left to shift as well as the [they] can . . .

Ampamit concluded the talks by emphasizing the deleterious effects that the often disadvantageous land deals of decades past had on his people:

> We have no more Land the Christians when they buy a small spot of Land of us, ask us if we have no more Land & when we say yes they enquire the name of the Land & take in a greater Bounds than was intended to be sold them & the Indians not understanding what is writ in the Deed or Bill of Sale sign it and are so deprived of Part of their Lands . . .

Subsequently, Governor Burnet did little to address the alcohol and land issues. His inaction was not surprising given his condescending note at the 1722 conference that the Mohicans:

> look better & are better cloathed than the other Indians that do not live among the Christians & therefore that they do well to stay among them. He beleives [*sic*] they live better since the Christians bought & improved their Lands than they did before then the Land lay waste & unimproved . . .[21]

The Mohicans continued their meager and deteriorating existence near New Baltimore for a bit longer.

The Local Connection

As is obvious, New Baltimore was in the midst of active Mohican centers, although pinning down exact dates and places of native habitation is difficult. We know that Indians and early colonists certainly made steady use of the Hudson and the parallel Catskill Indian Path, a primary track between Fort Orange (later Beverwijck and Albany) and points south that followed the eastward side of the Kalkberg. Researchers also are quite sure that the Mohicans' headquarters was for many years between the modern city of Rensselaer and New Baltimore.

A handful of early Mohican villages were believed to have been in Greene County at the junction of the Kaaterskill and Catskill creeks and at present-day Leeds, Kiskatom, and Freehold. Shirley Dunn, the distinguished historian of Mohican land dealings, has suggested that the mention in the 1662 Bronck Patent of cleared land away from the river indicates the remains of tilled fields by the Mohicans, if not an actual settlement. This also could infer that other inland settlements were within the modern bounds of Greene County.

On the north, the Hudson islands near the New Baltimore-Coeymans border were an integral part of Mohican life and history. With different names at different times, these small masses of land near the mouth of the Hannacroix Creek became known in popular usage as Aepjen's, Beeren, and Moesimus islands during the Mohican era. All of them are mentioned frequently in old deeds, maps, and in contemporary and modern narratives of the Mohican and early colonial periods.

On modern maps, they still are named even while ceasing to exist as freestanding entities. Beeren has slightly altered to be called Barren today and has become indistinguishable from the mainland on the west side of the river just north the Hannacroix Creek mouth. Beeren became a primary boundary marker for land purchased by Kiliaen Van Rensselaer in forming his patroonship in the early 1630s.

Aepjen's and Moesimus became Upper and Lower Schodack islands, respectively. These islands are across from Beeren Island and the Hannacroix. They have been incorporated through natural infill and the dumping of dredging spoils into one land mass that extends from near Castleton-on-Hudson to the southernmost tip of today's Houghtaling Island. Houghtaling probably was the land mass also called "Marten Gerritsoons Eylant" in early maps.

Schiwias, commonly called Aepjen ("Little Monkey") by the Dutch, was born in the Schodack area and ascended to be chief sachem of the Mohicans. Schiwias probably held the sachem role from the late 1630s into the middle of the 1660s and made his home on Upper Schodack Island. Upon the 1637 death of sachem Papsickene, the center of Mohican life had moved south to near Schodack after the chief's descendants sold the former headquarters on the modern Papscanee Island to Van Rensselaer agents.

Aepjen is believed to have had an engaging personality and was a born communicator, playing an instrumental role in negotiating and settling a long and violent dispute between the Indians and Europeans at Esopus (Kingston). The Dutch considered him to be the chief of all chiefs and cultivated a relatively amicable relationship with the leader.

This seemed a fortuitous strategy for the Europeans since he was a primary intermediary and principal in arranging and confirming land sales from as far north as the Cohoes Falls area to Catskill. For the Mohicans, regrettably, the lure of land sales as a source of income meant a dwindling homeland, which the Indians continued to sell off in bits and pieces in the coming decades in an array of confusing and often disputed transactions.

Aepjen's 1648 sale of land on a stream called the Paponicuck (now the Muitzeskill, just south of Castleton-on-Hudson) may have marked the start of the diminution of their Schodack holdings. His island seems to have gone into European hands for the first time in 1663. An Indian called Wattawit, who may have been Aepjen's nephew, and his mother Pepewitsie sold "their certain land lying on the goojer's kill on Apjen's island, or by the Indians called Schotack, their portion of said Apjen's island." Another transaction that day saw an additional allotment on the island go from Naspahan and his "squaw" Pasies to the same purchasers, Dutch traders Volkert Jansen Douw and Jan Thomas Witbeck.[22] Other deals followed.

As the sales progressed and intertwined, it becomes impossible to determine exactly when the Mohicans' presence ended on the Hudson islands or their near shoreline. In 1687, missionaries observed a number of Indians fishing at Beeren Island. By 1690, the colonial council at Albany invited the Mohicans there to relocate to Catskill to consolidate forces. Their resolution asked that "ye River Indians liveing at Beere Island and Catskill be Perswaded to goe all & live & Plant at Catskill who will be Ready on all occasions to be employed as skouts or oyrwise which will much Conduce for ye Security of our neighbours of ye County of ulster by there Continuall hunting and Rangeing ye woods."[23]

Apparently, the Indians, if they left at all, must have returned by the 1700s. There is no firm information about when or even whether Moesimus was sold back to the Mohicans in later years or simply rented to one or more of their members. Ampamit, apparently the last of the local sachems, lived on Moesimus Island starting at least from the second decade of the eighteenth century. His plaintive testimony to Governor Burnet on the plight of his people was cited earlier. Shirley Dunn mentions that, between 1730 and 1742, a Mohican village ("Ampamit's house") was listed on a map as being on Moesimus Island.[24]

As we reached the midpoint of the eighteenth century, reports of Mohican activity became even more infrequent. By 1737, at least one prominent source mentions a land sale on the Housatonic River in Massachusetts. The Mohican sellers were "formerly of Menanoke or the island in the Hudson below Albany."[25] By this time, the natives' council fire likely had moved eastward to near Stockbridge.

Toward the end of June in 1739, the missionary John Sergeant was called to preach "to the Indians on the Island in Hudson's River," a group of about "30 intelligent Hearers, who gave good Attention, and seem'd well pleas'd, especially some of them, with my coming." This location was Moesimus Island. Included among the flock were Dutch people whose request to Sergeant to stay at one of their homes was rejected, with the preacher opting to lodge with the Mohicans on the island to pray in the evening and the morning.

By his account, Sergeant was well pleased by the hospitality of the river Indians who plied him with "Entertainment, Tea, small and strong Beer, and a fat Lamb." In the end, the natives made a better impression than the Dutch, whose "Behaviour was much more disorderly than the Indians. And indeed by their Behaviour they seem'd to consider the Lord's-Day rather as a Season for Frolicing, than for religious Duties."[26]

Alexander Hamilton (not *the* Alexander Hamilton) was an adventurous Scotsman and physician who undertook a journey to America and settled in Annapolis, Maryland in 1739. Stricken by serious ill health in 1743, Hamilton decided the next year to trek northward for his health and some recreation.

One leg of the trip found him sailing the Hudson on his way to and from Albany. He is interesting for our purposes for two reasons. First, he was one of the last people to commit to paper his recollections of the presence of the Mohicans on the Hudson. Second, Hamilton's ship was grounded on the shoals between New Baltimore and Albany on both parts of his voyage, a frequent occurrence over many decades and a topic for later discussion.

On Sunday, June 24, Hamilton says that "Att five we sailed past Musman's Island, starboard, where there is a small nation of the Mochacander Indians with a king that governs them."[27] This was Moesimus Island, and the "king" would have been Ampamit. It could be argued that, given his stature as a leader, Ampamit was the figurative "Last of the Mohicans" on Hudson's river. Some individual Mohicans still were identified in Greene County and other nearby locations well into the mid-1700s but the integrated nation was gone.

2

Europeans Settle in Greene County

Cornelis Van Tienhoven, who was secretary of the New Netherland colony, wrote at length about the implications and responsibilities of putting down roots in the new world. Although the narrative dates from 1650 and focuses on the lower Hudson area, it gives a clear indication of what life was like for settlers in the rough country of Greene County and New Baltimore. Van Tienhoven advises that the newcomers should be prepared for the worst, going into detail about land clearing, farming methods, and shelter building. His directions for their literal survival were quite specific:

> All then who arrive in New Netherland must immediately set about preparing the soil, so as to be able, if possible to plant some winter grain, and to proceed the next winter to cut and clear the timber. The trees are usually felled from the stump, cut up and burnt in the field, unless such as are suitable for building, for palisades, posts, and rails, which must be prepared during winter, so as to be set up in the spring on the new made land which is intended to be sown, in order that the cattle may not in any wise injure the crops. In most lands is found a certain root, called red Wortel, which must, before ploughing, be extirpated with a hoe, expressly made for that purpose. This being done in the winter, some plough right around the stumps, should time or circumstances not allow these to be removed; others plant tobacco, maize and beans,

> at first. The soil even thus becomes very mellow, and they sow winter grain the next fall. From tobacco, can be realized some of the expenses incurred in clearing the land. The maize and beans help to support both men and cattle. The farmer having thus begun, must endeavour, every year, to clear as much new land as he possibly can, and sow it with such seed as he considers most suitable.
>
> It is not necessary that the husbandman should take up much stock in the beginning, since clearing land and other necessary labor do not permit him to save much hay and to build barns for stabling. One pair of draft horses or a yoke of oxen only is necessary, to ride the planks for buildings or palisades or rails from the land to the place where they are to be set.
>
> The farmer can get all sorts of cattle in the course of the second summer when he will have more leisure to cut and bring home hay, also to build barns and houses for men and cattle.[1]

The Greene County Arrivals

The land business was a going concern. It was not long before the Mohicans' interest in selling, and the Europeans' interest in buying, led a trail to Greene County. Second-generation newcomers needed acreage they could farm in fertile flatlands and on river islands, and streams on which they could build mills. Some were just interested in speculation, hoping that increasing numbers of émigrés would spend a good dollar to purchase wilderness property with growth potential.

The period of settlement to the south of Albany was an age of turmoil, the beginning of a hundred-year time of near-constant warfare—Indian versus Indian, Indian versus European, British versus French, American versus British—from the mid-1600s into the eighth decade of the 1700s. Then a brief respite of a generation's length came until the American and British were at it again in the War of 1812.

Although some brave souls may have sought to plant roots in Greene County earlier, it was Cornelis Antonissen Van Der Slyck who took the first recorded step forward in 1646. He secured a patent in the Catskill area from the New Netherland government and the West India Company as a reward for his good services. Hoping to establish a colony, Van Der Slyck had circumstances conspire against him, and he never followed up on his claim. Cornelis was the uncle of Willem Pieterse, the progenitor of the New Baltimore Van Slykes.

Brant Van Slichtenhorst, acting in the interest of the Van Rensselaers, purchased an extensive piece of property in 1649 near the junction of the Catskill and Kaaterskill creeks at modern-day Leeds. The cost was cloth, a beaver skin, and a knife. For some additional cloth, the Mohican leader Aepjen negotiated the deal for the sellers, the Catskill woman sachem Pewasck and her son, Supahoot.

In usual land exchange dialogues, the natives would travel to the patroon's house and spend several days celebrating the transactions with plentiful food and drink. Aepjen, in particular, was noted for ensuring that barrels of beer, bottles of brandy, and stores of food were emptied before his people departed back to their homeland.[2]

Van Slichtenhorst apparently convinced a few stalwarts to populate and farm the patroon's new acquisition. Van Slichtenhorst and New Netherland's director general Peter Stuyvesant, though, were caught up in an intense rivalry, largely over the ownership and settling of the land around Fort Orange. Catskill and some other remote places were caught in the middle. Stuyvesant successfully disputed the Catskill sale, leading to the downfall of Van Slichtenhorst and the diminution of the Van Rensselaers. But the settlement remained at the junction of the creeks despite several pioneers facing legal reprimand for their land intrusion.

Fort Orange court minutes make several references to people living or doing business at the little settlement that was called Catskill. On February 1, 1652, Paulus Thomasz was questioned by that judicial body as to the conditions under which he, Jan Dircksen Van Bremen, Pieter Teunisz, Compeer or Thomas Higgins, and others were able to obtain property at Catskill. Paulus responded that they were permitted to use the land tax-free for ten years with regular payments due thereafter.[3]

Van Bremen is mentioned on numerous occasions. Given his surname, he likely was from Bremen in northwestern Germany, providing evidence, along with the presence of Jan Andriessen from Dublin, of the diversity of population at even the smallest settlement.

The account in chapter 1 of the 1653–1654 liquor sales at Catskill and the trial of Jacob Clomp names several people who were either accomplices or witnesses to the dealings, including Van Bremen, Jacobus Theunisz Van Naerden, Willem Fredrixsz, Kit Davitsz, and Marten Martensz. Whether these individuals lived at or were just visiting Catskill is unknown but the context of the narratives makes one think that at least some of them were residents.

A 1651 survey of farm animals done for the Van Rensselaers shows that Van Bremen "at Catskil" owned four mares named "block," "Corlaer," "evert pels," and "sunijtgen," along with two colts, a stallion, and another unnamed mare. He also had "1 cow with a star, with her second calf," "1 heifer with her first calf," "1 cow with her second calf," and "2 calves of this year." A neighbor, Pieter Teunissen, "at kats kil" had an "old mare" and several more horses and cows of varying ages.[4]

The beginning of the year 1654 saw the Fort Orange court considering various events involving sums of money owed by or to Van Bremen. In one instance, the defendant's property at Catskill was subject to claim for the due funds. People participating in this proceeding were Arent de Noorman, Marcelis Jansz, and Pieter Bronck.

The interesting aspect about the latter's mention in this case and a couple of others was Bronck's close association with the Greene County area about ten years before his purchase of land there and assumed relocation of residence from Beverwijck. One case involved Bronck receiving grain at Catskill from Van Bremen and not paying for it.[5]

In the spring of 1654, court authorities had to address a distinctive economic and social concern at Catskill and other locations. A key element of facilitating commerce was being mishandled, the ability to adequately weigh items. There was an ongoing problem of shorting customers on the quantities of their grain and bread orders, which created a plethora of disagreements and money discrepancies. As a result, Fort Orange magistrates determined that:

> Whereas the people here, at Katskill, Esopus, and elsewhere are very short of schepel measures, whether whole, half, or quarter schepels, to measure grain or other commodities, your honors are requested to be pleased to order a reasonable quantity from patria to supply the people therewith, provided that everyone who receives one is to pay for it. Otherwise, one person and another measuring with a keg or kegs, great disputes are likely to be caused and to arise among the people.[6]

The court minutes mention a few other people with unambiguous Catskill addresses. In an August 1654 estate dispute, a complaint was made by "Catharina Liberis, widow of Pieter Theunisz van Brunswick, deceased, at Katskill." The court was considering the disposition of ownership of her farm residence that had been caught up in a family row.[7]

In another case demonstrating the ubiquity of women in the archival records, Femmetje Westerkamp was a baker's widow, probably a baker herself, and a prominent Albany landholder. The 1656 record of the dissolution of her marriage to Michiel Antonisz Van Uytrecht (he was married to someone else) mentions that she "is residing in Katskil."[8]

By 1657, the illegal sale of alcohol reared up again with the German-born Hans Vos, who was living at Catskill. He and his servant Michiel were accused of providing "anise water," a spirit, to both Indians and whites. Apparently not much of a gentleman, Hans also was accused of threatening that "if anyone denounces me or blabs that I sell, or have sold, any wine to the Indians, I'll tie a rope with a stone around his neck and throw him into the kill." Witnesses included Eldert de Gojer, Lourens Lourensen, and Gijsbert Teunissen. The latter person was mentioned specifically as living at Catskill.

Femmetje Westerkamp turned up again, at Vos's request, to testify that "the Indians, having come into his house at Katskil, wanted to force Jan Anderiessen, her brother-in-law, to get a bottle of brandy at Hans Vos's, which they said they had paid for."[9] The Irishman Andriessen himself was called to the docket in 1658 for selling brandy to the Indians.[10]

Hans apparently did not learn any lessons from his last run-in with the law. In the summer of 1658, he was imprisoned for the same offense, turned in by a crony, Poulus Janssen. The two of them were accused of selling brandy to the Indians. Denying the charge, Vos aroused the sympathy of his captors, who decided that rather than "putting him in irons he would be kept in custody in his house under a guard of two soldiers." Hans had bigger ideas and "escaped from custody during the night of the 22d of July, through a window, and ran to Katskil."[11]

Later that year, a case before the court saw Henderick Koeherder accusing Philip "de Brouwer" (the brewer) Hendricksz of attaching the former's money at Catskill. Philip claimed that Henderick owed an unpaid sum of money for an order from "Lange Marij" or "Tall Maria." The reference was to Maria Jansen, a Rensselaerswijck tavern keeper. One wonders if this infers that Henderick may have been operating a tavern at Catskill with Maria and Philip as his suppliers.[12]

In another instance, in the fall of 1659, Beverwijck's Reformed Church deacons arranged for the provision of shoes, stockings, cloth for clothing, and board for a young boy from "Kaskyel." The group also paid for services to the child from a surgeon called Gysbert Van Imborgh at Catskill.[13]

So, business and life stepped haltingly forward at the meeting of the Catskill and Kaaterskill creeks for the decade of the 1650s. Starting with the 1660s, people with more familiar names and a serious interest in establishing a homestead came to town. Even at that, the pattern of settlement was of isolated, self-reliant farms located in places of fertile bottomland. One tendency may have been to build homesteads away from the main highway of Hudson's river to avoid Indian attacks.

The 1662 Bronck Purchase

Pieter Bronck, a Scandinavian native, may have arrived in Beverwijck as early as 1646. He became a brewer and owner of a popular tavern tended by him and his wife, Hilletje Tyssingh. Early colonial records suggest that Bronck led an interesting existence. At least some of those experiences appear colored by his occupation. There are numerous accounts of his court appearances at Fort Orange, often regarding money that he either owed or someone owed him. Legal actions were common in those litigious colonial days and not necessarily an indictment of one's personality flaws. They also were rougher times, calling for rougher measures.

In one instance, in 1655, Pieter was called into court at Fort Orange for what some may have felt was a positive move of "tapping strong beer, for the reason that he brews the same . . ."[14] at his business establishment. An earlier law banned brewers from selling beer at retail and tavern owners from brewing same. "Strong" beer simply was a better grade of product.

Two years later, Bronck was back in court again regarding a case brought against him by the schout or sheriff for brandishing a knife in an alcohol-fueled brawl with Poulus Martensen. Pieter was again called for a Fort Orange legal session in 1658 for "repeated assaults" on a man named Barent Osterman.[15]

Falling victim to the uneven economy of the settlement days, and perhaps the added pressures wrought by onerous excise taxes on liquors, financial reversals forced Bronck to sell most of his Albany holdings to Reyndert Pietersz and Jacob Hevick, to whom he already was indebted. With Pieter looking elsewhere for income to support his family, the answer was to start a farm at the future Coxsackie.

Pieter contracted to buy from the Mohicans an area called "Koixhackung." The sellers had authorized Sioketas and Sachemoes to represent them in the transaction that was formalized at Fort Orange. A fee of 150 guilders in beavers was charged, "of which sum the buyer promises to pay the half next May, when he shall come to live there, and the other half on the first of May, A.D., 1663." The large parcel formally transferred to Pieter was situated:

> upon the north river, on the westbank between Marten Gerritse's island and the Neuten Hoeck, among the Indians, named Koxhackung; the cleared land being a parcel away in the woods (together with the kil), extending from said kil, which lies over against Martin Gerritse's island, westward unto the Katskil path, from thence southward along the path to the Stenekil, thence eastward until over against the Noten Hoeck, and thence northward along the river to the aforesaid kil, which lies over against Marten Gerritse's island . . .[16]

The Bronck land started from near the mouth of the Coxsackie Creek by Marten Gerritse's Island, subsequently known as Bronck's Island and now joined to the mainland in far southeastern New Baltimore. The boundary went in a slightly southwesterly direction to the Kalkberg, the rocky ridge paralleling Route 9W, and from there followed the route of the "Katskil path," the main Indian trail from their Catskill Creek settlements to the Albany area. The line then went to the "Stenekil," or Stony Kill, south of the overpass of Route 81 over the New York State Thruway and east "over against the Notan Hoeck." The latter feature was a point in the Hudson now off Coxsackie village, Nutten Hook being the nub of land on the Columbia County side. The Bronck boundary line then went back north to the point of origin.

As Bronck was pondering settlement of his new plot, he was walking into the tail end of an opened bees' nest. From 1659 to 1663, conflicts at Esopus (Kingston) put a damper on travel on Hudson's river and threatened the interests of explorers and settlers throughout the region. A mixture of suspicion, distrust, paranoia, and general misunderstandings owing to the clash of native and newcomer cultures led to flare-ups over the European intrusion into Indian life and land.

In mid-October of 1663, the Europeans were warned that Indians with bad intentions were on their way to Catskill and points north. In a special meeting of the courts of Fort Orange and Rensselaerswijck, the colonial administrators addressed:

> a certain ominous rumor, namely, that the Esopus savages intended to come up here in 2 or 3 days, to do harm to the country people. We have therefore gathered information from the Mahikanders, who thought we knew of it and informed us, that more than 15 days ago some Esopus had been at Keessien Wey's hook who wanted to come up, but had been

> prevented this time and in order to get at the truth of the matter, we have unanimously concluded, to send for 2 or 3 Sachems of the Katkils with Keesien Wey, and to see, whether they can give further news.

The helpful "Mahikanders" were the Mohicans. Court administrators sent "Jan the weaver with a savage called Tomas" south to convince "2 or 3 of the principal savages in Katskil" to come to Fort Orange to discuss the feared attacks. Toward the end of November, "Eldert Gerbertsen Cruyff appeared in the Court with the Indians from Katskil, namely Macsachnimanau, Sacsamoes, Keesien Wey, Sichano alias Teunis, and Aepje."

The sachem Keesiewey, with some reluctance, testified that he prevented the Esopus on at least five occasions from attacking Catskill and farms further up the river valley, exchanging wampum for their retreat. He protested about his usual reception when visiting Fort Orange that "the Dutch pull him by the ears and call him an Esopus rascal." In exchange for additional wampum, Keesiewey and his friends agreed to act as the Europeans' agents in warning the Esopus about the consequences of any adverse action on their part. The attacks never materialized.[17]

So, the Broncks avoided having the Indians pass their front door in an ill mood. After filing a certification in January of 1665 that the land had been properly surveyed by one Frans Pietersz, the Broncks awaited confirmation of ownership of their property under the new English government.[18] It took until June 1667 for Governor Richard Nichols to provide legal approval but the property "conteyning in all about two hundred & fifty two acres or one hundred seventy six morgen and one hundred & tenn Rod" rightly belonged to the family.[19]

Upon Pieter's death in 1669, the land went to wife Hilletje and younger son Jan—legend has it that an elder offspring, Pieter, was forced from the family fold for marrying an Indian woman. In 1665, neighboring acreage (mostly today's Athens) had become the property of Jan Clute, Jan Hendricksz Bruyn, and Jurriaen Teunissen. This Loonenburg Patent also was confirmed by Governor Nichols but the border between the two properties was unclear.

The aforementioned gentlemen believed that the Broncks' claim overlapped their Patent and took the matter to court. A July 1670 court appearance may have been the first trip by Hilletje and Jan into the legal domain to clarify ownership but certainly was not the last. The court's decision found in favor of the plaintiffs and advised the litigants to "regulate themselves according to their patents."[20] However, legal disputes boiled on for a number of years.

Interestingly, the Broncks also were in court more than once disputing the cutting of timber on their assumed property by Barent Coeymans,[21] who we will introduce as the first European owner of the bulk of the future New Baltimore. Given the boundaries of the Bronck and Coeymans lands, the timber in question very well may have been in New Baltimore.

In expanding the homestead, Jan Bronck built a sawmill, probably the first of its type in the region. There is record of him exchanging some beaver skins and other goods for the ironworks appropriate for such a task from a man named Albert Andriese Bradt. Bradt was the American originator of the family that became well known in the New Baltimore area as the Vanderzees.[22]

By late spring of 1681, the three Loonenburg patentees had sold the northern part of the holding to Marten Gerritsen, a Norwegian, ancestor of the notable Van Bergen family. Marten was a farmer, country magistrate, military captain, and diligent land speculator.

His immediate descendant, Peter Van Bergen, swapped land in an estate settlement with brothers Martin and Gerritt and gained title to a substantial plot near the mouth of the Coxsackie Creek. He erected a gristmill around the 1720s, almost certainly the first commercial enterprise within the environs of New Baltimore. It became the center of a small community now swallowed by the woods. The mill remained active almost to the twentieth century. The long-gone original road from Coxsackie's upper landing to New Baltimore hamlet crossed a bridge abutting the mill property.

Over the years, the senior Marten accumulated real estate in Catskill and Coxsackie, in addition to what were his primary holdings in and around Beverwijck. Given the ephemeral methods for marking boundaries in those days of untrammeled wilderness and vague legal precedents, the Broncks now believed that Gerritsen was infringing on their claim and went off to court again to do battle.

In July 1684, the opposing parties met in Albany. An interesting array of witnesses were called including the Broncks' hired hand Dirk Hendrixse and his wife Sarah, the 1665 surveyor Frans Pietersz, and even Mathys Houghtaling, who figures more largely in another thread of this story. Former owner Jurriaen Teunissen makes an appearance with one witness quoting him as decrying that "What does Jan Bronk know about it? He was at that time a snotty boy."[23]

The confusion reigned for some period longer. The Broncks and Gerritsen finally came to the mutual conclusion that everyone's needs could be met through cooperation. In the spring of 1687, Governor Thomas

Dongan decreed that he "Do Give Grant Ratifye Release and Confirme unto the said John Broncks and Martine Gerritse the Severall and Respective Tracts or Parcells of Land and Premises," combining the neighbors' holdings into one package afterward known as the Coxsackie Patent.[24]

Throughout the Bronck ownership years, Jan and other family members bought and sold tracts of land around their homestead and beyond. On one occasion, in 1675, they got acreage for free. The Mohicans Schermerhorn (also called Manueenta) and Sachemoes gave land near the settlement at Catskill (Leeds) "on the north side of the kil called Paskaecq," along with "free range for his cattle" to Jan Bronck "out of a liberality shown him [and] for friendship acknowledged."[25] A 1710 deed confirms the sale of a substantial fifty-acre parcel to Philip Conine near the intersection of the modern routes 9W and 385. Conine's family subsequently owned property northward of that original piece, up into the town of New Baltimore.

A core section of the Bronck Patent remained mostly intact for many years with direct family descendants inhabiting the original home and its later additions well into the twentieth century. Jan Bronck's 1738 will divides property among his sons, Phillip, Casparus, Jonas, Peter, and Leonard. This was the "Land near the Deep Kill at Koxsackie" along with shares in the family saw mill.[26] Their original house now is preserved by the Greene County Historical Society and is one of oldest buildings still standing on the east coast.

It is uncertain when any of the Broncks actually took up residence within the borders of the future New Baltimore. Perhaps it came as a result of the last-mentioned 1738 land transfer generated through Jan's estate. There is no doubt that Broncks inhabited several houses in the vicinity of the eastern outlet of the Coxsackie Creek. By 1812, Pieter and Jan's descendant, Judith Bronck, had married Teunis Van Slyke, the first supervisor elected in the new town of New Baltimore. We know he was born in 1787 and lived all his life within the bounds of New Baltimore.

1672 Coeymans Patent

Barent Pieterse Coeymans, known as De Molenaer ("The Miller"), came to Rensselaerswijck around 1636 with three of his brothers, probably from Utrecht in the Netherlands. Barent and his first and second wives, Agnietje and Geertruy (who may have been Devos sisters), had three sons, Andries, Pieter Barentse, and Samuel, and two daughters, Ariaantje and

Gerritje. The girls later married into the Verplanck and Ten Eyck families.

By 1645, after a period of apprenticeship in a mill owned by the patroon Kiliaen Van Rensselaer, Coeymans entered partnerships in saw- and gristmills at various locations near Beverwijck. Barent also may have been a vintner on the side as a Mohawk Indian was called before a Fort Orange judge in 1656 for having used wine bought by "three squas from Barent Pietersen, the Miller."[27]

In an interesting sidelight to the exciting times of those earliest settlers, on what must have been a boisterous 1649–1650 New Year's Eve, a great time was being had by all at the Rensselaerswijck home of Stintgen Peters and husband Louwerens Jansz. In the spirit of the season, Stintgen was entertaining several people, including "Baernt, the miller, and his brother, Lucas."

Regrettably, the evening ended in a later Fort Orange court date. While Stintgen testified that she coincidently was absent at crucial times, there were accusations of shots being fired at two in the morning. This aroused the attentions of Hans Vos, the deputy schout or sheriff (yes, the alcohol-selling Vos—he eventually was pushed out of his official position because of such transgressions). "Baernt" and Lucas did not take kindly to the visit and "tore Han Vos's baldric from his body and to pieces." A baldric was an over-the-shoulder belt used to carry a weapon like a sword.

Shortly after the first set-to, "Baernt" was confronted by Stintgen who was stirred from bed to find her visitor with six sausages in hand from her pantry. She quickly repossessed this apparently unapproved confiscation of her links, and no criminal sanctions appear to have been enforced against anyone.[28]

On December 26, 1672, Barent bought land along the Hudson River that ran twelve miles inland, with one goal being to create a milling enterprise. Maghsapeet, the sachem or chief at Catskill, was the lead in the transaction, representing a sizable group of other Mohicans.[29] In April of 1673, Governor Francis Lovelace validated the transaction by granting Barent letters patent on the purchased parcel:

> on the West side of Hudsons River to the North of a place by the Indians called Haxhaexks stretching in Length to the highest place where Jacob Flodder did used to roll down his Timber named by the Natives Sietkatm to the south of the Island belonging to John Reyerse and into the woods as far as the said Indian sachems right goes as also the wood Land Kills creeks Valleys & meadows . . .[30]

The problem with Barent's acquisition was that it was believed, at least by the Van Rensselaers, to overstep the bounds of their land. Another critical drawback was that the purchase was approved under governor's authority, a continuing nuisance for Barent as it was not done under royal authority. It led to various legal interchanges between the Coeymans family and the Van Rensselaers to secure the appropriate confirmation that would conclusively resolve the property dispute.

By the fall of 1706, the opposing groups "did come to a friendly & amicable agreement amongst themselves"[31] with the land being transferred from Kiliaen to Barent for a modest annual payment of nine shillings. By this time, the Kiliaen Van Rensselaer that was dueling with the Coeymans family was the grandson of the original patroon. The final settlement contained property that ran from the northern edge of the Bronck/Coxsackie Patent at the mouth of the Coxsackie Creek up the Hudson to a point at Jan Reyer's Island, also called Smack's or Sietpaghack Island. This latter land mass, now called Shad Island, is located just under the bridge at the western end of the Berkshire spur of the New York State Thruway.

When Barent the miller died, he left his eldest son Andries as the sole owner of his vast acreage. Queen Anne granted royal confirmation to the heir on August 26, 1714, which meant that the Coeymans family had as formal and final possession as one could get of the land along the Hudson from the Coxsackie Creek to the current-day northern border of the town of Coeymans and inland nearly a dozen miles. This covered most of the modern town of New Baltimore into Greenville, southeastern Albany County, and extending well into the town of Coxsackie to points across the west branch of the Potic Creek.

Andries apparently saw brighter horizons in New Jersey. He legally divided the homeland among his siblings, granting or selling acreage over a couple of fall months in 1716. He purchased a significant parcel at Raritan where he lived out his days as a prominent landowner. It was said that he left because of family dissatisfaction with his division of the land. One interesting provision of the land distribution was that further transfers could be made only to Barent's lawful descendants. Perhaps the effective prohibition of sale to outsiders was the impetus for the survivors' unhappiness.

The siblings, Samuel, Pieter, and Ariaantje, now married to David Verplanck, were left to deal with their father's legacy. Over the next few years, a confusing array of real estate transactions occurred among the children, their in-laws, and various newcomers.

In a couple of important permutations of the land dispositions for the Coeymans estate after Pieter's death, Geeritje, his daughter by second wife Charlotte Amelia Drawyer, ended up with the waterfront property south of the mouth of the Hannacroix Creek and a bit inland. This plot became New Baltimore's riverside hamlet and probably extended out nearly to where Route 9W lies today. Another relative, Elizabeth Coeymans Van Allen, sold her share just west of Gerritje's area to Thomas Houghtaling. Several Houghtaling homes eventually were built there and still stand in twenty-first-century New Baltimore near the main highway.

John Barclay, Gerritje's husband, had been sent to the Coeymans / New Baltimore area at a young age, and the two had been married in the 1740s. Gerritje died in 1753, leaving John to manage her properties, which he did for the next two decades, even after moving back to Albany around 1770. He subsequently became the first mayor of Albany under the new state government in 1777. The Barclays likely lived in the Coeymans homestead and not in New Baltimore.

By the post–Revolutionary War era, the Coeymans property had been divided into numerous plots inhabited by people with such familiar names as Blaisdell, Bronck, Houghtaling, McCarty, Verplanck, Springstead, Ten Eyck, and Van Dalfsen. These were both people who married into the family and outsiders, individuals seeking a home, a profit, or just some open space.

Houghtaling Patent

With land near the Hudson being gobbled up, there started to be a push inland. The last piece of the early land transaction puzzle for New Baltimore fell into place when a patent was granted July 8, 1697 by Governor Benjamin Fletcher to Mathys Houghtaling. The youthful Mathys is believed to have landed here from the Netherlands about the middle of August in 1655 on a ship called *De Waegh*. He had been rounded up with some other boys from the almshouse in Amsterdam to work for the West India Company and help populate the settlements. They were to "be employed according to their abilities for the best advantage of the Company and a proper advancement of themselves."[32]

Once here, Mathys moved around, residing at New Amsterdam, Kingston, Kinderhook, Albany, and perhaps other places. He showed somewhat of a rambunctious nature in Kingston. While chopping wood one Sunday morning, he was told by a passerby, "You joyously chop like a royal soldier." Not taking kindly to the remark, Mathys reputedly responded, "Damn the King, and the devil fetch the King," an accusation he denied. Conflicting witnesses may have held sway since no definite verdict was apparent when the sheriff hauled Mathys to court over his insubordinate manner toward royalty.[33]

Mathys leased a farm in 1675 from Marten Gerritsen at Coxsackie, where he resided for six years before going back to Kinderhook. In the midst of this peripatetic existence, Mathys married Maria Hendrickse Marselis in 1666. Among the Houghtalings' seven children, son Coenradt married Tryntje Van Slyke in 1688 at Albany. She was a daughter of Willem Van Slyke, another New Baltimore pioneer.

By 1683, perhaps pushed by middle age to look for a more permanent nesting, Mathys wandered back to Coxsackie. This was the same year that Albany County was created as a massive jurisdiction, stretching from the Sawyer's Creek (Saugerties) on the south to Saratoga. Catskill and Coxsackie, a single entity, was one of the subdivisions of the new county.

This was a time when war was again rearing its ugly head. King William's War began in 1689, the first of the four French and Indian conflicts that stretched over the next seven and a half decades. Mathys's neighbor, Marten Gerritsen, was appointed as a captain of the local militia.

In 1691, Mathys continued to build his kingdom through the purchase from Indian representatives Manueenta, Unekeck, and Kachketowaa of a sizable property comprising about 3,500 acres. The area, patented six years later, encompassed:

> a Certaine Tract of Land in our County of Albany Scituate and being behinde a Place within our said County Called kockshaughy beginning over the Path of Katts kill from the South side of the Deep kill or Creeke and along the Path to the Stony kill on the North side and along the Stony kill to the back side of a Lake Poole or Pond of Water and from the said Lake Pool or Pond of Water to the Deep kill Due North and Northwest from the said Lake and along the Deep Kill to the said Katskill path.[34]

This expanse of land covered the area from near the modern intersection of New Baltimore's Lime Kiln and Reservoir roads southward on the west side of the Kalkberg ridge. In Coxsackie, it took a path close to the Thruway to a point nearly west of the Bronck Museum complex then traveled straight back up to Jennings Road in New Baltimore and east to the aforementioned intersection. The combination of the land covered by this grant and the Coeymans and Bronck properties comprises the basic outline of the modern town of New Baltimore.

The Houghtalings became a well-established presence in New Baltimore. They intermarried with the Van Bergens, the Broncks, and other pioneering families. Their Lime Kiln Farm remained in the family for many years and has been listed on the National Register of Historic Places.

Who Came First?

The Beers history of Greene County reports that Albertus Vanderzee was the first European settler in the wooded wilderness of New Baltimore, soon followed by Andries Van Slyke.[35] Beers also says that Vanderzee lived on an 800-acre site overlooking the Hudson in what would become the middle of today's riverside hamlet. This proposition seems confused with a purchase from the Coeymans family made later by the Vanderzee brothers.

Local lore has given the distinction of first settlers to Teunis Willemse Van Slyke and his wife Jannetje Van Wie. The couple is recorded as having eleven children, one of whom was named Andries, perhaps the aforementioned. Teunis and Jannetje are said to have built a stone house in 1713 on the Hudson about a mile below today's riverside hamlet. Andries was only nine years old at the time. There is an indenture dated October 4, 1716 transferring land along the river from Samuel and Ariaantje Coeymans to Teunis but no firm record of a real estate transaction before that time.[36] It cannot be said with certainty then that Teunis and Jannetje occupied the property before the indenture was effective, although it was not uncommon for people to establish a homestead before actually taking legal possession.

The Van Slykes eventually owned several hundred acres that descendants shared as their holdings spread north and west from the original homestead. Teunis's 1746 will divides various plots of land to his sons, with the family homestead near the river going to son Pieter. Andries built a house near the intersection of the modern Route 144 and railroad crossing. The successor of that dwelling still stands. Andries and wife Maria Van Benthuysen's grandchild, Teunis Van Slyke (1786–1860), became New Baltimore's first town supervisor.

It is interesting to note that Henry Van Rensselaer's 1715 militia unit included "Samuel Coeyeman," "Conraet" and Willem "Hooghteling," Wouter Van Der Zee, and Storm and Albert "Brat."[37] This combination of names could mean that both the Houghtalings and Vanderzees were living in New Baltimore as early as 1715. Samuel and Ariaantje Coeymans sold land around this time in the area north of the border of modern New Baltimore near the Houghtaling patent. There is speculation that Ariaantje was buried on a farm owned by her relatives, the Witbecks, which was near the Coxsackie / New Baltimore Thruway interchange.

On the Vanderzee side, things get a little confusing since there were two sets of brothers named Albert and Cornelis in the area, making analysis difficult. Members of the Bradt family had come to Rensselaerswijck by 1630. The Vanderzees' ancestor, Albert Andriessen Bradt, known as "De Noorman" because of his Norwegian birth, was a miller and tobacco planter who established a farm on a stream named for him, the Normanskill. Albert's son, Storm Albertse, was said to have been born during a bout of foul weather on a ship coming to the new world. He later became known as Storm Vanderzee ("storm of the sea"), a name carried to subsequent generations.

On March 2, 1773, brothers Albert Storm and Cornelis Vanderzee bought the approximately 600- to 800-acre Barclay parcel, which included the area where the most-settled part of the town now is along the Hudson, plus part of the island across the river. This younger Albert Vanderzee was the person that constructed a log cabin on a knoll in the middle of the modern riverside settlement, a location that affords even today a picturesque view of the Hudson and the neighborhood. This may relate to the confusing Beers assertion. Albert's wife was Catherine Van Slyke, the granddaughter of Teunis and Jannetje.

Whether, for how long, and where his brother Cornelis may have lived along the Hudson is unknown, if he lived there at all. He and his wife Annatje Veeder settled in the section of the Van Rensselaer manor that evolved into the town of Bethlehem. The Vanderzees were leaders in that community, with Cornelis a founder of the Bethlehem Reformed Church. Both he and Annatje are buried near the church, in the Elmwood Cemetery along the modern Route 9W. Their farm eventually was sold and used in the creation of the Selkirk rail yards.

As for the Houghtalings, there is no evidence that the original Mathys and wife Maria ever established residence within New Baltimore's borders before his 1706 death, and it is unclear who the first of their family was to hold such designation. The majority of their patent probably lay in Coxsackie and ended up in the hands of their eldest son, Coenradt. He was listed as a freeholder at the manor of Rensselaerswijck in 1720 rather than with the Broncks and other individuals counted under "Coxhacky and Cats Kill."[38] His neighbors included the Coeymans and Vanderzees so the census-takers still may have been figuring in a portion of the Coeymans Patent as part of Rensselaerswijck.

All the children of Coenradt and his wife Tryntje were baptized at the Albany Reformed Church, perhaps owing to lack of a nearby option. Thomas, the firstborn child of their son Hendrick and his wife Hester Bricker, was baptized at the same place in 1731 but Hendrick and Hester's next three children were baptized at either the Coxsackie Reformed Church or the Catskill (Leeds) Reformed Church, starting in 1734.

The aforementioned Thomas is important because he certainly lived in the future New Baltimore. He married Elizabeth Witbeck, the granddaughter of Pieter Coeymans, in 1757. It seems likely that he was establishing his farm around that time in the vicinity of the modern crossing of the New York State Thruway with Route 9W. The family then maintained its residence on the bulk of the land in the shadow of the Kalkberg well into the twentieth century. Houghtaling or Hotaling is a name that has carried much weight in the region throughout history. Among other important commercial and political roles, six of their namesake descendants have been town supervisors of New Baltimore.

Government

As population grew and colonial law and circumstance dictated, community institutions began to develop. Throughout the Dutch period of governance, the upper Hudson area was under the loose authority of Fort Orange / Beverwijck administrators, with overseeing officers called "schepens" (magistrates or justices of the peace) and "schouts" (sheriffs or constables). As mentioned before, Hans Vos was a deputy schout with influence at Catskill for some period. In 1660, a court was created at Esopus (Kingston), and the Catskill area came under that body's jurisdiction.

When the English came into control, they kept this basic system in the Dutch-dominant locations for a number of years to avoid unnecessary disruption. As the years passed, more formal and complex local governing bodies made their appearance under colonial law.

Citizens in the precincts of Coxsackie and Catskill received a degree of self-rule in the summer of 1718 through legislative action allowing election of a supervisor. The holders of the existing positions of justice of the peace and constable were charged with arranging elections for the supervisor who then was authorized to represent Coxsackie's interests under the county board at Albany.

This system remained largely in place until 1772 when a law was passed allowing municipal entities or "districts""to be established and have powers to support the poor, superintend highways, raise funds, and have a variety of elected officers. The Coxsackie District was formed and could convene yearly elections for supervisor along with a tax collector, clerk, and dual positions each of assessor, constable, overseer of the poor, and fence viewer. The town of Coxsackie subsequently was authorized under state law in 1788. New Baltimore was part of Coxsackie until 1811.

Religion

Religion was an integral part of Dutch colonial life. Adherence to the Reformed faith was a key element in any of their settlements. Despite that essential relationship, the Zion Lutheran Church became the first congregation organized in the future Greene County, and that was not until 1703. The Reformed populations at Catskill and Coxsackie apparently were not sufficient to warrant the required investment in their own church beyond itinerant prayer sessions at individual homes. Marriages and baptisms of the era usually required travel to distant churches at Albany or Kingston, both of which date from the middle of the seventeenth century.

The transient nature of worship is reflected in the official records. One document dated January 14, 1650 records that Jan Dircksen Van Bremen has "leased and rented" for six years from Director Brant Van Slichtenhorst and his fellow commissioners "the old maizeland on the north side of Katskil, to wit the tract of land, where the squaw, who is chief of Katskil resides." A condition of the agreement was that "The lessee further engages to read on every Lord's or other Holiday for his Christian neighbors the holy Gospel or a sermon out of a homily, if it can be procured and to sing one or more psalms before and after the Christian prayers according to the custom of the Reformed Church."[39]

By the start of the 1730s, the population of the area was sufficient and the distance to travel to church at Albany or other locations great enough that the immigrants desired to have their own Reformed church. The miller Peter Van Bergen exchanged a small parcel of land for the nominal sum of five shillings, deeding the property to a group of elders, Abraham Prevost, Teunis Van Slyke, Pieter Bronck, and Philip Conine Jr.

The original meeting to organize the congregation was on February 25, 1732. At the start, it was a single congregation with one minister but two church buildings, one at Coxsackie and the other at Catskill (Leeds). A house of worship was constructed at Coxsackie near the intersection of the King's highway and the common road leading to the Hudson.

Dominie George Michael Weiss, a German Palatine, preached the first sermon to the new flock as fall unfolded in 1733. An array of familiar names—Bronck, Van Bergen, Vandenberg, Houghtaling—began to be recorded in church listings of baptisms and marriages. Dominie Weiss had married into the Bronck family.

The Specter of War

Starting in the middle of the 1600s, the Dutch and English and eventually the English and French had tumultuous relationships largely revolving around retaining or gaining control of land, the seas, and commerce, which easily spread a constant blanket of threat and outright violence over affairs in the colonies. Just less than two years after Pieter Bronck made his initial land purchase, the overmatched Dutch peacefully surrendered control of New Netherland to the English in 1664, regaining rule in 1673, four months after the Lovelace confirmation of the Coeymans Patent, only to lose it again in early 1674 during peace negotiations between the warring nations.

While many battles of the colonial wars occurred along the western frontiers of New York, in New England, on and over the Canadian borders, and even into Florida and South Carolina, local tension was palpable with important confrontations relatively close, including 1690 and 1748 attacks on Schenectady, the 1745 destruction of Saratoga, and a handful of calls-to-arms and unrealized plans to invade Canada. For decades, Albany was virtually a continuously armed camp.

In the earliest days of colonization, the Dutch and English employed a body of professional soldiers, with supplementary assistance from local militia companies. New York was the only colony that had an assignment of British troops throughout the time of their royal rule up to 1763. The men, though, were neglected and unsupervised by higher authorities and generally were inactive and ineffective. Much was left to the local militia. Any white or free black man ages fifteen to sixty had to enroll in their city, town, precinct, or manor company, providing at least a weapon and ammunition and participating in relatively infrequent training sessions.

The rules applied, of course, to Coxsackie's male population. Documentation of the extent of participation for the men of Coxsackie and southern Rensselaerswijck is sparse beyond a few muster rolls of troops. The meager evidence suggests active participation by local volunteers. For example, in 1700, "Andris Koyman" was assigned as an ensign in an Albany County foot regiment of 371 men under the command of Colonel Peter Schuyler.[40] Jan Bronck and Jan Van Loon petitioned the government in 1704 that their quit rent might be adjusted "in consideration of their services during the war."[41] No other details are known about the outcome of their plea.

In 1714, Pieter Coeymans was made an ensign for a company in the manor of Rensselaerswijck, and Jan Bronck appointed a captain and Samuel Coeymans an ensign for a company at "Katskill Coxhakki & Pathook."[42] The latter is curious. Does this mean that Samuel Coeymans was living on his patent allotment in Coxsackie? If so, he may have made his home within the confines of the modern New Baltimore and would enter the ranks of possible first residents.

There are lengthy lists of soldiers on 1715 muster rolls.[43] We see a broad representation of familiar names from Coxsackie breaking from their usual routines of farming and milling to be recorded among the valiant defenders in several militias, particularly in the Albany County companies of Henry Van Rensselaer, John Schuyler, and Jonas Douw. Numerous Conines, Coeymans, Broncks, Vanderzees, Van Bergens, Houghtalings, and Van Slykes are registered among the enlisted ranks. Also included were various Witbecks, Van Wies, Slingerlands, and Winnes, names common to the history of neighboring Coeymans.

With armed combat flaring up once again at the start of King George's War, Coxsackie's John L. Bronck was commissioned in 1740 as a captain of a company in a regiment under Colonel Sybrant G. Van Schaick. Van Schaick was a leading figure in eighteenth-century Albany County life, managing several family properties, including at Coxsackie, and rising to become Albany's mayor in 1756. He spent considerable time at the Coxsackie family homestead, calling that location his home in a 1772 will. His son, Goose, was a prominent soldier later in the colonial wars and in the American Revolution.

During the King George conflict, the third of the French and Indian Wars, the fighting hit much closer to home for the quiet farms below the city of Albany. In November 1745, French and Indian raiders attacked Saratoga, killing or capturing over a hundred settlers. A colonial force assembled once more in July of the following year in northern New York for a Canadian invasion that was short-circuited by a lack of support for the militia from British regulars.

The present danger was pervasive enough for fifty-three Coxsackie men to petition the colonial government for the right to establish their own militia unit. Among the signers of the July 14, 1747 pleading are dotted the usual array of representative Broncks, Houghtalings, Conines, and Van Slykes:

> As by all your actions since the Commencement of the present War, we are well satisfyed and convinced, that you have not only the Interest but the good and quiet of the people of our Country entirely at heart, We therefore beg leave to address you that you will be so good and speak in our behalf to his Excellcy our Govr and Commander in chief (for whom we have the greatest regard) That his Excellcy would be graciously pleased to appoint us Officers Freeholders residing in our own Ward. We take the liberty to set down the names of a few, out of which number be pleased to recommend two, the one to be second Lieutt and the other Ensign; recommend which you please, any of them will be agreable to us, and we are ready for ever to do our duty, and to obey His Excellcys Commands on all occasions, under whose Govermt we enjoy all the happiness we can expect in this troublesome and Barbarous War, and that we shall ever acknowledge this singular Favour, which if his Excellcy will please to grant will make our whole company satisfied and contented.[44]

By the fall of 1747, the colonies abandoned their defense base at Saratoga fort. Albany essentially was blockaded by the French. People scattered away from north of the city, deserting farms and villages. The effect had to be felt at Coxsackie with river-borne refugees floating south to safer territory.

The final piece of the decades-long series of conflicts came with the French and Indian War, the last of the four major colonial wars among the British, the French, and their Indian allies. As twenty-one-year-old Major George Washington fell into an unexpected and disastrous confrontation with the French in western Pennsylvania to start the hostilities, the Albany Congress of seven of the British colonies was discussing European-Indian relations and common defensive measures against the French.

The first part of the war saw a string of convincing French victories, including at New York's Fort Oswego and Fort William Henry. The colony became a focal point of military operations, particularly from Albany north to Ticonderoga. One major British success was in September 1755 at the battle for control of Lake George. The victory effectively secured a firm hold on Hudson's river valley and led to recognition of the valor of Goose Van Schaick, Coxsackie landowner Sybrant Van Schaick's son.

The nineteen-year-old Van Schaick had been appointed as a lieutenant in Captain Philip Schuyler's company of New York Provincials.[45] He later became a captain of his own company, which was present at the dreadful British defeat at Fort Carillon (Ticonderoga), an ultimately unwise attack on the impregnable defensive position of far-outnumbered French troops. At the battle, Van Schaick received a blow to his cheek from the butt end of a musket, perhaps causing a life-ending facial cancer years later.

Soon after, Van Schaick's men were among 2,100 New York soldiers at Fort Frontenac. Their victory on the northeast corner of Lake Ontario was the start of a turnabout, with British leaders hardening their resolve and committing new resources to the effort while French interest flagged in battling onward. British victories at Fort Niagara, Ticonderoga, and Oswego, the French abandonment of Crown Point, and the taking of Montreal in August 1760 led to French capitulation. The New York Provincials throughout this period moved from fort to fort with extended stays at base camps at Albany and Schenectady.

Even after relative peace came, military obligations continued for local men. The Albany County Regiment's First Battalion enrolled Philip Conine and Anthony Van Bergen on its roster in September 1762. Both men had been serving in the militia since 1757. Andries, Teunis, Johannes, and Gerrit Van Slyke turn up in a return of Captain Marten Hallenbeck's company in 1767, along with several Conines, Broncks, Van Bergens, and Houghtalings. Anthony Van Bergen and Philip Conine were serving as lieutenants while Johannes and Philip Bronck were sergeants.

A 1770 return of officers also exists for a militia foot regiment that covered the territory from the southern boundary of the manor of Rensselaerswijck to the southern limit of Albany County. In modern terms, this district stretched from the present Coeymans southern line down to Ulster County. Local men Sybrant G. Van Schaick, Marten Hallenbeck, Jacob Hallenbeck, Philip Conine, Anthony and Marten G. Van Bergen, and John L. Bronck were officers of varying rank.[46]

The maintenance of a ready military force would stand the local citizens in good stead in what remained hard, wild times. The tilling of their fields, grinding of wheat and rye, and tending of animals soon was to be interrupted again. War really was not over for long.

3

Revolution Opens the Door

Peace did not come easily or last long for the quiet farms and settlements along the Hudson. British financial woes from the French and Indian Wars resulted in a variety of taxation actions like the Stamp Act to pay off war debt and support continued military and civic functions in the colonies. These laws obviously angered many people and instigated armed resistance.

Coxsackie was near the crossroads of action. Albany remained for decades the heart of military and civil command and a constant target for the enemy. New York City was in British hands for much of the conflict. The Hudson and the rough land highways were ready paths for British and patriot troops with their animals and supply wagons. Leonard Bronk, writing in May of 1776, was amazed that "our Roads are lind with Waggons all a going up to Albany to ride provision for our Army in Canada."[1]

The Kinderhook region was a Tory stronghold just across the river. The more remote Helderberg area in rural south-central and western Albany County, and even the Catskills and their rugged foothills, were an attractive refuge for Tory agents, spies, and deserters. The pervasive threat of enemy intrusion created a palpable and constant atmosphere of stress for settlers and a need for military readiness. With the British on the march, the local citizenry was being called once again to serve in the face of an advancing enemy to protect families, farms, and mills.

Even before actual combat began, the colonial government authorized the formation of committees that would serve as local vehicles for opposing British rule. In New York, the Committee of Safety, Protection, and Correspondence, and its successor Commissioners for Detecting and Defeating Conspiracies, became the most important civil authority, including over operations in the Coxsackie District.

Local committees also were created to serve as conduits for tackling the orders and actions of government and military leaders. An April 11, 1775 letter from Samuel Van Vechten to Leonard Bronk indicates Coxsackie's participation in the quasi-governmental system. In speaking about the need to delay citizens' signing of a general provincial loyalty oath, Van Vechten suggests that "it would be best to Delay that till our New Committee was in force."[2]

As the British-American discord gained momentum, the committees became the wartime government structures for the colony, county, and district. Committee members at all levels had the general power to secure law and order for their assigned area, including apprehending and imprisoning loyalists and watching for enemy incursions from the Catskills and the Hudson. The members also were the coordinators for collecting assessments on residents for money, livestock, grains, clothing, and other supplies and goods ordered for the troops.

After a few preliminary meetings in early 1775 attended largely by Albany City representatives, the county committee expanded its horizons at a May session. A number of people were appointed to its ranks, including the newly designated "Cocksakie and Katskill" contingent of Hendrick Van Bergen, Philip Conine, James Barker, Mathias Van Loon, and Henry Oothout.[3] John Barclay played a continuing important role in the workings of the Albany County Committee, the same Barclay who owned much of the hamlet of New Baltimore through his marriage into the Coeymans family.

As the season progressed with the rides of Paul Revere and William Dawes, confrontations at Lexington and Concord, and the patriots' Ticonderoga triumph led by Ethan Allen and Benedict Arnold, one or more Coxsackie members regularly began to attend the committee meetings. The recorded minutes give brief insights into the contributions of the Coxsackie group to the countywide body as well as actions taken locally. For example, in late June of 1775, Coxsackie representative James Barker presented a list of local residents who had declined to sign the district's "association." A key vote occurred in July the next year on the disposition of gunpowder from the Albany City magazine. Coxsackie was among a plurality of districts supporting distribution of the stockpile of ammunition.[4]

One important early committee function was to serve as a vehicle for the newly convened New York Provincial Congress to distribute a "general association." This was a statement of loyalty and commitment that localities would have residents sign as willing supporters for pursuing freedom from the British. Well over two hundred Coxsackie men affixed names to their version of the oath, what has been called the "Coxsackie Declaration," affirming that the signers:

> Do in the most solemn Manner, resolve never to become Slaves; and do associate under all The Ties of Religion, Honour, and Love to our Country, to adopt and endeavor To carry into Execution, whatever Measures may be rendered by the Continental Congress, or resolved upon by our Provincial Convention for the purpose of preserving our Constitution, and opposing the Execution of several arbitrary and oppressive Acts of the British parliament, untill a Reconciliation between Great Britain and America, on constitutional principles, (which we most ardently desire) can be obtained . . .[5]

As expected, many of the signatures are from the most prominent citizens of the era, including James Barker, Henry and Anthony Van Bergen, John L. Bronck, Samuel Van Vechten, Peter Conine, and Thomas Houghtaling. The "Declaration" is noteworthy because it may be the only original of its type in existence, preserved at the Albany Institute of History and Art in New York's capital city.

Military Service

As spring progressed and summer arrived in 1775, the Provincial Congress was establishing its own regular military force as part of the national Continental Line under the overall command of General George Washington. The Albany County Committee passed a resolution to give renewed energy to a militia system that had existed in the colony for many years as a local defense mechanism. A third type of military unit also was organized, the levies, which entailed the periodic call of militia members or units to more formal service as a supplement to the Continental Line.

The New York Continental Line of four regiments was part of the Army's Northern Department commanded by Albany's Major General

Philip Schuyler. The Second Regiment's domain stretched from well north of the city of Albany down through Coxsackie and Catskill. Colonel Goose Van Schaick was the commander. An Albany resident, Van Schaick now owned the extensive homestead in Coxsackie that his father, Sybrant, had established. He apparently never lived there, leaving the workings of the compound to relatives.

In the spring of 1775, Anthony Van Bergen was busy tending his homestead on the north side of the Coxsackie Creek near the King's Highway. It was common for militia units to be commanded by notable local citizens, with regimental and brigade officers commissioned by the Provincial Congress. Anthony was an obvious choice to be drafted into a leadership role by his admiring neighbors in Coxsackie District. He responded affirmatively to the nomination, becoming colonel of the eleventh of eighteen regiments organized for Albany County.

The manor of Rensselaerswijck, which still existed as a jurisdiction of Albany County and included the Coeymans area, also had several militia units. Its rosters are dotted with Coeymans' descendants, including Verplancks, Vanderzees, and Whitbecks, some of whom may have owned property in New Baltimore.

Anthony was joined in the Coxsackie unit's leadership by, among others, his brother Henry and John L. Bronck. The final ledger of officers came after a spirited dispute with members of the neighboring Great Imboght committee with whom the Coxsackie men had joint responsibility for appointing people as officers. Eventually, at least a couple hundred men served in the local militia, in addition to the recruits who joined regular Continental army units.

Anthony and his men were called upon numerous times over the next few years. Their service included both duty on battlefronts outside of Coxsackie and frequent treks in and near the district to ferret out an array of disaffected parties, deserters, and Tory-inclined interlopers.

The Battle Heats Up

Fearful of the British presence in Canada in early summer 1775, the Continental Congress ordered Philip Schuyler and his Northern Department troops to invade Canada as a preventative move. This campaign evolved into the prominent but failed late December attack on Quebec commanded by General Richard Montgomery and the still venerated patriot Benedict Arnold. Over several months, Arnold's men were forced into an extended retreat to Montreal and various intervening points, ending up in the Lake Champlain region.

The Arnold retreat from Canada was chronicled by Coxsackie's Philip Conine Jr. in a May 1776 letter to Leonard Bronk. Conine now was a captain in Lieutenant Colonel Marinus Willett's levy regiment at Ticonderoga. Arnold's men were pursued during the spring through the Cedars, a Canadian post near Montreal. The captain also talks about the failing attempt by the Continental troops to secure the fortifications on the Richelieu River south of Montreal, including at Chambly or "Shembow." The Richelieu was the gateway to Lake Champlain and the south. Major General John Thomas and General John Sullivan are mentioned as seeking to help the escape effort. Conine wrote about "some Sad News from Canada":

> which we hear from there are Entirely Cut of [off] and taken prisoners afterward the [they] sent a major to Assist them with a Number of men Not knowing that the Regiment was Cut off and the [they] are also taken and kilt By the Regulars and Indians, we further hear that General Arnold is gone up there I suppose you have heard what price General Arnold has took from the Tories what the [they] designed to send to the Regulars there at the Ceders which is as we hear One Hundred and twenty six Barrels of Rum, and a great many Other things and some powder and Bawls which I Cant give an Exact Number of our army has possession yet of the point shembow which is forty miles on this side of Queback and we are In hopes that we shall keep a stand there which was thought impossible by the most of Gentlemen the [they] have made all the Fortifications that Ever the [they] could at the River St. CI. But we hear that General Thomas is gone Down to the point shambow again with Chief of the army to fortify that place General Sullivan Saild from here yesterday with his Brigade for Montreal . . .[6]

In June and July, the war also began to close in a little from the south for Coxsackie's farmers. General William Howe and his brother Admiral Lord Richard Howe sailed into New York harbor with a massive British war fleet that encompassed 30 battleships filled with 1,200 cannons, 30,000 soldiers, and 10,000 sailors, along with 300 supply ships. Following a brief journey up the Hudson by some of the flotilla bent on intimidating the natives, a series of battles began in and around New York City, leading General Washington to evacuate his forces to New Jersey. New York remained in British hands for the rest of the war, blocking trade on the Hudson.

American commanders also feared that the British could muster an invasion from the Canadian side of the border. In response to the northern and southern threats, the Albany County Committee decreed that district committees and local military commanders should muster troops to serve in both Canada and New York. Men were sent to both locations, with the Canadian contingent on the way to a posting at Stillwater. The plan for the Albany region, including Coxsackie, was for seventy-five troops to go to Canada and twenty-five to go to Ulster County. Districts also were required to provide a designated amount of money to raise and equip the requisite number of men. In the case of Albany, Coxsackie, and a handful of other communities, a total of $412 was due.[7]

In the meantime, Ticonderoga became a northern defensive front for the troops, in hopes of stemming the feared invasion by British reinforcements. Among the men stationed there were Captain Samuel Van Vechten and his company from Coxsackie District. Van Vechten supervised repairs to the damaged Fort Ticonderoga and built new fortifications nearby. The Van Vechten contingent soon was transferred to Skenesboro, present-day Whitehall.

Benedict Arnold also eventually ended up at Skenesboro. His charge there was to have his men build bateaux, the prime military vessel of that era, to be used in defending Lake Champlain. Many people believe that the small fleet resulting from this venture marked the birth of the American navy.

In a late September mailing from Skenesboro to Leonard Bronk, though, Samuel Van Vechten decried the pitiable camp conditions and seemingly intractable physical maladies facing the valiant troops:

> You will best be able to judge. I have this month Past been very much Troubld with the Fevour Ego [ague] every other Day which hes made me very week & Poor: it is the unwholesomet Place that Ever was known in this World their hes scarcely been a Men on this Ground for Two or three weeks but what hes head that Disagreeable Distemper or something worse But thank God I have got the Better of it for I have not head it these 4 Days last past & hope it may not lay hould of me again . . .[8]

Unfortunately, the local men's efforts were to little avail in an immediate military sense. Starting on October 11, an inexperienced patriot navy became engaged in a pitched battle on Lake Champlain and proved to be little match for the veteran British sailors, suffering a crushing defeat over a few days. However, their valiant effort, the strengthened fortress at Ticonderoga, and oncoming winter weather helped delay any further British threat, at least in the north. The battles continued down near New York City, with American defeats at White Plains, Fort Washington, and Fort Lee taking an exacting toll on the patriot forces.

In a more positive vein, at the turn of the year 1776, the Continental Congress ordered troops to march in the Mohawk Valley against enemy forces led by the infamous Tory leader, Sir John Johnson. Johnson and his men were believed to be mobilizing for attack, possibly all the way to the communities on the Hudson. The Americans assigned to the task included Samuel Van Vechten's company from Van Bergen's 11th Regiment. The local men trudged on foot and horseback over the near seventy-mile expedition from Coxsackie to Johnstown to join the main force.

The Van Vechten unit included Leonard Bronk, his cousins Richard and Ephraim, and other men with a litany of familiar names like Van Schaick, Conine, Brandow, Van Den Bergh, and Tryon. The operation resulted in the capture of Johnson and his Tory and Indian troops and reduced the immediate threat of any attacks on the Coxsackie District and surrounding locations.

As summer ended, the tensions back home were growing. Dissidents were at least imagined behind every tree around Coxsackie and the rest of Albany County. The Albany Committee, recognizing the need to placate concerns and ensure the safekeeping of local residents, detailed the Ranger company of Captain Alexander Baldwin "to march to such place of the District of Coxsackie as he shall conceive necessary to apprehend and secure such Persons in and about that District as are turbulent and Dangerous to Safety of the good People of that District and have concealed themselves in the Woods and are sculking about armed to the great Terror of the Inhabitants."[9] Colonel Van Bergen's local militia was ordered to provide whatever assistance the Baldwin men might need.

Apparently, the presence of the troops did not meet everyone's complete satisfaction. Coenradt Houghtaling went before the Albany Committee to complain about the Baldwin contingent. The visitors had "taken from him two Gammons, two Sides of Pork and forty odd Fowls, and that they had drove and made his Wife cook it for them, some of them paid what they pleased for it, and others not." Fortunately for Coenradt, the committee would accept an accounting of his losses if presented to the chairman.[10] This Coenradt undoubtedly was the great-grandson of Mathys, the original Houghtaling Patent holder. He married Saartje or Sara, the granddaughter of Teunis and Jannetje Van Slyke, New Baltimore's traditional first residents.

Despite the coming of a relatively peaceful fall season north of Albany, the American military leadership retained an enhanced sense of awareness about potential British movements. As a result, the New York administration ordered the Albany County militia, including part of Van Bergen's 11th Regiment, to Fort Edward as a supplemental defense force on that northern frontier. Following orders from Albany, which feared Tory action in Coxsackie, the colonel was to leave half the regiment at home. Those remaining behind were to keep a strict guard of the nearby woods for malcontents.

The Van Bergen troops must not have traveled far. Recognizing the threat to the rural settlements to their immediate south, the Albany Committee directed the Coxsackie militia to return home, to be joined by men from two other units, just two days after the initial orders. The soldiers were to "apprehend and take such Persons as they find in Arms, or suspect to be Enemies to this State, and keep them in safe Custody till farther orders . . ."[11]

The year ended quietly in the Hudson Valley. The British had a firm grip on New York City and focused their attention on raids into Connecticut and Rhode Island. Washington's men still were battling in Pennsylvania and New Jersey, with welcome victories at Trenton and Princeton. The Coxsackians steeled themselves for winter.

1777: The Tide Turns

As the new year arrived, the British were plotting a major push to capture the Hudson-Champlain and Mohawk valleys, ostensibly to split New England from the rest of the colonies and deflate the patriot cause. General John Burgoyne's 8,000-man force started marching south from Montreal toward Albany. Barry St. Leger was to bring his troops down from Oswego across the Mohawk Valley to meet Burgoyne. The army of William Howe was to sail up the Hudson River. Their hope was the ultimate meeting of the three arms of attack at Albany, which would form a crushing blow to the American union.

By end of June, Philip Conine Jr., still with the levies of Marinus Willet, was stationed at Fort Schuyler (formerly and later known as Fort

Stanwix), a bastion against the St. Leger force. He wrote to Leonard Bronk, reporting that "a Private soldier was Barborously killed by the Indians & a Captain shot threw the Body & Schulped" and was near death.[12] Shortly thereafter, the American general Arthur St. Clair surrendered the critical defense position at Ticonderoga to the British legions coming from Canada.

The enemy took an ultimately awkward and perhaps fatal step toward the end of July. Rather than sailing up the Hudson, the British commander, General William Howe, and his 15,000-man force set off from New York City to the Chesapeake Bay, aiming to capture Philadelphia, the American capital. This move soon served to leave Burgoyne and St. Leger in the lurch. Their rendezvous was neutralized as the trend of battle began to favor the revolutionaries.

From his Mohawk Valley post, Conine wrote again to Bronk in July, filling him in on efforts to repel St. Leger's advancing forces. In the next moment, he was:

> going Down to Onida Lake on a Scout and on our Return are to stop up the Passage of Wood Creek. Capt. Bleeker comands our Party which thus consist of fifty Continental Troops & Sixty Malitia. I hope no bad News Shall be heard from this Quarter our men are in high Spirits & dont make any doubt if the Enemy thus appear but what you shall hear the [they] shall meet with a Drubbing . . .[13]

In closing, Conine informs Bronk that, as he writes, an alarm has sounded, and some of the men were firing on a group of marauding Indians.

St. Leger soon laid siege to the fort. Militia units under General Nicholas Herkimer sought to aid the trapped Americans but were waylaid by the enemy at the Battle of Oriskany. With supply shortages and lost support from their Indian compatriots, the British were easily susceptible to a rescue effort. Benedict Arnold, with a small contingent of troops, managed to deceive the enemy into thinking a much larger force was on the way. St. Leger abandoned his post and retreated to Canada.

In the meantime, to counter the Burgoyne push from the north, rebel troops were ordered north up the Hudson. Part of Anthony Van Bergen's Coxsackie Regiment was posted first to Lake George, then quickly to Fort Ann and Fort Edward, then to Stillwater as the British took Ticonderoga and marched relentlessly southward. For their few-weeks stay at the forts, the men were assigned routine patrol duty to guard the fortifications.

At Stillwater, Van Bergen's men were reunited with their fellow Coxsackians from Van Vechten's company. As Burgoyne traveled down from Canada, these men lay right in his path. Their mere presence slowed the Britons' progress, which also were faced with dwindling supplies. One of Van Vechten's men, Corporal Andrew Dunlap, a Coxsackian, wrote to Leonard Bronk about their ongoing attempt to fortify the area and the anticipation that they "Expect every Minute that we Shall have a General Engagement as the Enemy is advancing Toward us."[14]

He was right. Three days later, the Van Bergen and Van Vechten men and their cohorts faced a massed British force 4,200 men strong. A pitched battle ensued over the next few hours during the first Battle of Saratoga. Action ebbed and flowed as each side took the attack. The fighting came to an inconclusive end as darkness fell, with the British holding favorable territory but sustaining double the Americans' casualties.

The sides recouped over the next couple of weeks until meeting again in combat at Bemis Heights, the second Battle of Saratoga. By now, the American force was up to well over 10,000 soldiers. The British were starting to lack sufficient numbers of men and supplies. In fiery advances, the Americans gained an authoritative edge over the overwhelmed British detail, which dispiritedly retreated. Over the next few days, the patriots gained strength with an increased army of 13,000, far outnumbering the Burgoyne contingent of fewer than 6,000 men.

The American commander, Horatio Gates, continued to apply aggressive pressure until Burgoyne was cornered. With no recourse, the British leader called for an end to the fighting. Coxsackie men were present at Burgoyne's momentous October 17, 1777 surrender to General Gates and the Americans. These Saratoga battles live on as the turning point of the war. It was a rousing victory for the revolutionaries and motivated French participation on their side, a critical alliance for future military progress.

Down the Hudson, Henry Clinton had been left in command at New York City with an army depleted by the Howe foray to Pennsylvania. As the British campaign crumbled, Clinton ordered a 3,000-man force upriver to divert patriot troops from the northern battlefield. This action prompted a general alarm.

Two days before the Saratoga surrender, the New York City reinforcements were anchored at Kingston, the seat of New York's revolutionary government and the place where the State's Constitution was born in April 1777. Highly motivated by this inviting target, the British proceeded to burn much of the place to the ground and, soon after, did the same to Livingston Manor across the Hudson.

At Albany and Coxsackie, panic set in. The burnings of Kingston and the manor were just too close and posed a more imminent threat to the locals. Richard Bronk rode from Coxsackie to Albany to relay the news of the British advance, an action for which he later received reimbursement of two pounds. Orders came for the residents to take every precaution to protect their livestock and other property, preparing for evacuation inland to the western wilderness. Local troops, probably including the now-returned Van Bergen company, were to assemble near the Hudson for ready transport. Cattle were to be driven away from the river to avoid enemy confiscation. Any available grain was to be shipped to Albany.[15]

Governor George Clinton believed that the British would not proceed after Burgoyne's Saratoga surrender. Indeed, in short order, Howe commanded Henry Clinton to abandon the Hudson campaign and redeploy the troops to Philadelphia. This was the end of strong threats to the Coxsackie area from the main Tory forces although guerrilla-type activities continued to be an ongoing concern, keeping local troops occupied. The British stayed in New York City from then on, leaving upriver to the Americans, who now controlled all the way to Canada.

Combing the Woods—Continuing Tory and Indian Threats—Frontier Duty

As 1778 came, the primary battlefields for the American regular army shifted south. Some local soldiers like Coxsackie's Andrew Dunlap and Tunis Van Waganen were on active duty with the Continental Line at Valley Forge. Three local men joined the forces protecting the Hudson Highlands. Peter Van Bergen, Ephraim Bronck, and Ephraim Bogardus were posted for a three-month tour at Fort Constitution across the Hudson from West Point.

Times were not good for the steadfast settlers and farmers out on the frontier of western Albany County and the fertile flatlands of the Mohawk, Schoharie, and Cherry valleys. They were a prime target for British raiders and their Indian allies. Some of Anthony Van Bergen's men were targeted for service out in the Mohawk Valley in the middle of June. The orders came from General Abraham Ten Broeck that "The depredations lately Committed by the Enemy to the Westward and in Tryon County and the Apprehensions of farther Incursions on the Inhabitants in those parts, it is become necessary that a Body of Militia of my

Brigade be Embodied for the protection and defence of our Brethren in those parts . . ."[16]

Real and rumored enemy incursions at home also had continued, demonstrating the need for frequent surveillance and pursuit tasks for the local military men and troops imported from further away. In May, Captain John Ryley and a fifteen-man force under the general command of Colonel Van Bergen were charged with patrolling the Kinderhook and Coxsackie areas. The practice of detaching militia or ranger units for such purposes was common. The troops spent considerable hours tracking real and imagined spies, deserters, and provocateurs, apprehending Tory-inspired thieves and Hessian deserters, trying to restore an ongoing sense of order to life. A month later, the Ryley men traveled by bateaux down the Hudson to Coeymans and from there trekked inland to investigate a complaint that a number of men were suspected of having gone over to the enemy's side.[17]

In another event in June, an enemy courier named Johannes Riemer was en route from New York to deliver papers to Tory officials. Albany authorities believed he was staying at the home of Albert Van Der Zee in Onesquethaw, one of those places in the shadows of the Helderbergs that was a hotbed of British sympathizers. This person may have been the cousin of the New Baltimore Albert and Cornelis. The Onesquethaw Albert was ordered before the board at Albany. In this instance, he came up to the commissioners' measure, responding satisfactorily to their queries and was released.

The Albany Commissioners relayed orders to both Colonel Van Bergen and Philip Conine toward the end of June to organize a party of troopers. They were to capture the enemy agent Riemer and bring him and whatever papers he held to Albany for interrogation and review. At this point, Riemer may have eluded the patriots' net.[18] The commissioners' minutes are quiet as to the rascal's fate but his wife later was ordered to be banished from the state.

The British and Indian leaders were focusing on putting a dent in the rich farming area west of Coxsackie that has been called the bread-basket of the Revolution for the Americans. Throughout the latter part of 1778, the Tories and their Indian compatriots carried out numerous bloody and fiery raids on the western frontiers, ransacking settlements, destroying crops, and confiscating livestock. In May, Cobleskill was put to the torch. In June, Springfield by Otsego Lake went up in flames. Residents at Andrustown near German Flats were massacred, and their settlement destroyed. Unadilla was next in the line of fire in October. Then, in November, 700 enemy soldiers attacked the small community of

Cherry Valley, killing or capturing dozens of civilians, including women and children.

During this progression of assaults, Governor Clinton ordered General Ten Broeck's Brigade into action. A quarter of each regiment was called into service, including Van Bergen's unit, as support. By September, sixteen of Van Bergen's men had been posted to Schoharie. Leonard Gansevoort Jr. of Albany reported to his cousin, Leonard Bronk, on the danger into which the Coxsackians had stepped: "We have nothing new at this Time but that two Men have been scalped at Fort Schuyler and three taken Prisoner at Cherry Valley by the Indians."[19]

In 1779, while the Americans designated General John Sullivan to lead a major offensive against the Indians who had posed a continuous threat to western frontier settlements, the local troops continued to patrol the nearby woods and fields. Van Bergen's men found themselves detached for duty around Schoharie, Johnstown, and other points west with little to show for their efforts. Calm generally prevailed.

Under the new state's laws, local men between the ages of fifty and fifty-five could petition the governor to organize a militia unit. On April 6, 1779, Coxsackie men exempt from military service organized a volunteer militia company that would be called for service only in cases of enemy invasion or "insurrections." John Bronk, Peter Conine, and Martin Van Bergen were among the group. James Barker was chosen to be the unit's captain. While undoubtedly providing steadfast moral support and dedication to the protection of the home front, it appears unlikely that the senior volunteers came under much, if any, enemy fire.

1780–1781 Home Front Tension

Frequent rumors and hearsay circulated among local and military listeners about unwanted Indian and Tory visitors. This is understandable since the enemy posed a continuing threat from the Schoharie and Mohawk valleys that were relatively close and easily accessible to Coxsackie. New levies were organized to defend New York's western frontiers. Colonel Anthony Van Bergen was called upon once again to furnish men for the effort. By June, a number of Van Bergen's men were stationed at Schoharie under the command of Isaac Bogart.[20] Another contingent quickly was shipped off to Fishkill.

Little did the Coxsackie settlers realize how close they were to a perilous menace to the viability of the whole revolutionary effort. On August 3, 1780, Benedict Arnold was appointed commander at West Point.

It was only a short six weeks before the capture of John Andre and the flight of Arnold as an exposed traitor down the Hudson to British refuge.

An Indian and Tory invasion into the Schoharie area and movement eastward remained dangerously plausible. Governor George Clinton wrote to Colonel Van Bergen August 10, 1780 about the imminent threat:

> that the Enemy may detach small Parties to your Settlements as well with a view of destroying them as to prevent your giving succour to your Neighbours. I have, therefore, thought it necessary to communicate the above Intelligence & to recommend to you immediately & without the least Delay to call out & station your Regiment on the passes [in the Catskill Mountains] leading to your Quarter until the further movements of the Enemy shall render it necessary.[21]

The area of Albany County in the shadow of the Helderberg Mountains also continued to be a flash point for Tories and their supporters, particularly in the hilly section at the bottom of the modern town of New Scotland. That was close enough to cause concern for the people at Coxsackie. Colonel Van Bergen sent a scouting contingent west in August of 1780 to seek out enemy representatives. The two-man expedition rooted out a suspected spy named John Sheerman and detained him for an appearance before the Albany court.[22]

The threat on the western frontiers remained active into the fall. Enemy forces under Sir John Johnson, Joseph Brant, and Walter Butler again were marauding in the Mohawk Valley. Patriot troops carried out frequent raids into the Schoharie Valley, with one unfounded warning that a party of 150 enemy warriors was headed to Catskill.[23] Additional levies from the Van Bergen company were called up in late November to answer concerns of Albany authorities.

Troubles continued into early April of 1781. The Tories and their Indian partners plundered the Catskill Creek estate of prominent settler David Abeel and abducted him, his son Anthony, and two slaves. In response, George Clinton mobilized troops from Coxsackie, Catskill, Schoharie, and Albany to the furthest reaches of Coxsackie District and into the Helderbergs and the Mohawk Valley to apprehend anyone they could find of dubious character. The campaign appears to have been relatively successful. Throughout this period, the minutes of the Commissioners for Conspiracies have a number of entries concerning the disposition of prisoners and people suspected of consorting with the British.

As part of the military maneuvers, Captains Philip Conine and Benjamin Dubois of Van Bergen's regiment were detailed to Catskill and Schoharie, respectively. The men were assigned to keep regular watch on trails. In Conine's case, this meant duty at a post at "South Cairo Great Plain." Lieutenants Peter Van Bergen and Isaac Van Valkenburgh were assigned in support of Conine.[24]

In late May 1781, Captain Conine wrote from his Cairo post to Leonard Bronk about his unit's scouting endeavors, lamenting that "the Inhabitants of this District are so neglectfull in Sending Provisions for there [their] men." He was hoping for support from Coxsackie. "Lieut. Van Bergen is this morning gone to Livingstons manor in order to receive some men at that place, how they will be furnished With provision I do not yet know I Every minute Expect Lieut. Van Valkenburgh in from a Scout that has been to Schoharry Kill and Betawvia or at Least the time they should return is to Day. I have Constant Scouts out but have not made no Discoveries as yet."[25]

The distressing times were luckily beginning to peter out for the war-weary New Yorkers. Tales of actual battle were at an end. In the middle of October, the British General Charles Cornwallis reached a breaking point after a disheartening siege of his troops at Yorktown, Virginia. He surrendered to the patriots' leaders, ending significant conflict in North America. A couple of weeks later, Leonard Gansevoort wrote once again to Leonard Bronk, congratulating him "on the great and glorious news of the surrender of Cornwallis. Yesterday we testified our Joy with the firing of Cannon, Ringing of Bells & drinking and eating plentifully."[26]

The Pension Evidence: Personal Stories

In June of 1832, the United States Congress enacted the last and what turned out to be the most liberal of the service-pension acts benefiting Revolutionary War veterans. The legislation allowed every officer or enlisted man who had served at least two years in the Continental Line or state troops to be eligible for a full-pay, lifetime pension. Veterans who had served from six months to two years could gain lesser remuneration. The law did not require applicants to demonstrate need.

The pension applications from local men provide interesting and important insights into personal affairs and military duties during the war for independence. In his application, Peter Brandow of the Coxsackie District gives a rare look at the typical routine of the troops on these duty tours. At various times, he was a soldier in companies commanded by Samuel Van Vechten, Philip Conine, and New Baltimore's Captain Thomas Houghtaling. Brandow served in the 1776 campaign against John Johnson but more routinely was involved in random reconnaissance patrols for the war's duration. He says that the militia:

> was divided into classes to guard a district of country extending along the North River about twenty miles, and west from the said river about thirty or forty miles—that the said classes were alternately called out in such a manner as to have a class out constantly and thus have a guard on duty every day & night—That the company remained thus classed and did duty for a number of successive seasons from the Spring until fall in each year . . . he was called out and did duty generally twice a week, sometimes once & occasionally once a fortnight. . . . That he was also called out on alarms, on special occasions, and on scouting parties.[27]

Ephraim Bronk of New Baltimore appeared before the Greene County Court of Common Pleas in early September of 1832 to plead his case for a federal pension. One of the witnesses signing the narrative of the proceedings considering Ephraim's application was prominent New Baltimore landowner Teunis P. Van Slyke.

After providing the date of his Coxsackie birth, March 1, 1756, Bronk went on to describe his moving to New Baltimore about the age of twenty to become a farmer, just as war was about to break out. In his detailed report, he talks about being a private in 1775 in a militia company commanded by Captain Thomas Houghtaling, part of Colonel Anthony Van Bergen's regiment. Lieutenant Henry Van Bergen and Ensign Ryckert Vandenberg also were officers. All the higher-ranked individuals had lived in Coxsackie and were now dead.

Bronk's company "received orders to be in readiness for actual service against the enemies of the country at a moment's warning, that they were then called minute men and were exercised and drilled almost every week." That effort was rewarded by the winter of 1776 when Bronk, John Van Schaack, Richard and Leonard Bronk, Philip Conine Jr., Ryckert Vandenberg, and other volunteers marched under the command of General Schuyler against the Tory forces of Sir John Johnson at Johnstown. Bronk, in commenting on his fourteen days of service in Montgomery County, registered a sense of accomplishment at being present for Johnson's surrender.

Ephraim's travels continued. He soon was posted twice to forts erected by the Americans in the Schoharie Valley. Both those sojourns lasted about fourteen days apiece, with Bronk serving on the first occasion under Captain Thomas Houghtaling and Lieutenant Henry Van Bergen. He soon volunteered again to travel off to a "place called Shingle Kill" in what became the town of Cairo "to defend the country against an expected attack from the tories and indians." John Witbeck of Catskill then was his captain.

In what Bronk believed was the summer and fall of 1776, he was stationed at Fort Constitution "in the highlands directly opposite West Point." His company had been ordered to provide two men to serve down the Hudson. Bronk and Ephraim Bogardus were the stalwart volunteers who made the journey.

Likely in the summer of 1777, Bronk was ordered for duty at Fort Edward and then on to Lake George for a total of about three weeks, returning "home shortly before the surrender of Ticonderoga." Back in Coxsackie, he claims almost continuous service "guarding the country against the Tories." Among possible other spots, Bronk had patrol duty out in Schoharie and at Loonenburg, in the modern town of Athens. Led by Captain Myndert Van Schaick of Coxsackie, Ephraim served between five and six weeks not too far south of home.

At that point in his narrative, Ephraim announces perhaps his most famous moment. He was not home for too long before moving out once again. This time, he was to "join the army against Burgoyne." He did not get to his Stillwater post until the first battle had been fought against the renowned British commander. While we do not know the details of his subsequent situation, "he remained there doing duty until after the surrender of Burgoyne to General Gates." Most notably, Bronk "was present at the surrender," spending in all thirty days on duty.

Other than these specific notations, Bronk maintains that from 1775 to the end of the war, he was "bound to military service" and "in constant readiness to do active duty at all times." He and his fellow troops were ordered to make frequent forays "in the adjoining wilderness and country, sometimes under one officer and sometimes another." These calls to alarms could last for a day or two or a week or more, depending upon circumstances, and happened every week for an extended period.

Under a general summary in his application statement, Coxsackie's John Van Schaack, a Bronk compatriot, advises "that the adjacent country was then almost an uninterrupted wilderness to the Canadas, infested with tories and Indians who were continually making depredations upon the property of the inhabitants friendly to the American cause and frequently murdered and robbed those inhabitants."[28]

The local militia men often had more routine assignments. In his pension materials, New Baltimore's Teunis P. Van Slyke, who in 1832 was sixty-nine to seventy years old, states that he "furnished himself with arms and ammunition." He and others then were "exercised and drilled" and "in the years 1779, 1780, 1781 appointed to guard a district of country on the west side of the north river extending for a considerable distance north and south & about thirty miles east & west." The men took turns on their scouting parties so a "constant guard was kept on foot. . . . The guard was kept on duty from the early part of spring in each year until sometime in the latter part of the fall." Depending upon the calling of an alarm, the service could encompass patrolling during daylight or at night and might be as often as once or twice a week or infrequent as "once a fortnight."[29]

Close Encounters: The Loyalists

Not everyone in Coxsackie may have been cast in the same clearly rebellious mode as Anthony Van Bergen, the Broncks, or Samuel Van Vechten. As we have seen, a constant threat was posed throughout the Revolutionary period by the activities of Loyalist sympathizers and people in the gray areas of noncommitment to the rebel cause. Support for revolution was not universal among Americans. One general theme is that the population was split with a third rebellious, a third committed to the crown, and a third minding their own business (or at least hoping to). So it was not uncommon for families to be divided by the war. Philip Conine's son Leonard was listed in 1780 for having "gone of [off] to and joined the Enemy."[30]

Around the turn of the year 1776, there is record of complaint before the Albany County Committee of Correspondence against William Rea, a merchant from the Coxsackie District. Over the years, Rea and his wife Maria Wells had acquired a substantial plot of land along the Hudson on the modern New Baltimore-Coxsackie border. Rea had been a regular, active member of the local militia for a number of years before the Revolution and even signed the 1775 Coxsackie Declaration. For unknown reasons, he became disenchanted with the cause.

Mr. Rea was accused of "speaking contemptuously and Casting severe Reflections on the Congress's & Committee's." After a period of confinement over the summer, Rea, along with several other Coxsackie men, subsequently signed a "New Association," paid a fine, and had their charges dismissed.[31]

William's troubles hardly were over. In early March 1777, he was among a group of "mutineers" who had "quit their work" and "took up Clubs & threatened others if they did not . . ."[32] He again was called on the carpet in July the following year regarding his loose interpretation of the new state law targeting people who were holding a neutral or equivocal position about the patriots' cause.

Rea and a handful of others were presented with an opportunity to take a loyalty oath but begged more time to consider their options. The Albany justice system granted them a brief interlude for thought, with an order to reappear. Regrettably, the recalcitrant group deferred their decision, and the government instigated the process to banish them to enemy territory.

By the first of August, the commissioners were ordering that Rea and the other transgressors report in two weeks to the Albany County Court House with fourteen days of provisions, clothing, and other personal items and whichever family members were to accompany them to banishment. "The Charges of Transportation to the Enemies Lines is to be defrayed by themselves." [33]

Rea disappears from the commissioners' minutes for an extended period. He may have spent the duration of the war in British New York City. In early 1783, a lengthy list was published of suspicious characters that had "been removed within the Enemy's Lines or detained by his Excellency the Governor for Exchange." Rea was among their number and not designated, as some were, of having hidden from capture.[34]

In 1784, the Whigs in government pushed hard to allow a certain number of exiles to return. As a result, the state legislature passed a bill for leniency for nearly thirty people to come back to their place of residence. William was among the chosen few.

Rea never had his land confiscated as did many convicted Tories and later led an apparently normal life. In 1785, Coxsackie supervisor Leonard Bronk and justices of the peace Philip Conine and Hezekiah Van Order granted William a preliminary license to resume his career as a merchant.[35] His children and grandchildren married into well-known families, including the Conines, Broncks, and Vandenbergs.

In another loyalty-versus-family case, nineteen-year-old Elizabeth Waltermire married John Garrett in the summer of 1766 at Rhinebeck, Dutchess County. Her sister Barbara married John Coonley. By the end of the 1770s, the Garretts and Coonleys were living in the New Baltimore part of Coxsackie District. Nearby was John's brother Simeon, who, perhaps in some good fortune, did not marry a Waltermire. All seemed fine and life went on until the Revolution. That is when the ladies' brother, Johannes, came to visit.

Johannes Waltermire also was known as Hans Waltermire, John Walden Meyers, and other variations thereof. In 1777, he joined the British army and recruited Loyalist forces. He also became the scourge of Albany County and other locations, serving as a frequent and uncatchable agent for the British and carrier of enemy dispatches. Most famously, in 1781, Hans led a spectacular, if unsuccessful, raid on the house of General Philip Schuyler, a featured topic for the tourists visiting that still-standing building in Albany.

In late 1780, John Garrett and John Coonley were called by Albany County's Commission for Detecting and Defeating Conspiracies for some transgression that is not specified in the corresponding minutes. An educated guess could be made about the charge. Brother-in-law Hans was in the neighborhood, and the authorities may have suspected some interaction among the men. Coonley was jailed and ordered before the commissioners to defend himself, only to be recommitted.

By this time, the two men seemed to be well-respected members of the community. Their bails were paid by Richard Bronck and Cornelius Conine, members of two of Coxsackie's most prominent anti-British families. The Johns were commanded to good behavior and to report to the authorities as ordered for the rest of the conflict.

At the same time, Simeon was victimized by accusations to the commissioners that he, while now living on Hans's former farm, was having "frequent Intercourse with the said Waltymier and harbours him when on his way through the Country." Simeon was discharged because of his diligence in reporting on occasion to the commissioners and paying a one hundred pound bail. Regrettably, his problems were not over.

In mid-January 1781, John Garrett and John Coonley asked that they be excused from further legal proceedings by promising to notify the commissioners about any reappearance by Hans in the future. This seems to have been a carryover from the previous event noted earlier. The board accepted their vow and discharged them.

By late spring 1781, Simeon was appearing once again before the commissioners. He said he had been imprisoned by Hans and kept captive for a period in the woods. Simeon's testimony also relayed the news that Waltermire had spent several nights in John Ver Planck's barn on Coeymans patent. Given Ver Planck's previous questionable behavior, he was brought before the commissioners where he testified he did not know that Hans was there. The commissioners accepted his excuse.[36]

Despite considerable efforts of many people from Governor George Clinton down, Hans never was captured. He later was a successful businessman and community leader in Canada. The Garretts and Coonleys became lifelong citizens of the New Baltimore area and never had any land confiscated, what should have been the ultimate penalty for people willingly consorting with the enemy. It seems just a case of having a problem relative.

Local residents also were victimized by the lawlessness and disorder that marked the war years. The Commissioners for Conspiracies met at Albany on July 6, 1781 to consider the case of Peter Van Slyke "residing near Cooksakie." Peter was one of the six sons of New Baltimore's traditional first family. His parents, Teunis and Jannetje, had transferred much of their real estate in 1741 to Peter and his brother Andries.

Peter had lodged a complaint that "a Party of Robbers headed by a certain Joseph Smith (formerly a servant of Walltimyer) did on the first Instant enter his House and steel a Number of Articles of him and that in attempting to make his Escape they fired at him and wounded him in the Arm and that they took Prisoner at his House Peter Clauw who has since made his Escape from them and is this day come to Town" to appear before the commissioners. The mentioned Van Slyck house likely was on the family homestead down along the Hudson, a site now in modern New Baltimore.

The original complaint started a chain of interviews of witnesses to the event or people who had aided and abetted Smith and his cronies in the larceny. Clauw volunteered important testimony, citing the participation of Adrian Bradt and others who lived in the Onesquethaw region just east of the Helderbergs. These individuals were called to task for harboring and consulting with Smith.

Eventually, Bradt and a number of coconspirators were judged guilty for their actions and sentenced to a range of punishments. Some of the defendants had to maintain appropriate behavior and report occasionally to the commissioners for the rest of the war or until the board released them. Some people were fined various amounts of money. The remaining culpable parties were subject to warrants for their arrest. The final disposition of the case of the main villain, Joseph Smith, however, is not noted in the commissioners' minutes.[37]

Home Front Duties

Throughout the war, the valiant warriors needed a constant supply of food, grain, clothing, blankets, arms and ammunition, horses, wagons, firewood, money, and just about any other supplies and equipment one could imagine. Without pack trains, rations, and the like, there was no army and no freedom. Local residents even could be called upon to provide food and shelter for traveling soldiers.

As ready and willing suppliers, the hard-working farming and milling men and women in the Coxsackie District were productive and valued contributors to the movement for independence from Britain. Many of the actions taken by them also illustrate that growing and harvesting crops had to continue even with the frequent absences of fighting men. As early as June 1776, there is record in the Albany Commissioners' minutes of Peter Van Ness of Loonenburgh (Athens) being paid to drive two sleighs full of lead and flint, weaponry ingredients, from his home area to Albany.[38]

In April 1779, justice of the peace Samuel Van Vechten issued a warrant for Philip Bronk and Edward Groom to collect a variety of agricultural products from Coxsackie farmers to help supply the army. Included were 20 tons of hay and 250 bushels of barley, rye, oats, Indian corn, and buckwheat. Van Vechten had urged cooperation, underscoring dire wartime shortages as "suffitient Quantity of Forage Cannot be purchased in this State for the use of the Army in the same or procured from the Naighbouring States."[39]

Local requisitions were a normal procedure when the government was unable to procure sufficient supplies from ordinary military sources. On another occasion, "with all convenient speed, duly and impartially," the "assessors" for the Coxsackie District had to cajole their neighbors into making or donating forty-five pairs of shoes and eighty-five pairs of stockings for the soldiers.[40]

The troops also needed sufficient and dependable transportation. There are several instances where Coxsackie people were asked to provide the use of their horses and wagons and the time to pilot the teams. In 1778, Commissioner Cornelius Wynkoop, then at Coeymans, wrote to Leonard Bronk for directions to obtain two horses "in best order & fittest for service." Later in the year, Albany authorities issued a warrant for horses, wagons, and teamsters to carry wood from Coeymans to Albany to build army barracks. In late spring 1779, there were at least two occasions when teams and drivers had to travel to Schenectady for about two weeks of service to move supplies into the Mohawk Valley.[41]

By 1780, Leonard Bronk had undertaken considerable responsibility for the war effort by becoming an assistant under Colonel Udny Hay, the general purchasing and payroll agent for New York. This position placed Bronk in the role of coordinating the flow of produce and livestock from the local fields, farms, and mills to the warehouses that supplied the troops. His orders from Albany could be of quite sizable nature and a considerable imposition on the local growers. For example, at one point, Leonard was ordered by Albany authorities to obtain ten tons of wheat and flour and "Twenty Thousand weight of Beef, or Fat Cattle."[42]

Not only did military requirements have to be met, but Coxsackie agriculturalists also had a degree of responsibility to friends and relatives who were in need because of wartime shortages and transportation limitations. Leonard Gansevoort's frequent missives from his Albany home to his cousin, Leonard Bronk, recall the effects of military absences and duties of the men in many households and the dependence within families for essentials like food.

Women and children must have been required quite often to undertake more than their usual responsibility in running farms when the men went off to war. In an August 1781 letter, Gansevoort, writing from Albany to Bronk, underscores the talents and indispensability of the farm women:

> As the Winter Season is approaching it becomes me like the Ants while it is Time to provide for a Supply for that barren Season, Polly says she wants Butter and reckoning you among the Number of her best Friends she has requested me to apply to you to procure it for her, your Mother is in my opinion the only Person who is likely to supply her Wants and she therefore begs you will apply to her for it I have a Butter Keg at Hanse Spoors which I would be glad you would when it is convenient send for and have it filled Polly also begs you would speak to your Mother for a Couple Pounds of Wool . . .[43]

Another interesting insight is provided into the presence and use of slaves or black servants in a colonial household when Gansevoort writes to Bronk toward the end of October 1783 that:

> Hard Times I have no Butter and am now obliged to send my Negro down to you for some . . . Polly says she wants some Vinegar if you can help her to some you will do her a Kindness, we want a great many Things for the Winter and I find a great Scarcity of those Things which are most necessary.[44]

Despite Gansevoort's concern about winter sustenance, a sense of joy must have been at hand. An earlier letter to his cousin Leonard noted an intention to travel down to a now-free New York City, an impossible venture for several years. He gleefully writes from his Albany home that "We live peaceable and happy every Thing is coming again into its old Channel. The Sloops come loaded from New York with every good and valuable article the Price of all kind of goods are low. . . . Remember me to the Old People I expect to find your Father grown at least ten years younger by the Peace and your Mother about fifteen. God bless you all."[45] The war was over.

4

New Baltimore is Born

The Revolution brought great change to Hudson's valley. The estates of manorial Tory dynasties were breaking up on the east side of the river. On the west, families of the original large land patent holders were expanding, with concomitant divisions of property and differing motivations about what they could, or must, do with their bequests. The developing senses of independence and democracy spawned a desire for personal ownership of one's farmstead, mill, shop, or tavern.

As the flames of war finally burned out, real estate became a premium commodity. A handful of local buyers undoubtedly were speculators but others—the Smiths, the Sarles, the Bedells, the Millers, the Powells, the Greens, the Wolfs, the Rundells, and the Palmers—were here to stay, some with descendants remaining on or near their adopted land up to the present day. A glance at old deeds and indentures shows that many residents bought and sold land on a regular basis, to expand their holdings, to accommodate their children, and to attract new neighbors (i.e., to make money).

From the outside, many people saw opportunities for residence, commerce, and agriculture on land once controlled by Indians, Tories, and settler families. The rich farmable acreage that soldiers and other travelers had seen or heard about during the peripatetic war years was a strong lure. Religious outsiders were looking for good farmland and more spiritual room to practice their beliefs. The Society of Friends, or Quakers, established a significant presence on the New Baltimore part of the Coeymans Patent—so much so that the area was characterized in some quarters as a "Quaker" place.

New Englanders were greatly attracted to the bounties of New York. Taxes were ranging upward in Massachusetts and Connecticut, and there also was a keen appetite in some places to escape puritanical religious constraints. An increasingly crowded Long Island opened the floodgates of emigration first into Dutchess and Westchester counties, then northward up the Hudson and eventually to many points westward.

By the start of the 1800s, New Englanders held the majority population in Albany, gaining control of city and river trade and transportation, and political and social institutions, much to the chagrin of the now outnumbered and outmaneuvered remnants of Dutch-era settlement. The newcomers were driven to organize formal town governments throughout the region, negating the power of the generally disliked landed aristocracy, and instilling democratic values, religion outside the Reformed tradition, and desire for an English-style education for the common good.

The area from Coxsackie up through the remnants of Rensselaerswijck that surrounded the city of Albany was pretty sparsely populated for a long time. A 1720 roster of Albany County and City freeholders contained twenty-eight names for the region called "Coxhaxky and Cats Kills" while the "Colloney Renselaers Wyck" had eighty-one.[1] By the 1790 federal census, the two-year-old town of Coxsackie, including the New Baltimore constituency, had a counting of 3,406, not a metropolis but certainly showing a substantial percentage of growth.

Many land sales are recorded in Albany County records throughout this period. Of particular interest is a September 13, 1791 deed transferring "Lot Number one on the map Drawn for the Regulating a Town . . ." from the Vanderzees to David Smith of Coxsackie for seven pounds, "Lying and Being In New Baltimore So Called . . ." This may be the first mention of New Baltimore in a public record. A little earlier, in the *Albany Gazette* newspaper, an August 10 public notice is given for auction of property owned at New Baltimore by probably the same Smith.[2]

These Vanderzees were Albert and Teunis, the original Albert who bought the land from John Barclay mentioned in the previous chapter and his younger brother Teunis. The two of them were in on a number of property transactions throughout this period. How Teunis supplanted his brother Cornelis as owner of the hamlet land is unclear.

Regrettably, there is no hint of why the place was called New Baltimore. Local lore has it that the name came either from land surveyors or visiting river traders. As strange as it may now seem, there was a marked visual similarity between the terrain of early Baltimore, Maryland and the little New York river hamlet.

After the war, civilization spread more steadily into the inner realms of New Baltimore. Large landholdings were divided to accommodate the newcomers. In one important instance, a local empire was further dismantled.

Barent and Gertruy Coeymans' daughter, Ariaantje, was survived by a twenty-three-years-younger husband David Verplanck who inherited her share of the family's estate. He later remarried and had several children. The burden of maintaining hundreds of acres with little immediate profitability led to David's borrowing a substantial sum from Jacob C. Ten Eyck, a wood-pile Coeymans relative and an Albany mayor.

This ill-fated association led to court action that resulted in the Verplancks losing a significant portion of the inherited property to the Ten Eycks. The families ended up with about a half each of the bulk of the territory now encompassing northwest-central New Baltimore, southwest-central Coeymans, and a good chunk of Greenville. Thus started a long string of land transactions between the two families and other interested investors hoping to set down roots or make a speculative fortune. This skein of sales led to the settling of the western part of New Baltimore.

Newcomers began to fashion little corners of civilization up and down the Hudson and into the hinterlands away from the river. Life around the primitive self-sustenance farms began to blossom into small hamlets that became centers of rural population.

A handful of houses and a school came into being near the Van Bergen mill on the banks of the Coxsackie Creek. A bridge that nearly touched the mill was a key landmark on the Albany and Greene Turnpike, the main highway between New Baltimore hamlet and the Coxsackie landing. Stanton Hill's Quakers formed the nucleus of another grouping. The Miller family homestead and a Congregational Church helped create Medway. The short-lived Sylvandale Methodist Church was the center of another tiny population grouping. And the Powell homestead and gristmill along with a Baptist congregation produced another rural neighborhood at Grapeville.

The first mill on the Hannacroix Creek likely was established by Salomon Skinner around 1780. Jeremiah Dean later took over the operation and carried out a thriving business, producing plaster and lumber and processing multiple grains. A cluster of homes and a school were built nearby. While it was common for farmers and property owners to run their own milling facilities, the Van Bergen and Dean businesses, the Croswell operation further down the Hannacroix, and the Grapeville Powell mill became popular commercial enterprises.

Noah Wheeler of Dutchess County settled in the New Baltimore area around the turn of the nineteenth century and built what likely was the first hotel in the western part of the town around 1808. Wheeler and his family maintained that business along with an active farm, helping to start a long history of boarding houses in the rural areas of New Baltimore. It was a necessary financial support to protect against the uncertainties of agriculture.

The Society of Friends

The Quakers had started a number of thriving communities in America as early as the mid-1650s. A variety of factors, including persecution and the lack of available land in many of their original settlements, pushed them into new frontiers. One stream of population came up along the east side of the Hudson to Dutchess County, crossing the river into what was still in the eighteenth century called the Coeymans Patent.[3]

The Quakers' arrival is chronicled in the journal of Elias Hicks, a prominent traveling preacher and farmer from Long Island whose future exploits would have a drastic impact on the faith. In late March 1781, Hicks journeyed upriver from Dutchess County to "Coeman's Patent" and met with a "few Friends, who had lately settled at that place, and some of their neighbors, who were mostly Baptists. It was the first Friends' meeting ever held there, and was a satisfactory season."[4]

Those "few Friends" undoubtedly were the multitude of Bedells, Gurneys, Hoags, Powells, and others with familiar New Baltimore names who settled on a patent allotment in the vicinity of Stanton Hill in the north-central part of the modern town. They must have been delighted to have had such an illustrious figure as Hicks attend their initial meeting. Hicks's journal describes several subsequent visits. By 1829, there were well over three hundred local practitioners of the faith.

The New Baltimore members held Preparative Meetings at which local matters were discussed. The next step up the organizational ladder was the Monthly Meeting, an amalgam of two or more Preparative Meetings. Then came the Quarterly Meeting, which usually was centered at a more established congregation. There are surviving minute books that describe Hudson as the site where New Baltimore residents would participate in Monthly Meetings.[5] New Baltimore's first Quarterly assignment was at Nine Partners in Dutchess County and later was under the

Duanesburgh Quarterly Meeting. Larger-scale Yearly Meetings were convened at New York City.

Nine Partners' minutes from 1788 describe the building of a meeting house on land in the Coeymans Patent. Another notation from 1794 describes the intention to build a meeting house that would be fifty by thirty-five feet and have two stories. Whether this building was a separate entity from the earlier structure or a replacement is uncertain.

The minute books generally are a good resource for small details about the daily workings of what many still called the Coeymans Meeting. The local designees for attending Monthly Meetings and holders of various official positions are named on numerous occasions. Edward Powell; Edward Hallock; Levi Hoag; Jacob Carman; Jeremiah Bedell; Benjamin and Charles Lisk; and Jacob, Joshua, and Benjamin Gurney were among the people who served as active participants in the meeting.

Important events and activities frequently are mentioned. The Stanton Hill members allocated a portion of their assessed monthly subscriptions to support a Quaker boarding school at Nine Partners and to help build meeting houses in other locations. There also were processes for helping fellow members who had been reduced to poverty, for removing troublesome parishioners, and for handling the relocation of people to other meetings.

The Coeymans or Stanton Hill Meeting was awarded the opportunity to convene a Monthly Meeting in late 1799, surely a momentous achievement for the locals. Small groups of people also were allowed to convene at other spots, particularly during wintry weather.

Around 1807, Friends in the western part of the Coeymans Meeting wanted to hold their own service. Consequently, a New Baltimore Preparative Meeting was sanctioned in the Staco area. It would be under the aegis of the Coeymans Monthly Meeting. In about five years, the Staco members had built their own meeting house on an acre of land, an edifice that had been proposed to be forty-two by thirty feet in size.

As early as the 1810s, the Quakers were lamenting the difficulties of establishing an educational system for their children. Once the Town of New Baltimore came into existence and created its own program of schooling, the Quakers generally sent the young people to the government-sanctioned common schools. Whether the exposure to the more secular ways of the town's other students contributed to the eventual dissolution of the Quaker faith in New Baltimore is subject to conjecture.

Elias Hicks reenters the picture in a big way as the 1820s progressed. He and numerous followers espoused a more liberal version of Quakerism that led to a split into two separate streams, the Orthodox and the upstart Hicksites. The New Baltimoreans leaned initially to the more traditional position. As Frances Dietz points out in her 1984 essay on the Quakers, there only are Hicksite minutes available from the summer of 1828 forward. This circumstance may well be due simply to lost records rather than indicate a trend in loyalties. The membership names of Powell, Lisk, Bedell, Titus, and Carman are mentioned on both sides of the schism, so intrafamily tension must have been disruptive or remarkably tolerated.

It may be difficult to confirm when either side predominated and to what degree but it seems that the Hicksites took over the old Stanton Hill meeting house. There is record of a new building erected by the Orthodox faction in 1833. The meeting went downhill from then on and was terminated in 1867, excepting for a couple of bursts of attempted reinvigoration in the next decades. That 1833 building had been converted into a hay barn and was destroyed by an arsonist in 1968.

Shortly after the Orthodox new construction, the Hicksites also commissioned their own new building near the intersection of the modern Roberts Hill Road and Route 54. It still stands today on private property. The Staco meeting came to an end on an indeterminate date probably soon after the mid-1850s. Their meeting house was moved and torn down in 1983. The Hicksites still were meeting almost to the 1880s before lapsing into inactivity and formally ending in 1898. Their demise likely was attributable to the pressures of a more modern world overcoming the traditional behaviors of faith.

The rich legacy of the Society of Friends is kept alive today by the neat rows of beautiful but simple tombstones at the Stanton Hill, Staco, and other cemeteries.

The Powell Mill and Grapeville

Close spaces and expanding families on Long Island forced an exodus of younger generations into Westchester, Putnam, and Dutchess counties. Moses Powell, one of fourteen offspring of Bethpage's Thomas Powell, a Quaker, found his way first to Westchester, then Dutchess County. His sons, Edward, Samuel, and Moses Jr., bought land as early as 1786 out of the Ten Eyck portion of the Coeymans Patent. Samuel's parcel included the land on which the New Baltimore hamlet of Grapeville now stands. Edward secured a plot along the East Branch of the Potick Creek just south of Samuel. Moses Jr. purchased acreage around the Staco cemetery.

The brothers built rudimentary shelters, outbuildings, and a sawmill, and cleared the fields needed to establish farmsteads. As the families grew and new settlers were attracted to the area, larger houses were constructed and a community was born. Grapeville eventually saw a store, tavern, blacksmith shop, wheelwright's shop, tannery, school, church, and cobbler's shop.

The Powells made a substantial investment in constructing a gristmill for processing home-sewn grain into flour and animal feed on an attractive and feasible site on the Potick Creek at Honey Hollow. The three-story structure probably was built around the turn of the nineteenth century. The elder Moses Powell had been part owner with brother-in-law Samuel Hallock of a gristmill in Westchester County, so the occupation may have been in the blood. The mill appears to have remained close to the Powells or their in-law Youmans family for much of its life span, up to its ostensible end around the beginning of the 1920s.[6]

Another important impetus for development of the modest little community came when Ebenezer Wicks, a Long Islander who had settled at Rensselaerville, Albany County, moved to New Baltimore around 1802. He was a farmer, carpenter, and Baptist minister with great initiative and ambition. He first held church sessions in his home before constructing largely with his own hands the first school house in the area. That dwelling served as a meeting place for the Baptist population before Wicks took another step forward by spearheading the construction of the Grapeville Baptist Church building, again at least partly by his own labor.

Today, the mill and all the other public or commercial structures in the hamlet have faded into history, except for the vibrant Baptist Church, which hosts the only school still active in town.

The Richest Man in Town: Charles Titus

Charles Titus came north from Dutchess County and invested in a substantial piece of land in the wilderness out near the modern Medway. Later purchases added to his real estate holdings. His name appears on a Coxsackie tax roll from the end of 1786 but the document offers no description of what he owned.[7] An Albany County indenture from June 1797 shows a transfer of property from Isaac D. Verplanck of Coeymans to Charles Titus of Coxsackie. The plot of over 126 acres lay in the eighth allotment of the partition of the original Coeymans Patent.[8] This would be in the vicinity of the modern intersection of Routes 26 and 51.

Forgiving an unrecorded or undiscovered transaction, it appears that this is the time that Charles bought the New Baltimore land where he proceeded to enlarge upon a commercial and real property empire that probably started in Coxsackie. Charles's brother Hollet came here at about the same time and may have been the impetus behind a gristmill in the area.

Charles built a house and, over the years, constructed a sawmill, a store (possibly the first in the Medway area), an ashery, and a blacksmith shop. He also became a justice of the peace for the town of New Baltimore. Titus owned at least one trading vessel, shipping and receiving a multitude of products from the landing at Coxsackie.

In May of 1807, Charles is recorded as receiving an annual license from the Coxsackie Commissioners of Excise to operate a public inn or tavern, location unknown. He also may have had a store at Coxsackie but certainly owned dockage there where he eventually had a brickyard. Charles and his first wife, Anna Mott, had one child, Martha, who married John W. Bedell, who became a partner and successor to his father-in-law.

A collection of Titus papers at the New York State Archives contains detailed lists of products that he bought and sold, much of which probably were imported from New York City through a prominent trading family, the Seamans. Among the many items handled were tea, snuffboxes, writing paper, beef, turkey, dog meat (for or from a canine?), hats, brandy, "India sugar," pepper, ginger, wire, "English powder," "temple spectacles," chintz, calico, flannel, muslin, gingham, thread, buttons, pen knives, house shears, raisins, tobacco, molasses, chocolate, butter, brandy, genever (Dutch gin), and rum.

Titus kept a steady supply of goods flowing to his neighbors. His day books note numerous sales locally to the Powells, Hallocks, Sarles, Lisks, Smiths, Bedells, and other Tituses.[9] By the time the 1837 New Baltimore tax assessment roll was compiled, Charles held $9,000 worth of real and personal property, almost double the valuation of the next wealthiest person, Teunis P. Van Slyke.[10]

All the Tituses were practicing Quakers with Hollet's son, Isaac, becoming a noted leader. After Anna Mott's premature passing, Charles married a widow named Prudence Rundle. While Charles is assumed to have been a member of the Society of Friends, his name is not listed in later member rolls. Some researchers believe he was put out for marrying outside the faith. Prudence Titus may well have been an Episcopalian, having married into a Rundle family that was instrumental in the founding of that type of church in Greenville. However, when Charles died at about ninety, he was buried among numerous Quakers in the Stanton Hill cemetery.

The Millers

Jonathan Miller and his wife, Lydia McCabe, were two more of the brave souls who made their way north from Westchester to the wilds of the future Greene County. Evidence varies as to the precise time of the Millers' arrival. In 1791, they bought land from Isaac D. Verplanck in the tenth allotment of the partitioned Coeymans Patent. One assessment roll lists a Jonathan Miller as being responsible for payment of taxes in Coxsackie as of December 1786.[11] In any event, the Millers purchased a sizable portion of property that eventually may have numbered in the range of a thousand acres.

First building a log cabin as immediate protection from the surrounding wilderness, the Millers also labored diligently at clearing forest and rock to uncover serviceable farmland. By the turn of the nineteenth century, the pioneers had built a larger, wood-frame home. Jonathan and Lydia's son Jesse established his own farm, also still standing just west of his parents' home.

Raising primarily livestock and fruit, the Millers made a prosperous life. The centerpiece of their farm was what many believed to have been the area's first commercial apple orchard, a forerunner to the fruit-growing industry that was to become very important in the town in later years.

The Millers were representative of the hard-working, socially minded families that came here in those days. Among other activities, the family was instrumental in developing a keystone institution that helped broaden their budding community. Around 1807, Jasper Hazen, an itinerant preacher from Vermont, came to the Miller homestead, hoping to promote interest in a religious gathering. The result was a service in the family's barn, from which the Medway Congregational Christian Church was born. The Millers strongly supported what is still an active parish.

After Jonathan and Lydia's passing, Miller children and grandchildren remained on the farm. The agricultural tradition was carried into the twenty-first century with the Miller-intermarried Woodhull family tending the land.

Paul Sherman

The riverside's denser settlement was growing into a little village with modest shops, two or three hotels, and a nucleus of energetic river trades. The lack of accessible roads to the interior and hilly terrain probably kept the place from becoming a more active shipping and commercial venue.

Neighboring Coeymans and Coxsackie had more viable early east-west routes for farmers to ship their wares from inland. Despite the shortcomings, a little community matured along the Hudson. John Maude, a well-traveled Englishman on his way to Niagara Falls in 1800, stopped along our shores and gave an early account of life. With a somewhat paradoxical tone, he entered into his journal that:

> The wind having entirely failed us, took the Sloop in tow, and at 7:00 p.m. had her moored alongside a Wharf in Baltimore, one hundred and forty-five miles. Went on shore; took with us Nicholas and his violin, the fiddle soon got the girls together; we kicked up a dance and kept it up till midnight. Treated with spruce-beer and gingerbread. Baltimore is a shabby place, every other house a tavern; in number about a dozen.[12]

While Maude may not have been enchanted entirely with the place, it was not unusual for people to "hang out a sign" on their homes, welcoming neighbors and travelers to a warm meal, a drop of drink, and maybe even a soft bed for the weary. Maude could not belie the fact that the place was lively.

There was progress in the little neighborhood along the Hudson. Among other new arrivals, Stephen Parsons came from Long Island around the time of the Revolution and built the still-standing stone house in the middle of the hamlet. His arrival spurred a long line of descendants who farmed, traded, and dealt land with great vigor.

After the war ended, anticipating an influx of new and adventurous investors, the Vanderzees, Albert and Teunis, enlisted the services of a surveyor, John D. Spoor, who produced a "Map Drawn for the Regulation of a Town at Said Place," probably as an enticement for interested buyers. New Baltimore (albeit not yet by that name) was on the planning map. The document is lost but references to it and its building lots are mentioned in various deeds. The brothers had started a trading post around the time of the Revolution that they undoubtedly hoped would be the economic focal point of a growing community.

By 1796, the Vanderzees and Paul Sherman were recorded as jointly owning a store house and dock on the Hudson. Sherman eventually became sole owner and built quite a compound at the trading station abutting his home. His granddaughter produced a wonderful watercolor of the complex, a work of art preserved at the Greene County Historical Society's Vedder Research Library.

Business and society were accelerating as the century turned. The first boat documented as built in New Baltimore was the *Sea Flower* in 1793. It set the pace for the hallmark industry of later years.[13] The 65-ton sloop was made for Salomon Skinner, the Hannacroix miller. Methodist services began to be preached around 1800 with the religion becoming established in nearby Coeymans a few years earlier. A church was not built in the hamlet, though, until 1855, outdone by the 1832 Methodist Church in Medway. Better transportation choices beyond the river began to come into being. The Albany and Greene Turnpike was constructed in 1806, providing more convenient hoof and foot access to the north and south.

Paul Sherman's history is a bit foggy before his arrival to a landholding along the Hudson River. He probably was born June 25, 1763. His immediate ancestors, the Sissons, were farmers whose property Paul may have shared in working. It is quite certain that he, his wife Bathsheba, and their children left Tiverton, Rhode Island and ended up in the soon-to-be New Baltimore around 1790.

A document signed that year by Mayor John Lansing Jr. granted Sailing Master and Trader Paul Sherman freeman status in Albany. So the family may have found themselves in Albany before purchasing land down the Hudson.

After finding the way to New Baltimore, Paul certainly took a wholehearted interest in buying and selling property around his new home. There are a plethora of deeds in the Sherman collection of family papers at the Vedder Library that attest to Paul's entrepreneurial skills.[14] Some of his real estate transactions were in partnership with the Vanderzees, David Dinsmore, and a number of other people, while others were sole moves.

In 1809, Sherman and Albert Vanderzee once again employed the ubiquitous John Spoor to map a development project. Spoor blocked out a web of 112 lots off the new central Albany and Greene Turnpike, crisscrossed by the mundanely named Main Street and roads commemorating war heroes, Greene and Washington, and a patriotic Liberty Street. There also is an optimistic notation that the location had "a fair prospect for the Mercantile & seafaring adventurer."[15] Several lots were sold but many remained in the Sherman family.

While all this real estate maneuvering was carried out, the other focus of Paul Sherman's life was his river trading and shipbuilding businesses. An account book of his activities is preserved in the Sherman papers and chronicles a steady circuit of transfer by sloop to and from New Baltimore of products ranging from wooden shingles, flax seed, and wheat to rum, clothing, and furniture. The Sherman wharf and warehouses dominated the local shoreline.

Sherman also hired men to build the ships on which he conveyed these various goods. All this activity meant jobs for locals and the construction of houses and storage space that might be sold or rented out. On the side, Paul devoted time to being a justice of the peace and did a little farming. He also provided a small bit of land for the extension of a school lot.

The Sherman papers help paint a vivid picture of life of the times. Through deeds, wills, letters, and other ephemera, we learn that John Plum Jr. was framing buildings in the little hamlet. Moses Gains was a mason. John Williams was a merchant of some undefined sort. Numerous other people were buying property and setting up homes.

It was an active world of exchange at the Sherman trading post. The family sloops would be importing vast arrays of food, drink, and goods. Local craftspeople, farmers, and millers would haul wool hats, furniture, barrel staves, clothing, hogs, grain, and anything else they could make or grow to Sherman to trade for the arriving items and future credit.

Paul passed away on September 10, 1820, leaving behind a well-established little neighborhood owing much to his commercial spirits. Bathsheba lived another dozen years. Their son Joseph and grandson Edward Ely and their families continued a vibrant Sherman social and business presence in New Baltimore well into the latter half of the twentieth century.

Birth of New Baltimore

After the Revolution, officers of the new state had to look toward creating more formalized structures for state and local governments. A major move in this direction was taken in 1788 with passage of wholesale legislation that divided New York's territory into counties and towns. The latter jurisdictions were very limited in their scope of authority, being created as instruments for local administration of state laws and generally having four major functions: highway construction and maintenance, crime control, fence maintenance, and animal regulation. Many of the municipalities already existed and were simply carried forward, including Coxsackie in Albany County.

The new Coxsackians were empowered to assemble at town meetings on the first Tuesday in April every year to select a roster of officers for one-year terms: a supervisor, a town clerk, three to seven assessors, at least one tax collector, two overseers of the poor, three commissioners of highways, and three constables. Overseers of highways, fence viewers, and pound masters could be selected in such numbers that the locals deemed necessary.

Laws following the pivotal 1788 county and town organization measure continued to refine and define local governance to allow increasingly independent action by officials right on the scene. A series of statutes in 1801 established the basic structures under which the Town of New Baltimore came into being, including specific provisions on the responsibilities of public officers for general administration and particularly for creating a system of courts, overseeing care of the poor, and constructing and maintaining highways.

With a renewed threat of war with the British looming ominously in the early 1800s, a group of local citizens were moving forward on efforts to declare the independence of their growing corner of Coxsackie. The progressive locals decided to mount a campaign to persuade the legislature and the governor to amend state law to create a brand new Town of New Baltimore. Regrettably, little information is available about the steps taken to start the process. The 1911 burning of New York's state capitol building destroyed the records for early town organizations. Any pertinent official accounts from the Town of Coxsackie also are missing. But legislative records provide a slender trail of insights into final consideration by the senate and assembly.

At eleven in the morning on January 30, 1811, the New York State Senate convened. One of the numerous actions taken that day was consideration of "the petition of John K. Brown and others, inhabitants of the town of Coxsackie, in the county of Greene, praying that the said town may be divided in the manner therein described, was read, and with the map and documents accompanying the same, referred to a select committee, consisting of Mr. Haight, Mr. Brett, and Mr. Hopkins." The petitioner, John K. Brown, was a New Baltimore hamlet innkeeper. The mentioned legislators were Samuel Haight of Catskill, who represented the Coxsackie area in the senate, Otsego County's Joshua H. Brett, in his last year of senate service, and David Hopkins from Washington County.

It was another week before the senate again brought the bill up for consideration. The next day, February 8, the pending measure ran into a little roadblock. "A number of remonstrances from the inhabitants of the town of Coxsackie . . . against the division of the said town" were referred for review by the body. There are no hints in the senate journal as to the content of the opposition's concerns but they apparently held little merit for the legislators. On February 13, the bill was reported from committee. The next day, the full senate passed the legislation, sending the text to the assembly for their action.[16]

Nearly a month later, members of that other legislative body began to consider the senate's Coxsackie division bill. The March 11 entry in the assembly journal provides our first glimpse of the boundaries that the town's planners intended to create between themselves and their soon-to-be neighbors to the south:

> Be it enacted by the people of the State of New-York, represented in senate and assembly, That from and after the passing of this act, all that part of the town of Coxsackie, in the county of Greene, beginning at Columbia county line, opposite a point of a rock at Hudson's river, near to a place called Planke Pat; thence running north eighty degrees west from said rock, six hundred and fifteen chains, to the west bounds of said town; thence seven degrees and ten minutes east, three hundred and twenty-three chains and fifty links, along the west bounds of said town of Coxsackie, to the county line which divides the counties of Greene and Albany; thence north, eighty-six degrees and thirty minutes east, along the said county line to the county of Columbia, in the Hudson's river; thence southerly along the Columbia county line to the place of beginning, shall be and hereby is erected into a separate town, by the name of New-Baltimore, and the first town meeting in said town of New-Baltimore shall be holden at the dwelling-house of Peter Wolf, now occupied by Matthew Setts, in said town.

There is little discussion noted in the record beyond mention of the usual procedural routine. By a healthy margin of fifty in favor and twenty-seven opposed, the Town of New Baltimore was voted into existence.[17] The April 10, 1811 edition of the *Catskill Recorder* posted an announcement for the appointment as justices of the peace for the infant New Baltimore, Benjamin Baker, Charles Titus, Simeon Garrett, and Anthony Van Bergen.[18]

The designated justices convened the first town meeting on Tuesday, April 2, 1811, at the tavern of Matthew Sitsers, probably located in the Peter Wolf house mentioned in the law and still standing at today's intersection of County Route 51 and Roberts Hill Road. After a printing of the law creating the town, the meeting's minutes are brief and to the point, laying out a framework for the local governmental functions and responsibilities allowed by the State. Elected as the first town officials were an array of old and new names in the area, some of whom appear to be doing double duty:

Supervisor Teunis Van Slyke;
Town Clerk Elisha D. Hall;
Assessors Samuel Youmans, Martin G. Van Bergen, and Hollet Titus;
Commissioners or Overseers of Highways Thomas Powell, Thomas Hallock, and Salomon Skinner;
Poor Masters Jeremiah Bedell and Peter Van Slyke;
Collector Jeremiah Bedell Jr.;
Constables Caleb Gage, Matthew Scott, Jeremiah Bedell Jr., and Levi Dewitt;
Inspectors of the Town Benjamin Baker, Simeon Garrett, Charles Titus, Teunis Van Slyke, and Andrew A. Vanderzee;
Pound Masters Peter Wolf and Noah Wheeler; and,
Fence Viewers John Armstrong, William Bedell, William Ray, Martin G. Van Bergen, Robert G. Palmer, and Thomas Powell.

The very first two actions written in the minutes are about the raising of $150 dollars to cover town expenses and the requirement that hogs were not to run in the streets unless they were yoked. The group went on to divide the people declared poor and related funding between New Baltimore and Coxsackie, create twenty-nine districts for overseeing and keeping highways, and certify election results and disposition of certain monies. The next meeting was to be held at Jonathan Miller's farm. It also is interesting to note the mention of several tavern keepers, likely for licensing purposes. Scattered across town, the purveyors of liquid refreshment were Jonathan Miller, Ephraim Garrett, Noah Wheeler, John Boom, Leonard Conine, John Brown, Jabez Bushnell, Caleb Gage, and Matthew Sitsers.

The hog rule underscored the critical importance of the more exotic jobs of Pound Master and Fence Viewer. The minutes also contain a list of the marks (e.g., a slit under the right ear) of individual livestock owners. The very existence of rural life hinged on the protected growth and harvest of livestock and crops. Fences and animal control were fundamental tasks throughout colonial and state life, and the earliest laws are precise and harsh in their treatment of anyone who, intentionally or not, might allow their livestock to roam free and destroy crops.[19]

Under state law, people with adjoining land parcels were required to construct and maintain agreed portions of partition fences between their properties. Any disputes about, or neglect of, these responsibilities were subject to enforcement and possible penalty by the town's fence viewers, including the payment of damages to neighbors adversely affected by the fence malfeasance.

As of the 1788 law, the pound master could take custody of any wandering or untended livestock, releasing them upon payment of a range of fees, "horse, gelding, mare or colt, and all neat cattle, one shilling each; and for every sheep or lamb three pence; and for every hog, shoat or pig six pence." Other provisions accounted for the disposition of the collected money, including defraying the costs of keeping and feeding the animal or providing for payment for damages caused by any wandering creatures. The animals might even be kept by the town in certain cases.[20]

State law over the intervening years granted additional responsibility, authority, and relative independence to local governments. The annual town meetings became biennial and finally monthly events. The sessions became board meetings in 1932, replacing what had been forums open to all citizens. Clerks and justices of the peace became board members and then not. Functions like fence viewer disappeared; pound masters turned into animal control officers and justices of the peace into town justices. Meetings became more frequent, and New Baltimore government well established.

War of 1812

As the split of New Baltimore from Coxsackie began to advance, the rest of the country was in the throes of rancorous diplomatic debate and combative turmoil. The British were fighting with Napoleon and his French legions, with consequences that quickly drew America to clash with the old mother country. One primary side effect of the European conflict was Britain's indiscriminate impressments over a number of years of thousands of American sailors into military service and the wanton seizing of commercial vessels of any supposedly suspicious nature.

On the United States' side of the increasing tensions were a number of authorities who wanted to complete the Revolution by taking Canada from the British and expand the borders of the country west and south into frontier and Indian territories. While the international disputes raged, the Indian presence was reinvigorated on the western frontier, with a discernible feeling that the British were feeding the discontent with supplies and arms. Many people were ready once again to go to war.

New Baltimore was motivated for a tussle. A group of patriotic citizens took the initiative of volunteering their fighting skills. A May 7, 1810 letter from Solomon Van Rensselaer, the state's adjutant general, sets the stage by announcing authorization for expanding the command of Lieutenant Colonel Jonas Bronk's Greene County militia regiment:

> The Commander in Chief having perused the petition of Benjamin Baker, Storm A. Vanderzee and others, praying the organization of a Company of Riflemen at the village of New Baltimore, in the County of Greene, and deeming it proper to grant the prayer thereof, hereby organizes the said Company of Riflemen, and assigns John Marshall Captain, Smith Dunning Lieutenant, and John Stone Ensign thereof, until the pleasure of the Council of Appointment be known in the premises. The said Company until further orders will be attached to and parade with Lieut. Col. Bronk's Regiment of Militia and will be uniformed as follows: Green Rifle frocks and Pantaloons with yellow fringe and buttons, black gaiters, round black hats, with yellow buttons, black loops and short Green feathers.[21]

While there is no clear record of what transpired next, Captain Marshall somehow must have announced his enthusiasm and impatience to confront the enemy. In a December 19, 1811 letter, New York's governor Daniel D. Tompkins was sympathetic to the captain's partisan zeal but had to apologize for there was "no authority at present to accept or to organize volunteers for actual service. It is to be presumed that such authority will be conferred before the rising of Congress, and whenever is shall be, I shall announce it publickly, & then it will give me great satisfaction to receive and accept the patriotic tender of your services."[22]

By January of 1812, war supporters nationally were winning the debate even though New York and New England were at the very least hesitant to join the battle. They greatly feared disruption of their established trade connections to both Canada and Britain. A modest consensus for battle held the day, and the Congress authorized an increase to nearly ten times the number of regular army troops that would include mostly recruits from state militias.

The New York State government set to work mobilizing its share of the fighting force. The governor recommended to Congressman Thomas B. Cook that appointments be granted to the army for several people, including John Marshall as a captain.[23] As conflict seemed inevitable in mid-April, general orders organized the militia forces. General Daniel Brown of Durham was to lead the 37th Brigade of Infantry with its component regiments and commanders, including several Greene County units.

As part of the mobilization, John T. Van Dalfsen of Coeymans was forming another outlet for the men of New Baltimore to fight the British. His 110th Regiment drew a number of local volunteers. Van Dalfsen married well. His wife, Charlotte Amelia Bronck, was the great-granddaughter of Barent and Geertruy Coeymans and a direct descendant of Pieter and Hilletje Bronck, the original patentees. The couple lived in one of the Coeymans family homesteads, a beautifully restored building still standing just north of the New Baltimore border on the bank of the Hannacroix Creek.

In a June 1812 circular from Albany to John Marshall and several other captains came a message regarding their ambitions and loyalties:

> I am instructed by the Commander in Cheif [Chief] to assure you that his Excellency has perceived with pleasure the devotion with which you and your companies court a participation in the honor of vindicating the violated rights of an injured and insullted people; and accepts with approbation and thanks, the tender of your services and of the corps under your command.[24]

Eight days later, America rendered a formal declaration of war against the British. It was not until its June 24th edition that the *Catskill Recorder* newspaper published a modest second-page announcement that "By accounts from Washington (per the Steam-Boat of Sunday) it appears that a formal Declaration of War, had taken place against Great-Britain, by a concurrent resolution of both houses of Congress."[25]

The battles of the War of 1812 generally took place in locations remote from the mid-Hudson, on the Great Lakes and into the western frontier of the country, in the deep south especially western Florida (including the Battle of New Orleans), and on the high seas (giving us some of our most famous national symbols, "Old Ironsides," "Don't Give up the Ship," and Francis Scott Key's "Star Spangled Banner").

There is little documentation of the participation of any New Baltimore men in actual battles. However, a sampling of veterans' records from the National Archives and Records Administration and other official documents and news accounts provide a flavor for the travels that local men undertook for the military effort. For example, in the latter half of the 1850s, survivors and widows were able to apply for reimbursement for clothing and equipment that a soldier had purchased that had been "depreciated, worn out, lost and destroyed" during military service.[26]

After the war formally began, about 2,600 militia men, a Greene County detachment among them, were called to go to the northern and western frontiers. Various companies and a handful of regiments of detached militia were to be dispatched to reinforce troops near the Saint Lawrence and at Sacketts Harbor. The latter location was a base of American military and naval operations throughout the conflict.

The war reimbursement application for New Baltimore's Michael Garrett notes his 1812 service at Athens and a journey to Sacketts Harbor. So, he appears to have been part of that first contingent traveling northward.

By the end of August, other units, including the artillerymen of the Catskill blacksmith Captain Jared Stocking and the light infantry companies of Isaac Dubois from Catskill and Silas Pierson of Athens, were on their way to defend New York City from the British threat. The plan was for the men to be stationed on Staten Island for ninety days.

John Marshall's riflemen and light infantry companies from Catskill and Athens were exempted from the New York City detail in anticipation of further general orders. Governor Tompkins from his quarters at Albany was growing concerned about enemy advances on the Niagara frontier, commanding General Stephen Van Rensselaer on the dire need to hold the lakes from British control. He comments in particular that: "The uniform Companies of this city [Albany] Hudson, Troy, New Baltimore, the Bocht, Lockwoo's Riflemen, some Riflemen from New York the Horse Artillery from Schenectady and Sullivan, two or three Companies of uniform Artillery etc will rendezvous and March as soon as possible."[27]

On September 20, 1812, Marshall still must have been in the vicinity of Albany, now posted under the command of Francis McClure, an Irish-born colonel from New York City. Governor Tompkins was issuing orders for the "keeper of the Arsenal" to provide McClure's men with the "muskets, Cartridge boxes, and knapsacks" that they need.[28]

Nine days later, Tompkins wrote to Henry Dearborn, commander of the army's northern department, about the lack of other sufficient critical equipment for New Baltimore soldiers: "We are much in want of flints for the State, and I beg leave to solicit that you will direct Mr. Merchant to deliver to John Vernor, our storekeeper, some flints & so many blankets as may be deficient in the New Baltimore Company, and Albany Greens, which are to follow the New York Greens to Onondaga, in a few days."[29]

As the end of September approached, orders came that: ". . . Captain Marshall's volunteer rifle company of New Baltimore, will immediately rendezvous and march with Col. McClure's New York Detachment and as part thereof, to Onondaga, or as soon after them as possible."[30] Marshall's service records at the National Archives show an accounting for his daily rations at Buffalo from October 3, 1812 to February 14, 1813 as a member of a company of volunteer riflemen in McClure's regiment. The period included an allowance for a fifteen-day march from Buffalo to Albany. Lieutenant Storm A. Vanderzee's subsistence and service records show service with the Marshall company at Buffalo for the same period.

An 1815 case before the Greene County Court of Common Pleas also sheds a little light on Captain Marshall's wartime whereabouts. Testimony places him at Sacketts Harbor from near the end of February 1814 until the second or third week in June that same year.[31]

Francis McClure's subsistence accounts verify his presence at Buffalo from September 23 to December 31, 1812 in one document. A later subsistence accounting shows him at Fort George from June 1 to August 17, 1813. McClure also documents travel of 450 miles from New York to Buffalo in November 1812; from Buffalo to Sacketts Harbor by order of General Dearborn in February 1813; from Sacketts Harbor to New York and back by order of General Pike in April 1813; and from Fort George to New York in August 1813. The American army had captured Fort George, an Ontario British stronghold, in late May 1813 and used it for a later ill-fated Canadian invasion.

National Strategy

A strategic goal for the Americans was to establish a foothold in Canada via a three-pronged assault before the beginning of winter in 1812. Brigadier General William Hull was to advance from Detroit in July. He was soundly defeated at the Battle of Fort Detroit. Henry Dearborn planned to travel across the St. Lawrence River to capture Kingston, Ontario, a key British outpost, but never gained the motivation to vacate his encampment near Albany.

Stephen Van Rensselaer, the heir and the "Last," or "Good," "Patroon" of Rensselaerswijck, and his Albany-area troops suffered a sound October defeat at Queenston Heights at the gorge of the Niagara. The American forces had been ordered to attack with the expectation that Brigadier General Alexander Smyth's force of 1,700 regular soldiers was available as support. Regrettably, the regular-army Smyth refused to obey the militia-man Van Rensselaer's orders or respond to his command to advance. The result was a disastrous thrashing.

Any role that the New Baltimore / Greene County men played in the battle at Queenston is unclear. Throughout the war, the *Catskill Recorder*, the main home newspaper, said little about the specific exploits of local warriors. Occasional letters were reprinted from larger newspapers, such as the *Albany Argus*, but those generally focused on more significant events and higher-level officers. Reports sometimes came from stagecoach or steamboat travelers who had firsthand knowledge of happenings on the western front and other locales but again with little detail.

However, a February 11, 1813 letter from Governor Tompkins commends the valor of Samuel Swartwout, who probably was from Poughkeepsie. Swartwout was "volunteer Adjutant to Col. McClure's regiment, that he was a volunteer in crossing with the detachment of sailors and regulars which prepared the way for General Smyth . . ."[32] So some Greene County troopers may have been involved.

Back Home

At the beginning of January of 1813, Captain Marshall's New Baltimore riflemen still were at Buffalo. In a letter from Governor Tompkins to Secretary of State (and later President) James Monroe, there are details of pay problems facing the troops including the New Baltimore men.[33] There were ongoing debates about the disparity in salary between regular troops and militia men. A shortage of paymasters to cover the large territory where soldiers were posted exacerbated the problem. The focus of American war efforts upon the new year was again at the Great Lakes and up the Saint Lawrence, harshly illustrated by the enemy burning of Lewiston and attack of Buffalo.

Back home, New Baltimore residents must have been concerned about their continuing physical and psychological well-being but some semblance of normalcy was apparent. People still had to meet their federal tax assessments on real and personal property, with payments due at the hotels of Henry Wheeler in the western part of town and John Brown in the hamlet. There were successful ongoing campaigns to convince farmers and other citizens to raise money and provide supplies and farm products for the support of the troops and relief for the families of absent soldiers.

Horatio Spafford's 1813 New York State gazetteer outlined the modest new town of New Baltimore as having an indeterminate population. The town of Coxsackie had 4,057 residents in the 1810 federal census, leaving a guess that New Baltimore had less than half that number as the gazetteer was being written. Spafford says there was a Quaker meeting house at Stanton Hill, a landing at the Hudson, and "a small Village of 15 or 18 houses, on the post-road from Albany to New-York," that road being the modern Main Street paralleling the river. A spring that appeared to rise and fall at regular intervals drew particular attention.[34]

A remarkable remnant of these times is preserved at the Vedder Research Library, the actual assessment roll that Greene County authorities completed in 1813. This is the only documented evidence of the 219 landowners who lived in the two-year-old town. Many of the names are familiar. As would be expected, the vast majority are men although Catherine Skinner, widow of the miller, Salomon Skinner, owned two hundred acres, three houses, and four outbuildings, which may have included the Hannacroix Creek mill. A handful of other women also are listed.

The person with the highest valuation of "lands, lots, and dwelling houses" was Baltus Van Slyke (800 taxable acres, 3 houses, 4 outbuildings) at $16,000. Anthony Van Bergen (769 acres, 3 houses, 5 outbuildings) was next at $15,500. Others with assets of at least $10,000 were Teunis P. Van Slyke (384 acres), Noah Wheeler (529 acres), and Thomas Houghtaling (500 acres). Jonathan Miller had 640 acres, four houses, and six outbuildings, but was assessed only at $8,500. Charles Titus's trading and milling enterprises likely are evidenced by his two dwellings and twelve outbuildings. He and Miller were at the top of the most buildings list. Van Bergen, Wheeler, and Jeremiah Bedell were next at eight apiece.

John Marshall, likely the same man who became the town's most prominent War of 1812 combatant, had a modest holding of a quarter acre taxable at $250 worth, one of the smallest assessments. Perhaps his military career put a dent in his financial well-being.

Twenty-two of the listed landowners owned slaves, none of whom are named. Thomas Houghtaling had the most, five, followed by Peter Houghtaling, Leonard Conine, and Tunis P. Van Slyke at four each. The slaves generally were assessed at $100 each in value, with a handful a little more and some a little less, in some cases apparently because of age (over fifty years old).[35]

The War Grinds to a Halt

By mid-summer of 1813, with pressure created by an advancing British naval fleet, the president again ordered mobilization of militia forces to defend New York State. The Greene County men were to be ready for imminent action. The county's Samuel Haight was to command one brigade. John Van Dalfsen also received an officer's assignment among the call-ups.[36]

On September 1, 1813, orders were given for the troops to convene at assigned locations. The men from Greene County plus Van Dalfsen's unit were to meet at either Athens or Coxsackie, with General Haight having the option to assign men to either site as he saw fit. The whole group was to proceed to Waterford. A number of troops then were shipped on to Plattsburgh, a key defense outpost that included a critical arsenal.[37]

Michael Garrett shows up on company pay roll and muster roll cards as a private in Captain Stacy Beakes's infantry company in Lieutenant Colonel Abraham J. Hardenbergh's New York militia regiment. A muster roll shows him posted at Plattsburgh from September 10 to October 27, 1813. Michael is noted as a Coxsackie resident but he likely was born, raised, died, and buried in New Baltimore. The pay roll is dated from September 10 to November 6, 1813 at an unspecified location, but Michael's residence is listed as two hundred miles from the point of his discharge.

Other of the men must have gone west at some point. In his war reimbursement claim, Van Dalfsen was part of the 12th Regiment of detached New York militia posted at Sacketts Harbor. He claimed subsistence payments from that location from October 14 to March 6, 1813, including a ten-day journey home at the end. The record, though, is a bit confusing. He also explains that he "commanded a separate Post at this time, therefore entitled to Double rations" and records a "New York" posting from January 30 to February 7, 1813. It could be that his regiment was split into separate details. He was paid throughout this period for his own rations and those of an unnamed personal servant.

New York City Service

The dawn of a new year saw continued action on the western and northern frontiers with the Americans making measurable progress. The British, though, created sufficient energy for a final burst of action.

By the end of May, they had blockaded the entire coast. Sensing the increasing American strength and no longer preoccupied with forces of the now-abdicated Napoleon, the British sent 15,000 troops to North America. One arm of their planned campaign was to launch an invasion into the New York-Vermont region, an attack that failed ignominiously at the naval Battle of Plattsburgh on September 11, 1814, giving Lake Champlain to the Americans.

From the south, enemy forces captured and burned a good portion of the city of Washington, the patriots' capital. Their success was relatively short-lived. The Americans repulsed them quite handily in September at Baltimore, where battling in the bay inspired Francis Scott Key's writing of the poem that led to "The Star-Spangled Banner." There was ongoing fear about a renewed British strategy to come across the western lakes, down the Hudson from Canada, and through New York City to divide the state into a defenseless posture.

Even with the Plattsburgh and Baltimore victories, New York City leaders throughout the period remained highly concerned about the need for military protection. President Madison responded by calling on the New York militia as part of a scheme to protect the Atlantic coastline. The September 14 *Catskill Recorder* reported that Lieutenant Colonel Van Dalfsen's regiment had sailed downriver from Coxsackie the previous Friday. Other Greene County troops readying for departure paraded to staging locations like Van Bergen's coffee house in Catskill. Cheering throngs of locals saw them off at the Hudson's docks. Men had to supply weapons and packs, cooked provisions for four days, and clothing for three months of service.

The *Recorder* also reported and shortly rescinded a story that the troops were called because the enemy was mobilizing in the waters off the city. In fact, the men spent most of their time further fortifying vulnerable spots, constructing defense structures at Brooklyn, Harlem Heights (the modern Morningside Heights around Columbia University), and on Great Barn Island (now Ward's Island in the shadow of the Triborough Bridge). The impact was felt at home as the call went out for handy craftsmen to build fascines that could be transported down the Hudson for city use. These were bundles of wood secured together and used militarily for reinforcing rampart walls around forts or arsenal batteries or for supporting trenches and ditches.

Things also seemed to be winding down for some volunteers. There were advertisements in the paper for the sale of military uniforms, perhaps to be used by new enlistees or to make some ready cash for people now finished with service.

A number of war records document the service of New Baltimore's men in a handful of locations at New York City during this period. In the 1870s, Anna Ten Eyck Vanderzee, widow of Captain Andrew A. Vanderzee, applied for a War of 1812 pension from the federal government. Vanderzee had passed away in March of 1829. These documents attest that the veteran had enlisted September 7, 1814 and was discharged at Harlem Heights December 8, 1814.

A subsistence account describes that Andrew, while serving under Lieutenant Colonel Ezra Post, was posted at Harlem Heights from September 7 to December 9, 1814 and paid for rations for ninety-four days. Andrew commanded his own company in the 29th Brigade's 61st Regiment of the New York State Detached Militia.

Joseph Bronk is listed on a muster roll in the middle of November 1814 at Harlem Heights. Bronk is described as having "joined Nov. 16 Coxsackie." He was a private in Vanderzee's company. Bronk later was awarded a $38 reimbursement for equipment and/or clothing used during defense of Harlem Heights around September 12, 1814. He also was claiming payment for transportation between Coxsackie and Harlem Heights.

Records of both George Van Slyck and Henry Wheeler show service in Van Dalfsen's regiment. Van Slyck was on pay rolls from August 18 to September 18, 1814 under Captain Ager Noble's company of detached militia and then September 18 to November 26, 1814 under Captain Charles Baker's company. Locations are not given. A muster roll for September 18 to November 22, 1814, though, has Van Slyck posted at Brooklyn in Baker's company.

This probably was the same George Van Slyck who was descended directly from the founding family and who lived for many years overlooking the Hudson along the Albany-Greene Turnpike south of the hamlet. In his reimbursement application, Van Slyck, now sixty-three years old, declared that he had been a private defending Coxsackie for over three months in Captain Baker's company in Van Dalfsen's infantry regiment. He claimed $69 in total for a hat, coat, vest, pants, stock, blanket, knapsack, canteen, two pairs of stockings, two shirts, a neckerchief, a pair of "Suwarrow" boots, and a pair of shoes.

Henry Wheeler is listed on payrolls from August 18 to November 26, 1814 when, for at least part of the time, he was posted at Brooklyn. Wheeler made reimbursement claims similar to Van Slyck's for various goods, while serving under Baker and Van Dalfsen. Wheeler's application also mentions Coxsackie service along with a petition for payment for transportation between Coxsackie and Brooklyn in 1814.

The Battle at Plattsburgh likely was the final blow to British military endeavors against their former colony. By the end of the year, crown authorities had had enough. British and American diplomats met around Christmas in Belgium and signed the Treaty of Ghent, formally ending the conflict.

Newspapers and the grapevine were alive with news of Andrew Jackson's smashing victory at the Battle of New Orleans, even though it was after the formal ceasefire. The *Catskill Recorder* was reporting dutifully about the intricacies of the treaty pounded out by the bitter rivals, including a February 21 full-page supplement announcing ratification and providing readers with the full text of the document. Life went back to normal.

5

Town Growth and Another War

In his 1824 gazetteer, Horatio Spafford described New Baltimore as having streams that "supply abundance of mill-seats." Perhaps he underestimated that the "village" still had only fifteen or eighteen houses but it certainly was not a booming metropolis. There now were two Quaker meetings. The town's population was 2,036, with "425 farmers, 60 mechanics, 2 traders; 5 foreigners; 79 free blacks, 29 slaves." By this time in history, there were ten schools, four gristmills, and nineteen sawmills, along with 2,180 cattle, 647 horses, and 3,214 sheep.[1]

So, at least from Spafford's perspective, the town depended on farming and milling for its economic foundation. Business related to the river apparently was insufficient to attract the author's attention even though at least the Sherman and Titus families were active commercially, and some ships were being made.

The 1825 New York State census counted New Baltimore's population at 2,171 people. Only Athens and Hunter of the ten Greene County towns had fewer people. Despite that, New Baltimore's farming community was productive. The town had the third highest acreage of improved land, was fourth in ownership of sheep and horses, had the third highest number of sawmills after Hunter and Windham, and was home to the primary producers of linen or cotton cloth.

Patrick Shirreff was a farmer and innovator in producing variations of cereal and was especially known for developing a number of new kinds of oats and wheat. Shirreff started out in April of 1833 from his home in Scotland on a journey to America to evaluate the potential of domestic agriculture as a guide to his younger, soon-to-emigrate brother. The Scotsman was a keen observer of people and places and on a lengthy tour from Philadelphia to Montreal and Boston to St. Louis, he took an enjoyable voyage up the Hudson. His description of the trip provides a look at the vibrancy of river life and the fertility of adjacent lands as the still-young town of New Baltimore approached the middle of the nineteenth century:

> The margins of the river Hudson, and islands in its course, assume a different character on approaching Albany; the islands being depositions of mud, susceptible of cultivation, and the banks rich soil, bearing good crops, and adorned with pretty houses. The tide flows up the Hudson to Albany, distant from New York 144 miles, admitting vessels of considerable burden, and sloops of small size penetrate much farther up the river. The waters of the Hudson, passing through a rich and populous country, forming the outlet of the Erie Canal, present a never-ending scene of pleasing industry. At all times innumerable sailing vessels, with extended cotton canvass, whitened by a bright sun, and pure air, float gracefully to and fro. Steam-boats, crowded with passengers, pass with rapidity, while cock-boats, loaded with fish, poultry, and fruit, rest in quietness. Sloops carrying well-formed hay and straw stacks, glide towards New York, while steam-boats tow canal barges and vessels of every description, up and down the river. The surrounding country is also full of interest, abounding in thriving villages and towns, each forming a depot to the country in their rear . . .[2]

In 1836, Thomas F. Gordon produced another gazetteer that, in a small space, captured a contemporary picture of New Baltimore. The town had two post offices, New Baltimore (the "village") and Four Corners (Medway), and an "agricultural vicinage" (i.e., farming neighborhood) at Stanton Hill. New Baltimore "contains a Dutch Reformed Church, 2 taverns, 4 stores, and about 50 dwellings upon one street, remarkable for their size and neatness." Perhaps a reflection of the 1825 opening of the Erie Canal, "It is a place of considerable trade, employs 6 sloops and exports large quantities of building stone to Albany." Four Corners, "a hilly country," had Christian, Episcopal, Methodist, and Baptist churches, a pair of sawmills, and about twenty homes. Stanton Hill still had two Quaker meetings and about fifteen residences.[3]

John Disturnell's 1843 gazetteer tells us that the town had 2,306 residents in 1840 and land that was "fertile, and mostly highly cultivated." The "village" still retained its 1836 character and now had "about 400 inhabitants, 50 dwelling houses, 1 Dutch Reformed church, 1 tavern, 4 stores, and 2 warehouses, 2 brickyards, 2 dry docks and ship yards for building and repairing vessels." Perhaps the same six sloops were plying the Hudson as in 1836, and the location was now noted as a steamboat landing.[4] The latter emphases may reflect the increasing commercialization of the waterfront that would be paramount in coming years.

The Prize-Winning Van Bergen Farm

Agriculture's history in New Baltimore is really the history of the town. The Van Slykes, Van Bergens, Houghtalings, and other settlers were first and foremost subsistence farmers who had to grow their own produce and livestock. As years passed, our many agriculturalists converted over to market-directed enterprises specializing in a crop such as milk or fruit or, even to today, hay.

In 1843, as part of a set of competitions for the Greene County Fair held annually at Cairo, a Committee on Farms visited several properties to examine the modernity of their agricultural methodologies and evaluate their productivity. The report of the committee's members described in depth Anthony Van Bergen's 700-acre spread near the King's Road in New Baltimore.

Van Bergen had been farming there for thirty-six years, starting with a tract of 150 acres and adding swaths more of land over the years. He was an ardent advocate of "scientific farming" and the latest techniques in animal husbandry and crop production. Anthony became a recognized farming leader locally and statewide. Among other achievements, he served as president of the New York State and Greene County Agricultural Societies and was a New Baltimore justice of the peace.

The Van Bergens' main crop was hay, but the farm also grew other products and had anywhere from twenty-five to sixty Durham cattle at any given time. The family cultivated about five hundred tons of hay the year of the committee's visit.

The visitors lauded the success of Van Bergen's operation, especially in overcoming the obstacle of poor clay soil that was prone to flooding. His use of ditches and stone drains to resolve the latter problem, the employment of plaster or lime to enhance soil fertility, and composting were innovations particularly worthy of comment.

The composting was intriguing enough for the committee to describe the intricacies of the preparation process in detail:

> First a foundation of top soil 16 feet wide and 50 feet long; next a layer of barn yard manure; next a layer of tan bark; next a layer of weeds; next a layer of muck; another layer of barn-yard manure; another layer of topsoil; a layer of marl; another layer of tan bark; and another layer of topsoil. These materials were in equal proportions, and remained in the heap through the months of July and August. They were then overhauled, beginning at one end and incorporating the mass more thoroughly. While in this state they underwent the process of fermentation so as to smoke. This heap contained 700 loads, and was drawn out during the winter, and spread as a top-dressing upon the meadows in April.

After complimenting Van Bergen on the order and design of his buildings, the committee rewarded him with a first premium among the examined farms in the county. Since the fair was held in October, perhaps the judges missed the most odoriferous days of the composting process.[5]

The New Censuses

A whole new world of information opened when federal census administrators started to ask people many more questions with the 1850 enumeration. The 1855 New York State census followed suit. All the people living in a household now would be listed, not just the head, along with any occupations of residents and other useful tidbits related to personal and property characteristics. Increasing categories of information continue to be a windfall for historians and genealogists.

In August of 1850, Luman Ramsdell took on the task of collecting census data for the Town of New Baltimore. Oddly enough, according to his own enumeration, Luman was a farmer in the neighboring town of Greenville. In a brief, one-page summary, he compiled a listing of the occupations of residents and how many people filled each job, a good snapshot of one aspect of life in New Baltimore at the midpoint of the nineteenth century.

Not surprisingly, 361 farmers were by far the winners in the numbers game. Next in line were 161 laborers. These people may have been farmhands or could have been associated with one of the other types of businesses in town. They may even have been involved in the soon-to-boom boat building enterprise. The census line for blacksmith Jeremiah Hyatt says his information was taken at the steamboat office.

It is certain that the five ship carpenters were busy on either building or repairing vessels of one sort or another. Given the proximity of the Hudson, the joint third-spot occupation unsurprisingly was boatman (thirty-three of them). This category of employment may have been an amalgam of different tasks. For example, the occupation of the wealthy river trader Edward E. Sherman is given simply as boatman. Others designated in that manner appear likely to have been boat crew or workers helping to build vessels.

The only other tasks in double figures were blacksmiths (also thirty-three), carpenters (nineteen), and shoemakers (ten). Given the proliferation of farmers, these numbers perhaps are not unexpected. The need for farmers to shoe their horses and themselves and to build and maintain wooden barns, houses, and sheds was routine. About one blacksmith for each eleven farmers seems a reasonable distribution. Then there were eight apiece of masons, millers, and wagon makers. A few tanners, drovers, coopers, and teamsters, and a harness maker also were around.

There were handfuls of jobs that generally supported a community just starting to demonstrate a little growth and movement away from a basic agricultural existence, including clerks, merchants, teachers, innkeepers, butchers, and single examples of tailor (Thomas Lockley, the burning of whose building would lead to the founding of the Cornell Hook and Ladder Fire Company), grocer, painter, and clothier. Frederick Green, Erastus Newman, and Theodore Cornell were tending the sick.

Paul Jones was a bit unique for New Baltimore. According to the 1850 federal census, the eighteen-year-old Paul Jones was making brooms while sharing a home in the riverside hamlet with his mother Clarissa, older brother Theodore, and younger sister Charlotte. Later in life, he was listed as being both a ship carpenter and caulker. Jones was on the roster of Baldwin shipyard employees as was Charles Jones, a "pitch boy" and probably Paul's son.

Illustrating how people often had to take up more than one job to survive in those days, Jones was written up in the February 6, 1878 *Coeymans Herald* newspaper for having been in an accident while working in an ice house. It could very well be that the winter was a slack season for the shipyard, necessitating alternate cold weather employment.

Jones's wife Sarah passed away in 1902. With Paul nearing seventy years of age, it perhaps was time for him to give up his dual careers and return to what may have been his first job choice. Local newspapers frequently reported on successful transactions of his broom business.

The *Recorder* of May 22, 1903 said that Jones was in New York City for a few days, "canvassing for his mops and dusters, and has received orders for considerable assignments to a number of wholesale and other houses." The January 18, 1905 *Coeymans Herald* mentioned that Jones had sent "yacht mops" to Havre-de-Grace, Maryland for the Pennsylvania Coal Company. A month later, the *Examiner* noted that "Paul Jones shipped twelve dozen of his patent mop heads to a New York firm the other day." Other reports crop up during the rest of the year. Paul died in 1918.

In the 1850 federal census, there were Quaker (Henry Halsted), Christian (Richard Moshier), Reformed (Staats Van Sandvoort), and Presbyterian (Joseph Tomb) clergymen. The latter was interesting because there is no record of a Presbyterian church in New Baltimore. This gentleman must have been ministering in another community or perhaps riding a circuit of places. There even were two brick makers, John and Henry Van Buskirk, and two lighthouse keepers, Jonas and Byron Parker. The three papermakers included James Croswell. The remains of a later mill of his are on a local walking trail, a site now included on the National Register of Historic Places.

The 1850 enumeration also counted over a hundred African Americans living in New Baltimore. One of the new columns in the enhanced census provides a demarcation of a person as "White, black, or mulatto." A black boatman, Peter Vandazee,[6] was living with Julia Vandazee who was described as a "mulatto."

The vast majority of the men of color were occupied as laborers. There were a few exceptions. Cato Vandaza was a farmer while William Vandazall was a carpenter. A number of people appear to have been staff in individual households, including Peter Houghtaling who was a laborer in the farming household of George and Ann Coonley, Elizabeth Vanderpool living with Baltus and Ann Van Slyke, and James Smith and John Houghtaling as laborers for farmers John and Elizabeth Bedell. The clergymen Staats Van Sandvoort and Joseph Tomb resided with Jane Van Bergen, in the first case, and Elizabeth Bregg and Samuel Van Slyke in the second.

A handful of the "black" New Baltimoreans lived in their own homes. There is an interesting congregation of people in what appear to be neighboring households. This grouping looks like it would have been in the south central part of town called Roberts Hill. Why they happened to live near one another is a mystery worthy of further research.

By 1845, the number of New Baltimore's citizens had grown slightly to 2,347. Only Greenville and Prattsville of the eleven towns in Greene County had fewer people. Despite that, it had the most barley-growing land under cultivation in the county at 262 acres, with Catskill next in line at 197 acres. New Baltimore was second in the acreage devoted to peas and beans, fourth in the amount of buckwheat raised, third in rye, second in number of hogs, and generally in the middle in total acres of improved land and in production of corn, potatoes, oats, and other crops and in number of cattle. The town was in the top half of grist- and sawmilling operations.

There also was one woolen factory that produced 1,250 yards of woolen and cotton cloth, one of three inventoried paper mills in the county (Catskill had two), and three tanneries. There also were Baptist, Presbyterian, Congregational, Methodist, and three Quaker churches/meeting houses (no Reformed Church was mentioned but perhaps the Presbyterian designation was misidentified) and sixteen common schools with 529 pupils. There was a single private or select school, two taverns, five retail stores, three groceries, 347 farmers, six merchants, five manufacturers, fifty-six mechanics, five clergymen, two physicians, and no lawyers.

By 1855, the population proportions of Greene County had been jumbled a bit. New Baltimore had risen to be the sixth most populous of the fourteen towns with a total citizenry of 2,402, 1,211 men, 1,112 women, 37 "colored" men, and 42 "colored" women. There were 455 families and 306 landowners. The town was third in the total number of gallons of milk sold and second in total yards of cotton and mixed cloth produced.

New Baltimore's agricultural propensity toward fruit growing was starting to come to the fore. The town came in fourth in the number of bushels of apples produced behind Durham, Greenville, and Cairo and fourth also in barrels of cider brewed behind Catskill, Cairo, and Athens.

War of Rebellion

Turmoil was the order of the day as the 1860s arrived. Relations between the northern and southern states were in complete disarray. New York State and Greene County were split politically and socially on the issues of slavery and secession. A good part of the state's commerce was transacted with southern businesses so many people could empathize with the need to continue an economy based on slave labor.

Catskill's *Recorder and Democrat* newspaper was quite emphatic in its editorializing on the need to maintain states' rights to do business as usual. The word "Democrat" on their masthead belies a certain political motivation that did not feature ready support for the programs and proposals of Republican president Abraham Lincoln. As late as 1864, the weekly still was publishing stories on the "Aromatic African" and referring freely to their perceived liabilities of the "nigger."

When Fort Sumter was attacked on April 12, 1861, a semblance of unity toward taking action prevailed among the masses, at least for the time being. The Congress had authorized Lincoln to call for volunteers. New York State immediately moved to provide requisite troops and dollars to support the war effort. The call-ups were centered on municipalities in state senatorial districts and targeted to men between the ages of eighteen and forty-five.

Both the Catskill newspapers, the *Recorder and Democrat* and the Republican-alternative *Examiner*, were keeping the locals well apprised of the rising tensions between North and South. Then, in its April 18 issue, the former broadsheet announced with appropriate gravity that Union troops at Fort Sumter had seen a blistering Confederate attack and subsequently been battered into an embarrassing surrender.[7,8]

20th/80th Infantry Regiment

In a few short days, the long-standing 20th New York State Militia Regiment was called into action for three months of service under its commander from the Catskills, Colonel George Pratt, son of the legendary Greene County tanner Zadock Pratt. This unit, nicknamed the "Ulster Guard," was based in Ulster County but drew a significant number of recruits from surrounding locations, including Greene County.[9] The war was on.

The men gathered to the strains of the Catskill Cornet Band before journeying to Kingston to board the Thomas Cornell Line's steamboat *Manhattan* and its two trailing barges for transport to New York City. The 20th eventually spent a brief campaign quietly on guard and performing drill duties in the Annapolis and Baltimore areas, at times protecting critical railroad links into Washington. Despite their longing to fight for real, our troops missed the First Battle of Bull Run that was fought practically next door to their encampment.

The expected civilian contributions to the war effort from back home started almost immediately. Private citizens and businesses were urged to action to support men called to duty. Soldiers' aid societies, relief agencies, and ladies' aid groups were quick to provide supplies and equipment for troops in the field. Toward the end of May, the *Recorder and Democrat* reprinted an article from the *Prattsville News* that "the Honorable Zadoc Pratt sent six firkins of butter to his son, Col. George W. Pratt, for the use of the 20th Regiment now encamped at Annapolis, Md."[10]

Back home and mustered out as August began, the men soon were called back to arms by Colonel Pratt, responding to national calls to address the widening conflict. Catskill became a ready and accessible point for troop deployment as men came on every stage coach from the west to set off for battle. The new Pratt unit, soon to be designated the 80th Infantry Regiment, was mustered in at Kingston between September 20 and October 20, 1861 for a three-year term. The troops, proud of their unit's history, strove to avoid use of the 80th name and continued to call themselves the 20th.

Joseph Bronk was among a handful of New Baltimore recruits to the unit. Bronk enlisted October 13 at Kingston and would remain in the regiment until its final muster out at Portsmouth, Virginia on January 29, 1866.

By the end of October, the valiant warriors were armed and equipped and on their way to picket duty around Washington and northern Virginia. As spring 1862 neared, the men marched and drilled around their encampments, skirmishing with the enemy on occasion and starting to sustain the harsh wounds of war. In late August, the Greene and Ulster County troops found themselves in the thick of the horror at the Second Battle of Bull Run at Manassas, where 279 of their number were killed, wounded, or declared missing. Leading his men on a gallant charge, Colonel Pratt was critically wounded, shot in the spine, injuries that proved fatal a couple of weeks later.

Other Units Join the Conflict

As the fighting intensified, other units quickly organized. A number of New Baltimoreans traveled to Albany in August and September of 1861 to join the renowned 44th Infantry Regiment or Ellsworth Avengers, named for Colonel E. Elmer Ellsworth, the first Union officer killed in the war. New Baltimore volunteers included Henry Huckens, Charles A. and John Burns, Almon M. Nichols, Daniel A. Burlingham, Frederick A. and Henry Mead, Silas Mansfield, and Henry Colvin. The unit was at such notable battles as Second Bull Run, Antietam, Fredericksburg, Chancellorsville, Gettysburg, the Wilderness, and the Siege of Petersburg.

Private Charles Burns may have been the unit's first casualty, albeit at first in a somewhat awkward manner. He sustained a hernia in his right side in mid-February of 1862 when his horse, struck by enemy fire, rolled over on him. Burns ended up in a regimental hospital. Back in action by the end of June, "at the seven days fight in front of Richmond he was struck on the head with a gun, in the hands of a Rebel soldier and rendered unconscious that while in this condition he was taken prisoner and was detained in the Rebel prison for six weeks when he was exchanged . . ."[11]

Burns was taken into Richmond and one of its notorious prisons, Belle Isle. He was extremely fortunate in being exchanged just six weeks after his capture. The system that the Union and Confederate leaders attempted to implement for trading prisoners was erratically applied and eventually generally abandoned.

The Rebel prisons were horrid snake pits that one hoped to avoid at all costs. Belle Isle is a low-lying island on the James River in the center of the modern city of Richmond. There effectively were no shelters beyond tents that housed the three thousand stated maximum number of captives. The rest of the six thousand men usually imprisoned at Belle slept on the tree-less ground in the intense summer heat and bitter winter cold, often without clothing or blankets. Human waste and garbage had no place to go so the island was saturated with filth. Disease was rampant and medical care minimal. Rations were scarce. At one point, the daily menu was three-quarters of a pound of cornbread.

Burns's New Baltimore compatriot, the 44-year-old Almon M. Nichols, was victimized by one of the largest killers of the Civil War. He had joined the 44th as a wagon driver at Albany on August 27, 1861. Just short of a year later, Nichols died of dysentery on a hospital boat moored at Philadelphia. His remains were interred at the Soldiers' Cemetery in that Pennsylvania city.

Two-thirds of the fatalities in the Civil War resulted from disease. Dysentery, measles, small pox, pneumonia, and malaria were common killers. Overcrowded camps, horrendous hygiene, inadequate or nonexistent sanitation facilities, weather extremes, lack of shelter and suitable clothing, and the poor quality of food and water were the routine of life for soldiers on both sides.

Nevertheless, the men of Greene County and New Baltimore enthusiastically joined a number of other regiments, traveling to Albany, Kingston, and other locales to answer the Union's call. Frederick Mead, the seventeen-year-old bartending son of hotelkeepers Stephen and Sarah Mead, entered Union service on February 9, 1864, enlisting with the 122nd New York Infantry Regiment. Alonzo A. Craw joined the 83rd New York Infantry Regiment and may have been the first local fatality, succumbing to disease at Sandy Hook, Maryland on August 4, 1862.

Horatio N. Badgley, a nearly fifty-year-old farmer from Medway, Edward Miller, and Abram Post signed up for the 156th New York Infantry Regiment. This unit was nicknamed the Mountain Legion because it drew men largely from the small communities tucked away in the Catskill and Shawangunk mountains and their foothills.

Andrew T. Hotaling, William Houghtaling, George Losee, James Mansfield, James L. Warner, and Charles Vickers took up the heavy guns of the 7th Artillery Regiment. Stephen J. Badgley (likely the son of Horatio mentioned earlier), George A. Powell, Newton Soule, and Robert Teel went into the 91st New York Infantry, or Albany, Regiment.

Eugene Van Sandvoort, a 26-year-old clerk, enlisted in the 169th Infantry Regiment at Troy on September 16, 1862. He was the son of Staats Van Sandvoort, the Reformed minister, and his wife Lucretia. Musically inclined, Eugene was appointed a drum major. His military records show him stationed in Florida and the Carolinas while being promoted to lieutenant. In October 1864, he wrote his commanders requesting relief from duty in the ambulance corps so he could accept a promotion to captain. This appears to have made Eugene the highest-ranking New Baltimore soldier in the war. Van Sandvoort was wounded in the knee at the Battle of Cold Harbor, buried alive, and survived an explosion at Fort Fisher with a badly wounded hand. After his July 1865 discharge, he died "suddenly" at Newburgh in November of that year.

Samuel Van Slyke, an African American, was born in New Baltimore in 1836. Among other jobs, he was a coachman for New Baltimore river trading magnates Edward Sherman and Henry Slingerland. He enlisted as a private in the 20th U.S. Colored Regiment on August 30, 1864 and ultimately was wounded and discharged as disabled at New Orleans' Corps d' Afrique Hospital in mid-June of 1865. Van Slyke came home and lived out his life on a pension with wife Mary at his Ravine Mill cabin on the Hannacroix Creek. He died July 19, 1889 resting on a chair in his garden.

120th New York Infantry Regiment

To facilitate the mobilization of troops, New York's counties and towns in mid-1862 were organized along state senatorial districts whose representatives would coordinate the meeting of recruitment quotas. New Baltimore was in the tenth district and had an initial requirement of twenty-five men to be gathered into one company.[12]

As a result, most town men ended up in the newly formed 120th New York Infantry Regiment.[13] The 120th was to become part of the Army of the Potomac that the United States Congress had authorized to defend Washington, D.C. from attack by the ambitious Confederate forces. It was the major Union fighting unit for the Eastern Theater of the Civil War that encompassed Virginia, West Virginia, Maryland, Pennsylvania, and North Carolina.

The recruitment campaign for the 120th Regiment was focused on Ulster County but also targeted Greene and other surrounding counties. Company D was the one drawn from New Baltimore, Coxsackie, Ashland, Prattsville, and Kingston. Captain Lansing Hollister and Lieutenant Minor H. Greene, Coxsackie farm boys in their early twenties, led the recruiting effort for the company under the overall command of Colonel George H. Sharpe.

Over a period of three weeks in August 1862, about twenty men enlisted at New Baltimore. There was the painter Stephen S. Mead, the Irish-born tailor John Francis Wright, and the boatman Joseph P. Smith, who was a neighbor and possible employee of the noted shipbuilder Jedediah Baldwin. The ages of the determined volunteers ranged from the eighteen-year-olds Francis W. Dedrick, Smith B. Dibole, and Martin A. Houghtaling up to the 56-year-old Baptist minister, Foster Hartwell, who was named regiment chaplain. A number of the men were in their thirties and forties and had families and established lives, including the Dutch-born quarryman Jacob Besley, Charles Deuble, John Langin, and Peter Sitser.

Before the war, Foster Hartwell had been the pastor at the Greenville Center Baptist Church. He started services for people in New Baltimore hamlet and later was instrumental in establishing a congregation there and building its house of worship.

Fathers and sons and brothers and cousins joined. Dedrick's older brother Hermance and the Reverend Hartwell's son Dwight were early recruits. Father and son Tunis P. and Philip Wolfe left wife and mother Ann and their jobs as painters and enlisted a week apart in early August 1862 as privates in the 120th Regiment. Philip was wounded at White Oak Ridge, Virginia March 31, 1865 in the Union's final push against the Confederates on the road to surrender at Appomattox.

The Smith brothers, Moses M. and Abram, volunteered. Both were working as caulkers in the shipbuilding business. The boys went their separate ways when war called. Abram signed up for the 120th in August of 1862 and drove wagons. Moses joined fellow New Baltimoreans Francis Church and John H. Marshall on the horses of the 2nd Cavalry Regiment. Smith and Marshall both were captured October 19, 1864 at the Battle of Cedar Creek. This was one of the pivotal fights for the Union to wrest control of the Shenandoah Valley from the Confederates.

Beyond the commitment of men for the military, the state's population now was called upon to underwrite the cost of the war effort. Funding was needed for troop salaries, equipment, and supplies. Soldiers had to be sheltered, fed, and armed. Bounties were paid to entice recruits, money that was to be derived from a variety of possible sources. For example, license fees required to practice various occupations were implemented or increased. Apothecaries would have to pay $10, bankers $100, livery stable keepers $10, surgeons $10, and on down a substantial list of producers and retailers, including $20 for jugglers! Theaters, hotels, circuses, eating houses, and steamboat operations also felt the licensing financial burden.[14]

Considerable anger arose in local circles when talk of a military draft came up. The First Battle of Bull Run took a huge toll on the troops through lost lives and debilitating injuries and fostered a growing disinclination for people to volunteer as readily for duty. Some felt that the Union should introduce a draft to ensure adequate staffing of forces.

The Greene County response to the rumors was clear. One local newspaper reported that "The citizens of the towns of Greenville, New Baltimore, Coxsackie and Athens, desirous to avoid the disgrace of a 'Draft,' offer, in addition to State and Government Bounties, a Town Bounty of $100 to each and every volunteer that shall come forward to serve his country, in a new Regiment now forming in the counties of Greene and Ulster . . ."[15] For the time being, the antidraft movement succeeded in stalling the effort.

Eventually, the dire need came to a head to ensure an adequate number of troops for a war that continued to drag on in ominous, deadly fashion. Governor Horatio Seymour led strong New York resistance, culminating in New York City riots of midsummer 1863 that resulted in more than one hundred people killed and fifty buildings burned.

Nonetheless, there were three drafts in total in 1863–1864. As the antiwar, anti-Republican, and most defiantly anti-Lincoln *Recorder and Democrat* dutifully but reluctantly reported on the September 7 and 8, 1863 ringing of the draft bell at Kingston for Greene County's men: "At about 10 o'clock, Marshal Fiero read the President's proclamation, by which it appeared that the number required from this district was 2006. Capt. McMahon turned the wheel and H. Van Buren, a blind man, drew the names. The utmost quiet prevailed." Sixty-eight New Baltimore names were drawn.[16]

As it turned out, few of the hometown draftees appear to have been pressed into duty. Chapter 690 of the State Laws of 1865 required Jedediah Baldwin of New Baltimore and other town clerks to make a record of the names of all the local men who served as troops during the Civil War. While not the final authority, the clerk's accounting only identifies one serving New Baltimore draftee, Irish-born laborer James McCabe.

Off to War

A couple of days after mustering, the 120th Regiment left their mid-Hudson home to the cheers of Kingston crowds, once again aboard Cornell's steamer *Manhattan.* By this time, there was a Union recruitment goal of 600,000 troops, including New Baltimore's quota of seventy-six. The volunteers sailed to New York City, ferried over to Jersey City, and boarded a train first for Philadelphia then on to Washington, D.C.

From their initial encampment just across the Potomac at Arlington, the men started on a series of marches, stopping at various camps, including cutting logs to help build corduroy roads to carry the artillery's wagons and guns. The usual picket duty and drilling practice also were daily routines. These vantage points gave an unthankful chance for the Greene and Ulster soldiers to see firsthand the scarred landscape of the battlefield at Bull Run and the bedraggled and wounded heroes who suffered through that recent Union defeat.

This period of relative inactivity and calm left the men with an anxious longing for action. Their first real taste of enemy fire came at the Battle of Fredericksburg, an initial step toward a push into the Southern capital, Richmond. Trying to regain initiative against an increasingly recalcitrant Confederate army, Union forces mounted a strong but futile frontal assault on Rebel defenders well dug into the hills above the city. While there were extensive casualties and the army suffered a humbling end to their planned campaign to take Richmond, losses for the 120th were relatively light. Exposed to some enemy shelling during their labors, the men generally were in a support position to the frontline troops, cutting wood to reinforce roads and fulfilling picket duties.

The Greene County soldiers spent their first dreary days and cold nights of winter service in Virginia just outside of Washington in a gigantic, troop-built city of tents and simple wooden huts. After a season of recuperation albeit while enduring harsh weather conditions in meager shelter, the opposing armies then were to clash once again at Chancellorsville. There, damages were much more critical. The Union army had more than twice the number of troops and was well rested and well supplied but Robert E. Lee enacted a remarkable Rebel battle plan.

It resulted in another striking Southern victory, with the 120th sustaining losses of sixty-six men killed, wounded, or missing. Consecutive, serious Union defeats invigorated the Confederacy, motivating General Lee to plan an invasion of the North. Pennsylvania was a ready target.

The Battle for Gettysburg

After a handful of preliminary set-tos and maneuvering in early June of 1863, the opposing sides drew together around Gettysburg. Lieutenant Colonel Cornelius D. Westbrook and Major John R. Tappen commanded the 120th Regiment in the 2nd or "Excelsior" Brigade led by Colonel William R. Brewster under overall authority of Major Generals Daniel E. Sickles and David B. Birney. Numerous other New York units participated in the battle, including the 20th and 44th regiments with their Greene County contingents of fighters.

As the fighting raged on the second day, General Sickles made the ill-advised, unilateral decision to move his corps from its initial defensive position on Cemetery Ridge forward a mile to a place known as the Peach Orchard. Regrettably, this location encompassed an area too large and indefensible for the size of Sickles's unit. The men became sitting ducks for two Confederate divisions that proceeded to bombard the corps who nonetheless bravely held their ground and extracted significant Rebel casualties.

Colonel Brewster provided some graphic details of the battle, noting a particular illustration of the heroics of the Greene County regiment:

> At about 1 o'clock on the afternoon of the 2d, I received orders from the brigadier-general commanding the division to move the brigade to the front, and form line of battle in rear of the First Brigade (then going into position on the right of the First Division), and send one regiment to the crest of the hill, about 250 yards in advance of the First Brigade, with instructions that, should the enemy attempt to take it, to hold it at all hazards . . . [Note: at this point, the 120th was assigned to support the first line of battle of the division.] At about 4 o'clock we advanced our line of battle, and in our new position were exposed to a most terrible fire from the enemy's artillery on our left, which was most destructive, killing and wounding many men . . .
>
> Up to this time we had not been engaged at all, but now the troops on our left being obliged to fall back, the enemy advanced upon us in great force, pouring into us a most terrific fire of artillery and musketry, both upon our front and left flank. Our men returned it with great effect, and for some time held the enemy in check, but the troops on our left being, for want of support, forced still farther back, left us exposed to an enfilading fire, before which we were obliged to fall back, which was done in good order, but with terrible loss of both officers and men.
>
> Seeing the enemy in possession of three of our guns, I made a charge at the head of about 150 men, from the Second, Third, Fourth, Fifth, and One hundred and twentieth Regiments, and succeeded in recapturing them, taking from one the colors of the Eighth Florida Regiment, and bringing in as prisoners the major of that regiment and some 30 of his men . . .
>
> As the sun set, the men were reinforced and allowed to reform and rest for the night. The next day saw the 2nd Brigade subjected to severe artillery fire and further personal damages but the end was near. The troops sadly were left to collect their dead and wounded from the field of battle.[17]

On the third, while fighting raged on various fronts, the main event occurred on Cemetery Ridge. General Lee ordered an ill-advised, futile charge of 12,500 Confederate troops to take the center of the Union line. The Northern regiments were well ready and exacted a staggering toll of destruction. The massive casualties of this infamous Pickett's Charge forced General Lee to retreat back south to Virginia and turned the tide of the war.

The 120th Regiment listed over two hundred of its full complement of troops as killed, wounded, or missing, about a quarter of its total war casualties. General Sickles lost a leg and left his command and military career behind in tatters. The demoralization of their losses perhaps was a little leavened by the eventual striking Union victory, crushing the Confederates' northern campaign and pushing them in the direction of ultimate defeat.

The *Recorder and Democrat* at Catskill was reporting that the 44th New York or Ellsworth Regiment came out of the Battle at Gettysburg with 111 men dead, wounded, or missing out of a total of three hundred troops. "The recent terrible battles in Pennsylvania, attended with such fearful slaughter, have sent mourning into very many of our households, to be repeated many times, we fear, ere 'this cruel war is over.' "[18]

Despite the North's victory, the boys of the 120th Regiment had to lament the outcome. Their casualties were too many, 30 men killed, 154 wounded, and 19 missing. The beloved young Captain Lansing Hollister was fatally wounded. Among New Baltimoreans, Francis W. Dedrick, the eighteen-year-old farm boy originally from Athens, was killed. The German-born, 32-year-old laborer Charles Deuble was wounded. He and Dedrick were recruited by Hollister at New Baltimore the same day almost a year before the battle.

Abram Smith, the 24-year-old ship caulker, was shot in the left arm at Gettysburg, putting him in the hospital for much of many coming months. The Canadian-born ship carpenter John Langin had left his wife Catherine and three small children at home. He was wounded, as was a likely workmate, Robert Hilton, a 29-year-old ship carpenter and native of Hackington, England. John Wright and Jacob Besley also sustained minor injuries.

Back home, as the Gettysburg battle unfolded, the state of New York enacted legislation permitting the local governments for New Baltimore and other places to convene a Board of Relief to grant assistance as needed to the families of soldiers from their municipalities. They could provide locally decided amounts of support. The Town Board minutes and local newspapers are silent on any official action New Baltimore may have taken to organize such a group. In fact, the only time the annual meeting of the board recorded consideration of anything regarding the war was to report on a vote to change the Constitution to allow people absent for military service to vote. Otherwise, the meetings were used pretty much to verify election results.

After their retreat from Gettysburg, Confederate forces gathered by the Rapidan River in northern Virginia, with Union officers criticized for their failure to immediately and sufficiently pursue the enemy. The Northern commanders responded by planning several new offensives in Virginia, the earliest of which at places like Bristoe Station were stalemates. Coincidently, this location is quite close to the unincorporated community of New Baltimore, Virginia. Perhaps the Greene County boys felt a little the pangs of homesickness.

Andersonville: Martin Houghtaling, George Gage, and Frank Church

Martin A. Houghtaling was an eighteen-year-old New Baltimore–born farmhand. Martin probably is the young boarder on Robert Nelson's farm counted in the 1860 federal census. Barely into his adulthood, Martin must have had understandable second thoughts about volunteering and perhaps even a bout of homesickness. He was recorded as a deserter on a September 5, 1863 list of prisoners at Castle William on Governor's Island in New York City. He had run away in May at Falmouth, Virginia and was arrested in late August at Coxsackie.

Desertion was a major problem in the morally vague arena of a Civil War. It also was defined loosely and did not mean that the soldier was evading service for good. A man just may have been lagging behind, separated from his troop, or gone home to help with the family farm's harvest. Things were easily forgiven, understood, or overlooked.

Houghtaling was back in the ranks by fall and marching with the 120th to James City, Virginia where the men hoped to corner General Lee's forces. Regrettably for the Union troops, confusion reigned, and the Confederate cavalry overwhelmed the desperate New Yorkers. Accounts may vary as to exact numbers but well over one hundred soldiers of the 120th were captured on that fateful October 10, including Martin Houghtaling.

He was confined ten days later at Richmond, likely at the infamous Belle Isle prison, then sent on to the Camp Sumter prison at Andersonville in southwest Georgia by early March of 1864. What became known simply as Andersonville was hell on earth, even compared to Belle Isle. During its fourteen months of operation, of 45,000 total captives, 13,000 died from malnutrition.

The prisoners faced minimal rations and nothing to cook them with, with no wood for heating or cooking. Only crude shelters self-made from cloth, mud, brush, and branches offered protection from the weather. The men's torn and tattered clothing had no replacement unless something could be salvaged from the dead. Newcomers described the captives, once "stalwart men," as "now nothing but mere walking skeletons, covered with filth and vermin. Many of our men, in the heat and intensity of their feeling, exclaimed with earnestness. 'Can this be hell?' 'God protect us!' "

The Stockade Creek running through the middle of the prison was the water supply, laundry (sand substituted for soap), bathtub, and repository for runoff from the latrines of both the prisoners and guards. The central area of the compound was described as "a swamp, occupying about three or four acres of the narrowed limits, and a part of this marshy place had been used by the prisoners as a sink, and excrement covered the ground, the scent arising from which was suffocating."[19]

If a prisoner did not waste away to nothing before release, he died by the curse of multiple diseases. After about six months of what must have been a tortuous existence, Martin Houghtaling was admitted to what there was of a hospital at Andersonville on August 18, 1864 and died the same day of diarrhea. He lies in grave 6094 at the National Cemetery there.

It seems likely that he knew George Gage and Frank Church. George was the teenage son of steamboat pilot David Gage and his wife Abigail. He had traveled to New York City to enlist in the 2nd New York Cavalry on New Year's Day 1862. Gage was wounded and taken prisoner in early June 1863 in Virginia at Brandy Station, a precursor to the Gettysburg campaign and the largest cavalry-dominant battle in American history. Like Martin Houghtaling, he first was taken to Richmond but fortunately was released at City Point, Virginia after less than a week. His short confinement perhaps resulted from an extensive parole campaign then underway at Belle Isle.

Promoted to corporal in November, Gage's run of bad luck reappeared just into the New Year in 1864 when he was recaptured, this time in the vicinity of Ely's Ford, Virginia, a key crossing of the Rapidan River. George was imprisoned once again at Richmond. Regrettably, early release was not to happen this time. He was put on a train to Andersonville. George lasted two months in the squalid conditions before being admitted to the hospital where he died of diarrhea or scurvy or a combination of both three days before Martin Houghtaling's passing. He was laid to rest with his fellow townsman in the grounds of the prisoners' cemetery at Andersonville.

Francis M. Church, or Frank as he was called, endured captivity the shortest time. He had enlisted at New York City two weeks before Christmas of 1863. The son of laborer William Church and mother Ann Eliza, Frank left four younger sisters and a brother behind to join the Union cause. He was captured June 29, 1864 at Reams Station, Virginia, an early battle in the Petersburg-Richmond campaign, or the so-called Siege of Petersburg. Frank Church died from diarrhea at Andersonville three days before George Gage. He joined his New Baltimore neighbors for eternity in Georgia soils.

Petersburg and the Boydton Plank Road

By the beginning of June 1864, the warriors of the 120th, with its Company D New Baltimoreans, had marched their way to points south of Petersburg, Virginia. Their goal, as part of a combined Union force, was to squeeze the life from the Confederate capital at Richmond, cutting the city off from its critical main supply and reinforcement route from the south. Initial assaults on the Rebel fortifications generally were repulsed, resulting in the Northern army digging trench lines that ran over thirty miles along the southern and eastern outskirts of Petersburg, a neighboring city a few miles below Richmond.

Frequent jousts between the opposing sides over the next nine months led to possibly the most hurtful confrontations of the war for the New Baltimore men. The first casualty for the 120th may have been Frederick Waggoner who had enlisted as a private two years earlier. He was wounded close to the end of July near Petersburg.

Andrew T. Hotaling, the 24-year-old New Baltimore-born farmer and son of Ephraim and Emma Gay Hotaling, enlisted in late 1862 at Guilderland in the 7th New York Heavy Artillery and eventually reached the rank of sergeant. A poignant March 15, 1864 letter sent from Andrew at his Delaware encampment to his sister observes that he "will be home the 5th day of November 1865 if I live to see it." A gunshot wound fractured his left foot "near Petersburg, Va" on June 22, 1864. He died a little over a month later in Ward 12 of the Lincoln Hospital at Washington, D.C., "of gunshot fracture, exhaustion, hemorrhage."[20]

On October 27th, the men of the 120th marched to the Boydton Plank Road, southeast of Petersburg City, and joined its brigade. The troops were posted in an open field east of the road in support of a unit that was to take higher ground across a stream. Then all hell broke loose. Van Sandvoort's history of the 120th quotes the diary of one soldier:

> we were startled first by the rattle of musketry at our right, and then nearly in our rear. A sudden and furious attack had been made on General Pierce's brigade, who, thus assailed unexpectedly by an overwhelming force, fell back in disorder, leaving two cannon to fall into the enemy's hands. Egan abandoned the projected assault against the heights, faced about, and, assisted by our brigade and some other troops, made a countercharge, retaking the guns General Pierce had lost, and capturing about one thousand prisoners from the enemy. We soon found ourselves facing about south, in the direction from which we had marched. A rain was falling, and without breast-works we were subjected to a severe fire of artillery, which caused serious results to the regiment. We moved forward a short distance to the woods, where, with our hands and tin plates, we dug in the ground to protect ourselves from the enemy's bullets, which seemed to come from every direction. We were surrounded by the foe, and the prospect was anything but agreeable. Late in the afternoon our regiment and the Eleventh Massachusetts were ordered to charge the enemy in front of us. We moved forward, capturing a number of the pickets and driving their skirmish line before us. After getting through the swamp we could see the enemy's forces rallying, and they were soon advancing and pouring into our ranks such a stream of musketry as to force us back to our position in the edge of the woods, from which our volleys held them at bay. Captain James Chambers and seven enlisted men were killed during the day, and thirty-three members of the regiment were wounded and sixteen missing. Lieutenant-Colonel Tappen's horse was killed by a solid shot or shell as he stood by it, waiting for orders. About dusk we heard a Union cheer in front of us. The enemy had been attacked from the rear, and were soon compelled to withdraw, losing a number of prisoners. The bullets from the attacking columns whistled over our heads, and we soon joined in the loud cheers that followed. Our part in the battle of Boydton Plank Road, or the "Bull Ring," as it was called, was ended,

> and after dark, through the cold rain and the mud, we commenced our march back toward the front of Petersburg, and on October 31st we arrived once more at our old quarters, the bomb-proof camp near Fort Morton.[21]

The Greene County men in the 120th took their share of the losses on October 27. Robert Hilton, the English-born ship carpenter had been wounded at Gettysburg but survived to gain promotion to first sergeant in mid-October. Just over two weeks later, he was shot in the head and killed instantly at Petersburg, leaving behind Mary, his wife of nine years. The Baptist minister's son, Dwight Hartwell, was killed the same day.

Hermance Dedrick was wounded. His younger brother Francis had been killed at Gettysburg. The brothers Moses and Abram Smith had gone their separate military ways only to wind up together in dire circumstances. Moses Smith was captured October 19, 1864 at the Battle of Cedar Creek, a pivotal conflict in the North's campaign to cripple the economy in Virginia's Shenandoah Valley by cutting off a key supply base for the Confederates.

After his Gettysburg wounding, Abram Smith found himself in a hospital at Newark, New Jersey. After a long recovery, he was back in action only to be taken prisoner at Jerusalem Plank Road during the waning days of the Petersburg siege. Both young men ended up as captives in the Confederate's infamous Libby Prison at Richmond, an institution noted for its horrendous overcrowding, unsanitary conditions, and numerous prisoner deaths. The Smiths were released from confinement on February 5, 1865 at Cox's Wharf, Virginia. Both brothers were mustered out with their companies near Washington the following June.

The losses for New Baltimore servicemen, though, still were not over. With the initiation of conscription in 1863 by both the Northern and Southern armies, draftees were allowed to hire substitutes to fulfill their service requirements. One young local man, Darius Salisbury, appears to have taken advantage of such a financial arrangement. Darius probably was the twelve-year-old youngster who shows up in the 1860 federal census as the son of laborer Benjamin and his wife Eliza. The family was neighbors of papermaker James Croswell, prompting the thought that Benjamin was working in the Hannacroix Creek paper mill.

Salisbury was mustered into service with the 10th Infantry Regiment in August of 1864 at Kingston. The New Baltimore town clerk's register of Civil War participants lists him as a substitute. It also reports his wounding at the Battle of Hatcher's Run that took place in early

February 1865 as part of the Petersburg campaign. While there are no details about his injuries, the adjutant general's 10th Regiment roster describes Salisbury as being mustered out of service at Mower United States Hospital in Philadelphia at the start of the following summer.

By the beginning of April, General Lee saw the end of the road, yielding to the unrelenting Union pressure on his remaining stronghold. He abandoned Petersburg and Richmond and started on his ultimate retreat to surrender at Appomattox Court House. The 120th Regiment was there to witness the combatants' final lay down of their swords.

Postwar

As New Baltimore's brave warriors returned back up the Hudson, nursing wounds and illnesses and mourning the handful of mortally lost colleagues, they found a world that had seen the usual ebbs and flows of life. The Medway Congregational Christian Church had been built, and its dedication was held the day after Christmas during the war's first year. The Baldwin brothers steam mill near their shipyard had burned as had Henry Wolf's barn and stored farming equipment. The shipbuilders also had launched their largest vessel ever, the 253-foot steam freighter *Nupah.* The soldiers had left town with one Democratic supervisor in charge, Peter Stover, returned to another, Daniel Miller, having missed a third in between, Edgar Halstead.

The 1865 New York State census reported concerns about local farming production. The town had two election districts at the time, the first covering essentially the hamlet and its close environs and the other comprising the more rural central and western acres. Two farmers, Levi Bedell and David Williams, were the enumerators for the east and west districts, respectively. They were asked to poll local agriculturists for their production output for 1864.

The first district was hampered by a severe drought that limited the hay, oats, and corn crops by about a third less of a usual output. The second district was claiming a bit less of a downturn with potatoes, rye, and buckwheat at par levels but corn and hay were at two-thirds of regular output. Oats were the western part of town's biggest downfall with only about a quarter of the usual crop.

To compound harvesting issues, the price of farmland had risen about 25 percent since 1860 in district 1 and $10 an acre in the west. Pay for farm laborers also was up considerably. First district costs for summer workers had gone from an average of $16 monthly wages in 1860 to $25 in 1864, and the second from $28 to $33. One wonders if the higher salaries were the result of supply issues due to working men away to war. One also wonders about the statistic that crime in the western part of town had been cut in half!

On the business front, the Hudson-side area had three "inns, hotels and taverns," four retail stores, and five groceries. The west side of town had one hostelry and two groceries. The census lists James C. Sherman, Joseph Sherman, William Raymond, William C. Hinman, Herman Hinman, John Rowe, George Van Slyke, George W. Smith, James Trego, David Hallock, Albert Hallenbeck, and Albert Miller as merchants who either were operating the noted establishments or were trading on the river.

James Ostrom was a saloonkeeper. The young Civil War veteran, Frederick Mead, was back in town working as a bartender for his father, hotelkeeper Stephen Mead. Also residing at their establishment was wife and mother Sarah, ship caulker George Everson, Irish- and German-born laborers Barney Flynn and Henry Long, ship carpenters William Phillips and Allen Tobias, painters Lyman Diefendorf and Edward Scott, and the Meads' daughter-in-law Augusta, grandson David, and nieces Jane and Carrie Whitbeck.

Handfuls of butchers, shoemakers, wagon and harness makers, teachers, and dressmakers also worked hard to support the community. It was not uncommon for careers to be intergenerational within families. Thomas Huckens and his sons Henry, John, and Samuel headed a small coterie of tailors. John B. Marshall and his sons Leonard, Constantine, and John H. all were working on the Hudson as were Gillet Van Zandt and his sons Richard, Robert, and Melvin. Another Stephen, Henry, and Caleb Mead joined a second Frederick as painters in the same household.

Doctors Theodore Cornell and Isaac Van Hoesen met the medical needs of the eastern and western parts of town, respectively. There even was a sawyer (Edward Raymond), undertaker (William M. Scribner), taxidermist (William Davis), and a couple of fishermen (John Anderson and Dan Shepley).

The clergy was represented by Robert Strong, Staats Van Sandvoort, Foster Hartwell, James A. H. Cornell, and Warren Hathaway. Some local churches, though, may have taken a hit in attendance because of the war. In the hamlet, the Reformed Church had a capacity of 250 and average attendance of 220. The Methodist-Episcopal congregation only saw 70 attending of its 200 capacity.

In other parts of town, there was a mixed bag. Grapeville's Baptist Church routinely had 150 of its 250 members at services. Medway's

Christian congregation was at a healthy 350 attendees of 400 members. The Methodist Church in the western district appears to have fallen into disfavor with only about a sixth of its parishioners coming on Sunday. The previously popular Quakers must have been approaching their lowest ebb. The Orthodox Friends branch was at 20 of 300 worshipers while there are no attendance figures provided for the Hicksites beyond the listing of a 200-member capacity.

The vast majority of New Baltimore workers were registered in the census as either farmers or laborers. The latter group of people may have been common farm workers, particularly in District 2, the largely rural, agricultural western part of town. There is little doubt that this class of worker also was employed on building vessels at the shipyard of the Baldwin brothers, Jedediah and Henry, laboring in the grain mills of John Van Bergen, Jeremiah Dean, Garrett Sickler, and Richard Powell and the paper mill of James Croswell, and assisting the plethora of carpenters, masons, painters, and blacksmiths. The western district blacksmith, Charles Smith, employed three helpers, as did the wagon maker, Lewis Simmons.

The Hudson River trades were well represented with the occupation of "boatman" taking the third place in numbers. Ship carpenters, pilots, and engineers also were plentiful. Noted river freighters Edward E. Sherman, Henry Slingerland, and James Reynolds were hamlet residents. The Civil War Smith brothers, Abram and Moses, are working as shipyard caulkers.

Perhaps one of the more interesting groups of census-counted residents was a sizable number of people whose occupation was given en masse as railroad worker. Most were single men although Charles and Mary O'Neil had a brood of five youngsters encamped in what the census described as shanties. Mostly Irish-born with a handful from New England and nearby counties, these folks had come to New Baltimore to participate in a big postwar event in town history, the coming of the steam-driven train.

The wealth of the census data provide a view of life to come for New Baltimore. The period after the Civil War through the end of the century was to be the high point of the town's commercial history as shipbuilding, ice making, and farming sparked excitement, anxiety, and sustenance with much of the economic passion centered on the mighty Hudson.

6

Life on the River

The Hudson River quite naturally played a pivotal role in the settling and development of the town of New Baltimore. While rudimentary Indian paths may have provided rough access, it seems more than likely that the original settlers floated here on the river's waters. While most of the shoreline was a bit steep and hilly, those early wanderers saw potential for hacking a living out of the wilderness. For many subsequent decades, a multitude of residents managed to draw all or part of their living from the Hudson.

We have spoken a little about the trading and other entrepreneurial skills of the Shermans, Vanderzees, and Tituses. For many decades, travelers also could catch a ride on the *City of Hudson*, *Lotta*, or another of an array of sailing or steam vessels docking behind the Imperial Hotel just down the short hill from the hamlet's center crossroads of Main and Mill streets. Regular runs went from New Baltimore to Albany, Catskill, and other locales. River industry, though, probably met its economic height in the years after the Civil War, revolving largely around the manufacture and repair of vessels and the harvesting of ice.

A mass of people may not have become rich from the river but they had new jobs that provided pretty steady employment for a long time. We should not overstate the scale of New Baltimore's place in the maritime world of the nineteenth and early twentieth centuries. But the Hudson and its world played an important role in the lives of local workers and their families who often had to scrape to earn a living. New Baltimore still was a modest community with a modest economy but it might have been different.

The Canal to New Baltimore

New Baltimore almost was a twin to the port of Albany—sort of. The first inkling of why came in 1609 when Henry Hudson and crew were making their way upriver in search of the riches of the east. One of the stalwart shipmates, Robert Juet, kept a journal of the trip. In September of that hallmark year, just above New Baltimore, their small sailing craft, the *Half Moon*, "grounded: so we layed out our small anchor, and heaved off againe. Then we borrowed on the banke in the channell, and came aground againe . . ."[1]

The Hudson north of New Baltimore was an unpredictable stretch of shallow water prone to frequent shoaling that would prove a problem to many voyagers. The area was given the Dutch name of Overslaugh, which more or less means an impediment. There are numerous accounts of boats being stuck there into the twentieth century, and a long history of dike-building and dredging to solve the barrier to trade and travel.

John Maude, an English traveler of 1800, gave an early account of what had and would befall many a vessel attempting to traverse the treacherous reaches south of Albany. Embarking from Albany about 4:30 p.m. on October 2, Maude's sloop *Magdalene* did not get far on its voyage to New York. By five that afternoon, they were hung up on the upper Overslaugh, just three miles downriver. At seven, they were grounded on the lower Overslaugh, eight miles from Albany:

> As there was no prospect of our getting over this shoal till the tide had attained its highest point, we took in all our sail and carried out an anchor into deep water. This lower Overslaugh has seldom more than eight feet of water upon it even in Spring tides, and our Sloop drew seven feet, though a great part of her lading was on board a Lighter, and not to be shipped till we had passed these shoals, which are a severe interruption to the navigation between New York and Albany, and which might otherwise be carried on in vessels of larger burthen than are now employed in this trade. There are a variety of channels among those beds of sand called the Overslaughs, and the main channel shifts almost every year. The remedy is easy; block up all the channels except one, and the water will accumulate there and keep it ever free.

Settling in for an indeterminate delay, Maude and his companions enjoyed a good meal and pleasant conversation in waiting out the low tide. By the next morning, the level of the water was high enough for another attempt at pushing free: "Being high water, we endeavoured to warp off the shoal; we succeeded only in part, and were obliged to wait another tide." Not one to waste a good opportunity, Mr. Maude did some sightseeing ashore while buying eggs and milk. Finally, by six that evening, the crew was primed for another attempt at freeing the *Magdalene*: "Being high water we succeeded in warping off the Overslaugh." They then were able to take on their full cargo and proceed south.[2]

New York State had sought formally to remediate the river's obstacles as early as 1797. From then to the 1830s, the main palliative was the construction of wing dams that sought to prevent the flow of effluents from streams and other sources from clogging the channel. This effort was supported by sporadic dredging of materials. This tactic was not particularly successful in securing an adequate passage for increasingly larger draft vessels and heavier river traffic.

The federal government soon took over authority for the Hudson. From then on, there was a near yearly plan and appropriation of funds for navigation improvement. A big push came around the Civil War years when a concerted program was implemented to confine the currents by building longitudinal dikes along both shorelines. The diking system would both limit the flow of water and keep side deposits of silt, sand, and stone from entering and blocking the main channel.

New Baltimore's William Fuller became a major player in working on the dikes. He and his son, also William, operated a thriving business for many years building dikes, docks, wharves, and other works, much of it under contract with the federal government. A good portion of the wood, stone, and concrete dikes that still are visible along the Hudson today from New Baltimore north was at least partly their handiwork.

Starting with various sailing vessels in the 1840s, the Fuller group owned several barges, pile drivers, and steamboats, including the tugboat *Lydia*. The latter vessel carried Fuller to his final rest after he passed away at eighty on a Delaware and Hudson Railroad train at Whitehall, New York, while returning from his Lake Champlain summer cottage. Another of his three sons, Howard, published one of two short-lived newspapers in town, the *New Baltimore Sun*.[3]

Despite diligent maintenance and rebuilding efforts over decades by the state and federal authorities and the Fuller company, the dikes did not do the job. Throughout the twentieth century up until today, the chosen alternative, dredging, continues to clear a path for ships and boats traveling to the port of Albany and other places. The spoils from that work have filled in behind dikes and made various islands whole cloth rather than the hodgepodge patchwork of lands that existed for previous centuries. A few times, the rocky bottom of the river was blasted away to gain ground. Gradually, a not-so-small fortune has been spent to deepen the channel north from New Baltimore from four or fewer feet up to a current maintained depth of thirty-two feet.

One of the most interesting alternatives suggested to resolve the Hudson's navigational woes was to construct a ship canal from New Baltimore to Albany. Perhaps the first proponent of this approach was Edmund Charles Genet, the Citizen Genet of French Revolution notoriety.

Genet had come to New York City in 1793 as French minister to the United States to try and convince the Americans to alter their neutrality toward the new French republic. Unsuccessful in that effort, he chose to stay here, fell in love with, and married Cornelia, New York governor George Clinton's daughter. Fearing reprisals from home with the creation of a new government, Genet was granted asylum and became a gentleman farmer, never really becoming involved in international politics again.

In 1804, Genet had moved from Long Island to Greenbush (now Rensselaer), across the Hudson from Albany. He was greatly perturbed by the obstructions to navigation that his sloop encountered on the way upriver, particularly between Kinderhook and Albany. Sand bars and shoals were a major inconvenience to the northward progress of the sailing ship.

At that time, he had the seemingly distinct advantage of being the governor's son-in-law. He made his concerns about the river known to Clinton, who subsequently advocated in addressing the state legislature the critical need for improvements in the Hudson's accessibility, but did not mention a canal as a possible option—so much for familial influence. The legislature, for its part, deferred to the experts on the topic, and a board of commissioners was appointed to examine the need for rectifying the still extant obstructions.

To Genet's dismay, the state found the "common method of damming and contracting the channel" to be the most prudent and effective means of addressing the problem. This basically was the use of wing dams and jetties projecting from the shoreline into the river to redirect massing of materials.

Genet's response to this approach was to insist that the work only succeeded "to transfer alluvions from one place to another, to add artificial obstructions to the natural ones; to dam up the ice at the breaking up of the river . . . and finally, as fatal experience has evinced, to make the river worse than she was when suffered to force her own ways through channels of her own choice." While Genet seems to be taking things rather personally, the fact was that boats were still getting hung up, and the need was intensifying to improve access to the increasingly important shipping center of Albany.

The initial setback did not dissuade Genet from pursuing the topic further, albeit several years later. Next in line for persuasion was his wife's cousin DeWitt Clinton, whom Genet approached upon his ascension to the seat of gubernatorial power in Albany. He claimed that the Hudson used to be a much wider and deeper waterway and that "an immense body of alluvial land, extending from the village of Greenbush to Kinderhook, occupies the old bed of the river."[4]

As mentioned, Greenbush lay across from Albany, and Kinderhook was at the head of unobstructed navigation across from northern Greene County. Through these so-called flats, Genet aimed to construct a canal that could accommodate oceangoing vessels of minimum 132-foot width and 21-foot draft. The passageway would have a lock or gate at each end and a dike on its east side, to serve as a protection from the river and as a tow road.

Unfortunately for Genet, the reaction was much the same with the younger Clinton as his uncle. The governor stated that an engineer was being employed to evaluate the situation, and he would review Genet's plan. In addressing the legislature on the topic of travel on the Hudson, DeWitt was noncommittal about the means for effecting change.

The argument proceeded for another few years as the State devoted more money to damming and diking as a remedy to the sailing impediments. A law enacted in 1819 authorized appointment of seven commissioners to determine "the best and most efficient plan for improving the navigation of the tide waters of the Hudson river." The men were to report their findings to the next session of the state legislature and were given the authority to procure the services of any professionals needed to complete the assigned task.[5]

In the spirit of governmental efficiency, the committee, which included DeWitt Clinton, reported to the legislature in March of 1820. Their prime recommendation was that the canal would be the most efficient means of solving the problem. In fact, Genet drafted an appendix to the report that was quite specific about the dimensions and path of the proposed waterway, which was to run from Albany on the east side of the river to the Schodack Creek then obliquely between two islands below the border dividing New Baltimore and Coeymans.[6]

By 1824, the proposal still was nursed along. Governor Joseph C. Yates in his annual message to the state concurred with the canal commissioners who were supporting the New Baltimore project. He urged, however, that the federal government authorize tonnage duties on vessels using the canal to pay for operations.[7] Unfortunately, the State Senate committee with jurisdiction believed that ongoing canal work elsewhere took precedence, and no further projects should be undertaken for the time being.

Shortly thereafter, the legislature began to consider measures to support dredging of the trouble spots. Included was at least one bill to purchase a dredging machine. There also was discussion of a privately funded canal to New Baltimore, with associated legislation to incorporate a Hudson Ship Canal Company.

Once again, the idea slept for a while. Then, chapter 240 of the state laws of 1834 directed the canal commissioners to engage a "competent engineer" to survey the Hudson from Albany to New Baltimore and Albany to Troy as to the obstructions to navigation and the practicability and cost of their permanent removal. The law also directed the commissioners to survey and estimate the cost for a ship canal route from Greenbush to New Baltimore, as outlined in the Genet plan. But, alas, the canal still could not merit sufficient political and financial support to come into being.

By this time, the federal government officially had taken jurisdiction over the Hudson and now had a tremendous say over how things were run. Unfortunately, the Congress did not provide the needed funding for any work at removing obstructions. Note the use of the word "removing." They were not inclined toward a canal but rather looking to a system of longitudinal dikes along shorelines and dredging. Diking and dredging together was pretty much the tack taken when the work was intensified in later years.

A bit of attention still went into channel improvement in the next few years. However, ships kept getting bigger while remediation efforts, particularly by federal authorities, were minimal and virtually nonexistent for a long period from about 1839 to near the Civil War.

The canal proposal though was not quite dead. In a February 11, 1853 report to a committee appointed by the city of Albany "to inquire into the expediency of constructing a ship canal from Albany to New-Baltimore,"[8] engineer William J. McAlpine laid out a detailed analysis of the proposed canal's path, dimensions, cost, and potentials.

Such a project supposedly would alleviate New York City of some of the strain on their overburdened shipping and receiving facilities, thereby reducing costs. Albany seemingly would be a fine substitute, but only if the vessels of oceangoing nature could get there.

There essentially were three options for resolving the Hudson obstruction problem: improving the channel of the river itself, extending the Erie Canal to a point beyond where the shallows were, or building a ship canal to connect the end of the Erie to the Hudson near New Baltimore.

McAlpine suggests that channel improvement was favored by many interested parties and that remedy already was being implemented. However, current efforts were to establish a depth of nine feet, which McAlpine felt was inadequate for projected need and that further work in that vein might be cost prohibitive.

Extension of the Erie Canal seemed even more disruptive. You essentially would be bypassing the port infrastructure already established at Albany and reestablishing it in a different location. That seemed unlikely to occur.

So the issue at hand, the one that McAlpine was charged with investigating, was a new ship canal. McAlpine was proposing to evaluate the efficacy of his suggestion that there be a canal elevated above river level to avoid costly excavation and protect against destructive freshets that commonly occurred and greatly affected Albany. The twelve-mile structure was to be fifty feet wide on its bottom, not less than 120 feet at surface, and twenty feet deep, with locks at New Baltimore and Albany.

The engineers' research found that there generally was a channel fifteen to thirty feet deep at low tide from New Baltimore south to Four Mile Point about four miles north of Hudson. The rest of the way to New York City was not in question. The stretch from New Baltimore to Albany was the continuing sore point: "the channel is very uneven, and at several points does not exceed 7 or 8 feet depth of water; and that depth is frequently diminished by the formation of bars during spring floods. The deeper channel is at many points both narrow and crooked, and frequently changing its location by the moving of the sand in the bed of the river, rendering it no uncommon occurrence for boats drawing not more than 5 or 6 feet of water, though managed by experienced and skilful pilots, to be run upon the ground."[9]

Shortly after the McAlpine report, in April of 1853, a new law was enacted to create a corporation called the Albany and New-Baltimore Ship Canal and Basin Company. This entity was to construct and manage a canal with associated wharves, docks, and other facilities on the west side of the Hudson, running from near the south border of Albany to New Baltimore.[10]

However, Governor Horatio Seymour's 1854 annual message to the state legislature talks at length about New York State's canal system but fails to mention any proposed waterway from Albany to New Baltimore.[11]

Again, during this period, severe financial problems had caused suspension of critically necessary modernization and enlargement work on the Erie and other existing canals. This was due largely to the huge debt incurred by the state in undertaking various public works. So, the commencement of additional projects was unlikely.

The 1853 statute was revived and updated in the spring of 1858. By that time, though, the federal government was deeply involved in inland waterway operations on the Hudson, and all parties were well along in investing in improving the existing river channel. Depressed conditions of state finance also again came into play, limiting their immediate participation. The possibility of New Baltimore being a key to marine shipping as a canal terminus on the busy river finally went away for good. River dredging as the main palliative continues today.

Shipbuilding and Repair

As we have noted, sand bars and shoals just north of the current hamlet of New Baltimore made the Hudson impassable for larger ships, especially at low tide, transforming a good section of the waters into the shallowest spot in the river between New York City and Albany. The natural little bay at New Baltimore and the beginning of deeper water made a ready spot to wait for a higher tide or to transfer cargo and passengers between larger and smaller vessels for continuing passage north or south.

The location probably also helped foster local businesses. Paul Sherman's trading exploits were mentioned earlier. There are records of the Vanderzee brothers shipping goods from New Baltimore in the 1790s aboard their sloop *Friendship*. At one point, Charles Titus and a handful of other men owned the same boat and operated it in a commercial venture.

As the middle of the nineteenth century approached, river activities intensified. The Paul Sherman empire, as it reached its second family generation, had transformed into a four-way partnership among son Joseph Sherman, William Southwick, Andrew Mull, and Jacob Reynolds. In 1854, Henry Slingerland joined the reorganized firm as sole partner with Reynolds.

In 1867, the company sold its New Baltimore dock and buildings and moved to Coeymans where it established the main base of the freighting operation. Eventually, Slingerland consolidated efforts to his Coeymans docks and transferred the New Baltimore freight building and operations to Andrew J. Vanderpoel. Vanderpoel devoted a large part of the premises to expanding his longtime ice harvesting business. He also continued freighting, employing the vessels *Redfield* and *Walter Briggs* to haul goods up and down the Hudson. At various times, Andrew also ran a grocery store and was captain of the passenger- and freight-carrying *City of Hudson*, a notable side-wheel steamboat.

In the middle of September of 1897, though, an all-too-common calamity struck when a blaze ignited in the northeastern corner of the main Vanderpoel building, which housed an office and space for storage of grain. The alarm was given at 11:45 p.m., and local firefighters were on the spot in quick order but still too late. The steam pump of the tugboat *Lydia* was pressed into service attempting to halt the escalating catastrophe. The flames were way too far ahead of everyone's valiant efforts, leaping to the abutting Baldwin shipyard and destroying a stock of lumber and the paint and oil shop.

The fire service concentrated attentions across the street on the house of the noted shipbuilder William Baldwin and the general store of R. H. Goldsmith. Both buildings were saved but the other affected areas were a total loss. Favorable winds may have kept the flames from spreading to much more of the hamlet.

Vanderpoel and Baldwin lost about $4,000 to $5,000 worth of property each, with just a little insurance in place. Each businessman managed to survive the event but the New Baltimore waterfront now had a sizable hole. This was one of a string of fires in the neighborhood thought to be the work of an arsonist. A reward of $500 was posted for sufficient evidence to convict anyone implicated in setting the fires.[12] The heyday of commercial freighting out of New Baltimore though effectively was over, except for the shipping of ice.

Coming of the Baldwin Shipyard

Boatbuilding also started up in those days around the Revolutionary War. New York's governor George Clinton and Colonel Cornelius D. Wynkoop exchanged several communications in the spring of 1778. The colonel was encamped at "Coeymans" commanding a large crew of ship carpenters and laborers in fabricating vessels for the war effort. In early April, the colonel advises that he has "about 50 Carpenters at work here, a Building Boats of Forty Foot Keel & Sixteen Foot Wide . . ." and hoped that additional workers could be ordered to the site.[13]

Given the inclination for people in those days to identify New Baltimore hamlet as part of Coeymans or the Coeymans Patent, Wynkoop's boatbuilding operation could have been located anyplace between the Coeymans and Coxsackie creeks. It is plausible to speculate that the work was being done in what became New Baltimore's landing.

Anthony J. Gambino, in his thorough study of New Baltimore's maritime industries, comments about having spent valuable research time at the National Archives and Records Administration in Washington, D.C. There, he identified the *Sea Flower*, a 57-foot sloop, as the first registered boat built in New Baltimore. This vessel was put together in 1793 by Nathaniel Dunbar for the Coeymans and New Baltimore miller Salomon Skinner. Gambino then documents a number of other sloops and schooners assembled in the later 1790s and earliest 1800s.

Gambino gives valuable insights into a variety of men who built, owned, and/or piloted craft at New Baltimore from those earliest days through the peak years of the industry. Among numerous individuals, he writes about ship carpenter Peter Hull, Paul Sherman's son Joseph, a one-time Sherman partner James Keeler, the colorfully named Adam Oysterbanks, James and Allen Plum, Edward Hallock, and Stephen and Darius Parsons.[14]

In 1830, a dry dock was built in back of the Eagle Tavern right in the center of the hamlet. Leander Sheffield, Stephen Ayrault, Henry L. McKinney, John Parsons, and William Wheat repaired sloops there. McKinney may have been the first professional wheelwright in the area. His share of the yard ended up in the hands of Joseph Sherman.

Ayrault had built the hostelry a couple of years before. The building has lasted to present days as a finely preserved private residence. At one time, it also was the home and office of Percy Waller who was a prominent and beloved town physician for over half a century.

Five years later, John G. Raymond built another yard just south of the tavern. Raymond operated there until 1846 when John Burlingham took control of the business. Raymond also owned at different times various dry goods, grocery, and other stores in the hamlet. The property over the next several years was bounced between operators, from Burlingham to brothers Jedediah R. Baldwin and Henry S. Baldwin, back to Burlingham and William Wheat, then to Ludlow T. Goldsmith and John Ten Eyck who worked it for a year, when it was discontinued.

Goldsmith and Ten Eyck built a yard about three hundred feet south of the freight dock. They continued to repair vessels and began building barges. Around the beginning of the 1850s, a group of these gentlemen built the New Baltimore Steam Mill adjacent to the shipyard to saw lumber for their construction projects. They also installed machinery for grinding plaster and buckwheat. Subsequent owners rebuilt and continued to operate the mill after the original building burned in 1864. It appears to have been used solely as a sawmill from that time, primarily for the ship operation but also doing custom work and selling lumber to people in the area.

By the late 1850s, the Baldwin brothers had bought the Goldsmith and Ten Eyck yard, and the business started to hit its economic stride. Over the next twenty years, they built numerous towable barges, paddle-wheel and propeller-driven steamboats, and a handful of sailing vessels.

The men's brother William North Baldwin's oldest son, William H. Baldwin, was born in 1846. At twenty-one, he labored for a year with Raymond and Company, a general store in Coxsackie, where he learned bookkeeping. William next became a clerk in his uncles' office at the shipyard, working there for eight years until the partnership dissolved. The younger Baldwin diligently involved himself in learning all details of the shipbuilding industry.

The business declined in the late 1870s before it essentially closed. The property went through a sequence of ownership arrangements. In 1882, the whole operation went up for public auction, and William H. bought it. He reestablished the shipyard with great success, employing nearly one hundred men at one time.

Under the keen Baldwin eye, the workers over the next decades built and rebuilt steamers, barges, and other vessels, gaining a reputation for honesty and integrity and good workmanship. An adjunct activity was the lumber business.

Baldwin was held in high regard throughout the boating industry. Insurance companies, some from out of state, often took advantage of his knowledge and experience to appraise and adjudicate on damages to vessels. He also was at one point co-owner of a Main Street hardware store with James G. Turner who served as a blacksmith for the shipyards and ran a stagecoach line.

William also was a key town leader and a major supporter of the Reformed Church. The shipyard lay on both sides of Mill Street directly south and east from his home in later years, where he could keep a close watch on daily activities.

Among other achievements, the yard turned out what became known at the time as the world's fastest and most mechanically sound dredge for its size. Baldwin had contracted with John P. Randerson of Albany to build the machine for use along the upper Hudson. The vessel was 90 feet long, 34 feet wide, and about 9.5 feet deep and incorporated about 140,000 feet of yellow pine and 5,000 feet of oak timber. The final cost was about $25,000.

The high point for the Baldwin operation may have been 1905 when eight vessels were registered as being built, the screw steamers *Joel D. Smith*, *Passaic*, *Chas. C. Wing*, *Sara E. Carroll*, *Thomas J. Johnson*, *Walter B. Pollock*, and *Easton* and the oil screw *B. F. Huntley*. Screw means the type of familiar, underwater propeller that motors the modern pleasure boat. This was the technological successor to the old-time paddle-wheeler. The *B. F. Huntley* was one of the few non-steam screw vessels ever built by the company. Most, if not all, of the 1905 ships probably were tugboats. Over the years, the yard workers also built a significant number of barges for hauling goods and people.

The importance of the shipbuilding industry in New Baltimore during the years from the nineteenth into the twentieth centuries is clear from a look at the 1905 New York State census. The homes on Main Street, Mill Street, and the other byways of the Hudson-side neighborhood are liberally populated with a crowd of shipyard or river workers. There are about a dozen each of people who state their occupation as ship carpenter or steamboat engineer. Many are called day laborers. A good portion of this latter group probably was doing the more unskilled tasks in the yard or associated businesses. Then, there are an assortment of undefined "boatmen," along with steamboat pilots and firemen, deckhands, boat builders, and captains.

The center of the hamlet where Main and Mill streets met must have been a busy place. Townspeople could fill many of their household needs right nearby. At least five local women identified themselves as dressmakers in the 1905 census. Daniel Vincent, Leonard Colvin, and Joel Nelson were grocers. Shoe dealer John Patterson, meat and fish merchant Edward Bristol, general store merchants David Hinman (sister Mary was a telegraph operator) and Stephen Whitbeck, hotelkeepers Evelyn Pettit, Edward Powell, and Frank Dietz, and bakers William and Edmund Burlingham all were serving the community.

There also was a watch repairman, three blacksmiths, two barbers, numerous house painters and house carpenters, and coal merchant Edmund Albright. Percy Waller was at the start of a medical career that saw him doctoring local patients into the 1950s. Clergymen were preaching at the Baptist, Reformed, and Methodist churches.

Outside the hamlet, agriculture was still by far the predominant occupation. Farm and farm labor families lived and worked side by side in adjoining properties. You can identify where centers of rural population were sufficient to sustain some support businesses. Morgan Wildey had a blacksmith shop at the Medway Four Corners with Daniel Davis's grocery store as a neighbor.

Charles Badgley was postmaster at Grapeville, sharing a household with his brother Jesse who was a butcher. Volna Titus was a grocer in the neighborhood near the railroad station where Clarence Albright ran a barrel factory and sold coal and Harry Albright was a blacksmith. J. Wesley Gray was a railroad station agent, probably working with railroad mail clerk Howard Forman.

Scattered among the farms were the homes of a variety of people who made a livelihood as well as they could in the rural parts of town. Thomas Hotaling was a meat dealer, Orma Garrett a cooper. Fannie Smith and Alfred Cramp ran boarding houses. Elijah Hudson made harnesses. William Muller and Edward Roberts were rural mail deliverers. Lauren Powell pressed hay for an occupation while Harvey Truesdell operated a threshing machine for local farmers. In a somewhat mysterious vein, Emerson Miller manufactured "extracts." His daughter Bertha was a milliner. Jane Moore and Catherine Lezette were dressmakers.

The Later Years

In September of 1919, the aging William H. Baldwin sold his yard to an entity initially called the New Baltimore Shipbuilding and Repair Corporation. William J. Wade and his wife Bertha assumed roles as lead officers of this group. In later years, with a refocusing of its work, the name of the business was changed to the Wm. J. Wade Sand Company, Inc.

The Wade enterprise sold washed and screened sand and gravel; rented tugs, scows, and derricks; painted and stored yachts and other craft; sold shipyard and marine railways; and built and repaired boats. Anthony Gambino has identified the *Kittanning* built by Wade in 1922 as the last vessel produced in New Baltimore. It was a nearly ninety-foot passenger steamer.[15]

Ill fortune started to dog the Wades beginning in the early morning of November 30, 1925. William was starting across the New York Central tracks at Castleton on the way to his moored boat. A speeding train struck him, tossing him twenty feet, crushing one leg, and fracturing his skull. Clinging to life, he was transported to Albany where he succumbed to his drastic injuries. The business carried on for another decade. His wife Bertha succeeded him as the capable president of the company.

William's death was compounded by two subsequent major blows that spelled the essential end of the remnants of the riverside hamlet's vibrant commercial life. Fire has always been a curse of any community's existence, particularly wherever there was a supply of old, wooden buildings. What many would consider the worst blaze in New Baltimore's history came suddenly in the early hours of May 14, 1929. All the buildings on the east side of Main Street were lost from the Sherman house still standing today at the intersection with Washington Avenue to the modern Cornell Hall Park.

Jennie Miller discovered the well-underway conflagration between her family's store and Herman Schillenger's Imperial Hotel. It may have started in the latter's garage. Miller's husband, Lewis, scrambled to ring the Cornell Hook and Ladder Fire Company alarm, a sledge hammer and a locomotive wheel. The fire company was headquartered at Cornell Hall just across the street from the Miller place. Coxsackie, Coeymans, Ravena, and Selkirk companies soon joined the effort and fought fearlessly as dawn came.

Before the firefighters could make much headway, the flames had spread through the hotel and its barn, Charles Stott's garage, Charles Bortle's plumbing and radio shop, another garage owned by Town Supervisor Levit Powell on a neighboring dock, and old sheds and lumber near the Hudson. All were rapidly destroyed. A particular crisis arose when a 200-gallon fuel tank at Miller's went up in an explosive burst.

Courageous, hardworking firemen prevented the blaze from crossing the street, but the intense heat badly damaged Cornell Hall, scorching paint and breaking many windows. Panes of glass also were shattered and paint peeled right away from wooden siding across Main Street at Platt Wheat's post office and general store and the Nelson confectionary store next door. Charles Stott's tall brick structure south of the stores also was damaged. Sparks floated several hundred feet, and the diligent firemen barely kept the inferno from taking a much wider path of destruction. Half a dozen automobiles were burned. Small blazes flared in the shipyard just south of the main fire site but were quickly extinguished.

Much of the damage was believed to be covered by insurance, and several property owners expressed enthusiasm about rebuilding. Just a week after the destruction ended, Levit Powell had Irving Vanderzee hard at work rebuilding his garage. In the meantime, it was reported that more than two thousand cars and five thousand people visited the site during the seven days following the devastation. A new building eventually rose where the hotel sat, becoming a hotel again for a short time then a nursing home and now a private residence. The Miller building also was reconstructed, eventually housing the post office, which moved from across the street. It now has been converted into apartments.[16]

It also is interesting to note that the Cornell Hall in this story was the second such building, the first being destroyed by fire in 1905 along with Leonard Colvin's neighboring grocery. This first hall had been constructed to house the newly formed Cornell Hook and Ladder Fire Company through the beneficence of the Reverend James Cornell and the efforts of local business leaders such as William Baldwin, James Carhart, and William Gay. These gentlemen had been concerned greatly about protection since the property of tailor Thomas Lockley had gone up in smoke in the middle of the hamlet. The Wheat (then Whitbeck's) and Nelson stores had burned in 1912 and were rebuilt. These were torn down in more recent years.

The year 1936 was a fatal one for Wade's company. Toward the end of April, shortly after midnight, sparks ignited in their complex of buildings. By this time, the business had evolved into an entity for shipping sand and gravel and accommodating a handful of nautical supporting activities like boat storage, equipment and boat rentals, and small vessel repairs. Disaster shadowed disaster. The misfortune came about a month after a spring freshet severely damaged buildings, equipment, and vessels owned or stored by the company.

The newspapers reported that there was no insurance to cover the estimated $15,000 loss from the blaze. Gone were the boiler room, business offices, paint and oil warehouse, blacksmith shop, and garage. Investigators found that a safe in one of the buildings had been bothered, leading them to believe that burglars somehow may have set the fire.[17] Other than a marina later established at the site of the McCabe and Smith ice house and the mushroom-growing remnants of the ice industry, that was it for the center of New Baltimore's hallmark business connection to the Hudson River.

The Ice Industry Begins

New York City needed ice. The pleasures of cool drinks on hot summer days and the desire for dependable and healthy food storage were strong motivators. The city's booming population along with its bustling hotels and restaurants were outstripping demand. Boston businessman Frederick Tudor had been shipping ice from a Massachusetts pond to numerous locations starting in 1805, even to New York.

Some entrepreneurs saw the promise of the burgeoning market and the availability of more local supplies. They began harvesting and shipping ice from Rockland Lake near Nyack. The industry expanded as partners were added, new companies began, more markets were opened in the city and down south, and more sources were required. Tapping the wintry, frozen expanse of the Hudson was an obvious next choice.

Immense, hangar-like buildings, often double-walled and filled with sawdust for insulation, were thrown together by an army of carpenters and laborers. As the heart of winter came, teams of men and horses would arrive from well before first morning light to clear any fallen snow and mark the ice field for cutting. Some workers would come from homes just up the street, some from rooms at Schillenger's or Colvin's hotel. Idled during the winter season, a number would come via foot, hoof, or wagon wheel from the farms in outlying parts of town or from places further afield like Greenville or Westerlo, flocking to the Hudson's shore for life-sustaining cold-weather income.

The men would work into the night marking, sawing, and hauling smooth-shaven frozen blocks, usually about two feet by three feet in size, to conveyors stretching up into the mammoth houses. Inside, workers would labor to pile the chunks into neat stacks that would await loading onto 100- to 150-foot wooden barges that were strung together in multiple numbers and floated to their assigned destinations, often to New York City. A lesser number of more permanent staff would manage the houses after harvest season, maintaining buildings and equipment and continuing to load barges until supplies were exhausted.

The frigid, wet job meant long hours and many dangers. With sawdust as filler between ice layers and within walls as insulation, the wooden-sided buildings were potential tinder boxes. Slipping on the ice could mean a fractured arm or leg. Impalement or jagged cuts resulted from sharpened saws and the iron hooks used to grasp blocks. Many a man and horse had to be roped out of the drink chilled to the bone. Ice jams, thaws, and spring floods took a frequent toll on equipment, supplies, profits, and workers' wages, even to the extent of severely damaging buildings.

One noteworthy victim, Martinus Mulder, had his foot cut by an ax while working on an ice dock. The Dutch-born Mulder became widely known as the inventor of several useful ice-handling tools, including a horse-drawn scraper that allowed ice to be dumped from its grasp. "It is almost automatic, a child four years old having strength enough to work it."[18] Another Mulder innovation was a mechanism for extracting from the bottom of a storage room:

> Everyone familiar with ice-handling knows that taking out the last courses in a room is attended with serious difficulty,

> often calling for the services of six or eight extra men, according to the incline. All this trouble is obviated by the use of this machine, which is in the form of a gig, large enough to hold one cake of ice; this gig is fixed in a frame and attached to a stout crossbar; on the top is the hoisting-line, which passes through a pulley fixed in the top of the frame and thence through a snatch-block at the foot of the frame, and thus a horse can with comparative ease hoist the cakes to the necessary elevation, where by an automatic arrangement they are dropped into the run above and by their own volition pass along to the boat. Attached to the towing-line is a whip-tackle, which makes it much easier for the horse, and, as the distance traveled by him is very short, ten or a dozen cakes can be hoisted every minute.[19]

In 1911, Jeff Boice, a teamster for local entrepreneur Arthur Wicks, was drawing ice with a wagon one afternoon. While approaching the shoreline by the shipyard, the horses fell through the ice and were drowned. By the use of grappling hooks, workers managed to retrieve the wagon and harness.

An indicator came the following week of how people in those days had to diversify their work to keep bread on the table. The newspaper reported that Arthur had bought a new draft horse for his coal business, which probably was his primary income source. At one point, Wicks also provided a horse-drawn taxi service to transport people across the frozen river.[20]

Two of the most dreadful incidents occurred later in the life of these massive buildings, some of which now had been converted to mushroom growing. In mid-June 1927, four young New Baltimore men were crossing the Hudson in a dilapidated rowboat. They had finished their day's work at the Knaust brothers' mushroom operation in a former ice house on Schodack Island.

A hard wind and accompanying high waves swamped the craft about two hundred feet from shore. Two of the passengers, Theodore Groben and Theodore Fryar, managed to cling to the overturned vessel. Two others, Thomas Williams and Harry Onisk, fought for their lives attempting to swim to shore. It was too far. Both perished beneath the swift-flowing waters as scores of onlookers watched helplessly. Thomas was nineteen, and Harry seventeen.[21]

A couple of weeks after New Year's in 1930, Arthur Mosley walked into another building that the Knausts now used to pack mushrooms.

The structure was next to the former Vanderpoel ice house south of the hamlet and had been used as a boarding house for ice workers. Mosley apparently was carrying a lantern to search for gasoline to fuel a truck. Somehow, an ignition occurred, setting the building ablaze.

Mosley was badly hurt. He was transported to the hospital in Albany but shortly succumbed to his injuries. Continuing the tragedy, despite the valiant efforts of the Cornell Hook and Ladder Fire Company to quell the blaze, the sawdust insulation in the walls in the nearby ice house must have caught some sparks and smoldered overnight. The building burst into flames the next day and was destroyed.[22]

Ice harvesting was an industry acutely prone to corruption and manipulation almost from start to finish. The profiteering combining of companies led to numerous incidents of price-gouging and employee abuse. New York City's William Hagedorn, who had ice interests in New Baltimore, was stabbed in the chest by two of his employees.

Ice worker strikes were not uncommon. In one instance, in the winter of 1883, employees at the Smith and McCabe and Knickerbocker houses were in a decidedly unhappy mood about the state of their wages. The men resolved to strike, seeking daily increases from $2 and $2.25 to $2.25 and $2.50. Fifteen or so of the Smith and McCabe force took up ranks and marched as planned to the Knickerbocker house. Regrettably, there the would-be recalcitrants apparently could not reach a consensus and fell to bloody blows with one another, deflating their plans. "Black eyes and bloody noses were all that was left of the resolutions." The men returned to work at existing pay rates.[23]

New Baltimore's First Ice House

While local farmers and others were cutting and storing their own private supplies of frozen blocks for years, the first larger-scale, commercial ice house did not come to New Baltimore until the mid-1850s. Greene County deed records show the creation in September of 1854 of a partnership among Teunis Chadden, Andrew Mull, and Joseph and Edward E. Sherman in a dock and an ice house just east of the modern intersection of Mill and Main streets. Joseph Sherman was the son of Paul and had succeeded to the helm of the family's longtime seafaring and trading company. His son, Edward Ely Sherman, worked for his father's shipping business, including as a boat captain. Chadden was listed in the 1860 federal census as a carpenter but had a long career in the ice industry. Mull was a veteran river man.

Reflecting the monopolizing instincts of the ice industry, the New Baltimore men only kept ownership of the facility for a very short period. County records show various transfers of properties along the river first from our principals to the People's Ice Company and, ultimately, to the giant Knickerbocker Ice Company. By this time, the property was cited as containing a "dock & two buildings for storing ice."[24] Whether Chadden and the other investors intended to build for their own ends or to make a quick profit by turning to the larger business is open to question. At any rate, the men appear to have gone back to their own devices, save for Chadden who became a long-term Knickerbocker employee and ran the facility.

The initial capacity of the house was 6,000 tons but a series of expansions into the 1860s enlarged the operation to 27,000 tons. The *New York Times* gave a brief glimpse of New Baltimore's productivity and the vagaries of harvesting. The nearing of spring brought a fierce rain and wind storm followed by a cold period and a couple of mild days that sapped the strength of the Hudson's ice fields: "The ice-men have been using every opportunity, night and day, to 'make hay (ice) while the sun (cold snap) shines.' Extra forces of men and teams, the farmers and every available hand has been used. No rest has been allowed on Sundays, and at night, by the glare of calcium lights and kerosene bonfires, they have worked unremittingly."[25]

The *Times* credited New Baltimore with a total available supply of 36,000 tons. At this time, the Knickerbocker place was the only large house in town. Smaller suppliers or ice stored in a warehouse or two along the waterfront may have accounted for the difference reported between capacity and the *Times*-reported measure.

By the end of the 1890s, the Knickerbocker interests had been swallowed by the Consolidated Ice Company, a nationwide ice trust, which now owned the original New Baltimore house and a multitude of others. Misfortune arrived around midnight on Thursday, October 19, 1899 when

> a blaze broke out of the roof of the Consolidated Co's ice house here and in less than ten minutes the whole lower section of house south of the elevator, was in flames. Luckily a few people returning from the fair being held at Coeymans saw the fire at the outbreak and the fire alarm bell was rung. The firemen arrived in quick response and in less than half an hour had the flames under control, the cut-off being close along the south side of the elevator. The north end of the south section having fallen to the south helped to preserve the elevator which

> was saved. Fortunately as on former occasions the wind was from the northwest which carried the sparks and flame on the river, thus preventing the spread of the fire to other buildings and which would probably have been destroyed had the wind been from the south. The stack buildings on the north of the elevator were saved, also the engine-house which was within twenty feet on the west. Repairs had been going on about the house for the past week or more but no one had been in the loft. It may be a case of tramps' lodging and a careless use of matches, or incendiarism. There was no insurance.[26]

The Boom of the 1870s and 1880s

By the mid-1870s, the Hudson River ice houses could store 1.4 million tons, of which the Knickerbocker Company controlled the vast majority, shipping the ice on their fifty-seven barges. The middle of the 1870s to the late 1880s were boom construction years in New Baltimore for the huge ice storage edifices, their loading wharves, and auxiliary buildings for feeding and sometimes sheltering employees, storing tools and equipment, and housing the steam engines to drive conveyors and other mechanical apparatuses.

The giant buildings popped up north and south of the hamlet down to the Coxsackie line, at Mathews Point, on Houghtaling Island across from the hamlet, and on Bronk Island at the mouth of the Coxsackie Creek. The Horton Ice Cream Company of New York City was the first entry in the boom period, building a 22,000-ton-capacity house a quarter mile below the hamlet in 1875. By the 1890s, there were over seventy ice houses between Castleton and Catskill, a distance of about twenty-five miles, with as many as nine larger operations in New Baltimore alone. Various members of the Vanderpoel family, brothers Edward and Peter McCabe, and Peter Smith were among key local builders and operators. Outsiders like the New York City based Scott and Company also entered the highly competitive business with houses on both islands and other locations along the Hudson.

Van Orden, Vanderpoel, and Sherman Ice House

In the middle of June 1881, local businessmen Andrew V. S. Vanderpoel, Edmund H. Van Orden, and Augustus Sherman formalized a partnership to conduct an ice business. Their intention was to construct an ice house on property across from the hamlet on Houghtaling Island. Vanderpoel was a stone merchant in his early fifties and member of a longtime commercial family in town. Van Orden had been a farmer but was listed as retired in the 1880 federal census. Augustus was the latest edition of the ubiquitous Sherman family and son of Edward Ely, the original local ice magnate.

Luckily for future historians, the Shermans, and Augustus in particular, were inveterate keepers of family business records. Among many other documents, the Edward Ely Sherman Collection at the Vedder Research Library contains what is undoubtedly the preeminent archive from any Greene County ice house.

The records provide a detailed paper trail starting with the initial transfer of the land for the operation. As July of 1881 came, a hulking steam dredge motored up from New York City to begin excavating for the works. A gravel-filled, oak-piling dock had to be assembled both for handling building materials and later for ice shipments. Sherman ran the construction operation.

Albany firms provided cement and wheelbarrows and shovels for the workmen. The biggest source for lumber was H. C. Burleigh of Whitehall who shipped 115,896 board feet down to New Baltimore on the canal boat *C. J. Brunelle*. Vanderpoel provided some of the rock from his own quarry for the dock and other purposes.

The steam engine and associated equipment came from English and Best of Castleton. Catskill's Wiltse foundry and Athens's H. F. Dernell and Company sold the partners' ice elevating machinery, ice chain, pulleys, ice saws and hooks, canal hooks, and other pieces and parts. New Baltimore's own Baldwin shipyard and steam sawmill and blacksmith James T. Turner were among several local vendors that also provided various services. The company owned by William Fuller, who lived in the hamlet, did some pile driving. As mentioned, Fuller was known up and down the river for his long career in quarrying and the building of docks, wharves, and dikes. Paint, coal for the steam boiler, and salt hay to insulate harvested ice were shipped in via steamboat.

Upon completion, the ice house structure spread 150 by 100 feet. There were four storage rooms with ceilings rising 37 feet and a storage capacity of 11,237 tons. The entire operation was powered by steam with a smokestack rising an impressive 45 feet.

The ice house became one of the economic stalwarts of the town. One 1889 weekly employment roll lists sixty-six names. The business also had its obvious ups and downs, starting with the first harvesting season.

Normal maintenance was a routine expense. Vigorous storms during the houses' first winter led to an unexpected expense for roof replacement. The spring thaw also damaged the dock, necessitating repairs. By 1885, the owners were employing William Fuller and his company once again to drive new pilings with required gravel backfilling for the loading wharf. The principals stuck it out until 1896 when the operation was sold to the Hyer and Watson firm of Brooklyn.

New Baltimore's Last Ice House

About halfway through 1882, Teunis Chadden must have been getting restless as the New Baltimore foreman for the Knickerbocker Ice Company. He joined with his neighbors, William R. Gay and James E. Bronk, to build a new ice house down the Albany and Greene Turnpike from the hamlet. Construction went fairly quickly. By the middle of August, masons had completed half of the foundation for the building, which would have an initial capacity of 12,000 tons.

In mid-January, the *Coeymans Herald* newspaper could report that the Chadden, Bronk, and Gay facility was operating full speed "with Teunis at the helm, issuing his usual proclamation, 'Let the ice come.' "[27] Chadden did not survive to see his house expand to its fullest extent. He passed away June 27, 1897 at age eighty-two.

James Bronk and William Gay carried on in generally successful fashion, expanding the facility as the years passed. Right before harvesting season in 1898, the partners built a barn and a mess room for the convenience of their men during harsh wintry ice-cutting season. The ice house's capacity eventually reached 26,000 tons.

In the darkness of very early morning on January 15, 1905, the ultimate disaster came to the Bronk and Gay operation. An uncontrollable blaze broke out at the site, devouring the entire building in the face of a strong south wind. One consolation was the timing of the fire. Barely into the harvest season, the men had only laid up about a third of the house's full capacity.

The good news was that the loss was covered partially by $13,000 in insurance derived from several different providers. Adjusters were quickly on the scene, and the principals made plans to rebuild in time for the next harvesting season. The summer of 1905 saw a flurry of construction activity, and the ice house was ready to go again. By the turn of the new year, crews were hard at work tapping a new crop.

Three years later, the local owners gave in to the entreaties of the ambitious New York City ice magnates. James Bronk and William Gay and their wives Mary and Lizzie sold the property to William Hagedorn, the knife-wounded coal and ice dealer mentioned before. But the days of the booming ice business were long gone with the advent of electric refrigeration in the early 1900s. There also was a strident campaign about how polluted the Hudson was getting, making any ice crop unfit for human consumption. A succession of owners followed Hagedorn until the property was sold to the Knaust brothers mushroom farming enterprise, under whose domain the facility remained for about thirty-five years.

Time and nature took its toll on the great ghostly ice buildings in New Baltimore until just this one had survived. On one February Friday afternoon in 1961, mushroom plant workers became decidedly leery of the continuing stability of their work space. Nearly a hundred of them worked diligently to remove the winter's stored crop while installing cables in a vain attempt to keep the walls from falling. The retrieval effort succeeded but the old building could not stand the strain. The walls came crashing apparently outward since many of the tall westward planks still recline against the cliff beneath which the ice house sat.[28] The ice age was over.

The river will always provide beautiful scenery. Locals and passersby can watch seagoing ships from exotic locations carrying cargos that we all guess about. A myriad of tugs pull barges hauling scrap metal and fuel. In good weather, pleasure craft zip back and forth, avoiding a handful of kayakers and canoeists and fishing boats. Fire, age, and the changing landscape of economic progress took their toll. Stores and hotels disappeared. Other than a few foundation remnants, deteriorated dikes, and the odd wharf piling here and there, the average person today sees no evidence of the commercial bustle that the hamlet of New Baltimore once enjoyed.

7

The Train Arrives in New Baltimore

On April 5, 1864, the New Baltimore Town Board held its regular annual meeting at the house of William S. Cary to certify the election of town officers.[1] We can only wonder if the new supervisor Daniel S. Miller, town clerk Jedediah R. Baldwin, and the rest of the newly elected locals knew what was happening in the hallowed halls of big business. The railroad was coming through town.

The Saratoga and Hudson River Railroad (SHRR) filed articles of association less than two weeks later to construct a track from Saratoga Springs to Schenectady, and then to a point on the Hudson River, in the town of Athens. In New Baltimore, the planned route from the Coxsackie line north would traverse land of Andrew Vanderpool, Francis Mathews, James Houghtaling at the Hannacroix Creek, Benjamin Houghtaling, George G. Wolf at the New Baltimore turnpike, Jerry Springstead, Edmund Van Orden, Andrew Houghtaling, and Garret Houghtaling at the Greene-Albany county line.[2]

The 1860s were a fertile time for the creation of small railroads. They grew out of a desire to link the larger roads with more remote locations that had critical products or natural resources or to fill gaps in service. Some companies more cynically were organized simply to provide a source of competition for existing roads or to make ill-gotten gains through stock manipulations and other chicanery. Many of them never got beyond paper or survey.

The robber baron and steamboat magnate Daniel Drew had several reasons for building a modest line out of Greene County. Drew wanted to establish a terminal for his People's Line steamboat operation that might remain ice-free for a longer period in winter and bypass the infamous "Overslaugh" shoals between New Baltimore and Albany. He also wanted to be able to run his trains right to the Hudson's shore, avoiding delays that often occurred at Albany in transferring people and freight between boats and trains. Finally, Drew likely saw a financial gain to be made in linking his line with the proposed Schenectady and Saratoga Railroad to exploit the tourist industry at the latter location.[3]

Drew also may have been trying to be a nuisance to his archrival, Cornelius Vanderbilt, who had been building his own rail empire on the east side of the Hudson through the New York Central and Hudson River Railroad. The irony is that Drew somehow managed to persuade Vanderbilt to invest in the Athens road, a move the legendary commander later claimed as the worst decision he ever made.

One of the first tasks for Drew's new company was to survey the properties along the planned route. Henry A. Whitbeck completed this job for at least some of the lands in question in New Baltimore from the latter part of the summer of 1864 into the fall. Interestingly, the 1860 federal census lists a Henry A. Whitbeck as being a farmer in New Baltimore. Given the frequency of having more than one occupation in those days, perhaps this is our man. But whether he would have been doing surveying in the summer and autumn prime farming periods, as was the case here, gives one pause.

Management filed the legal paperwork for the new railroad with the Greene County Clerk on June 23, 1864. They proposed a near 38-mile, single-track road from a new Athens terminal on the Hudson, traveling slightly northwest then straight through the flats at West Coxsackie, into New Baltimore, Coeymans, and on toward Schenectady. The New Baltimore section generally followed the path of today's freight line.

The purchase of rights-of-way appears to have gone relatively smoothly until the company got to Coxsackie and New Baltimore. In New Baltimore, some landowners were so displeased, they went as far as forming a "club" to fight the compensation decided for them.

If a price settlement could not be reached with the affected property owners, the railroad could petition New York State's Supreme Court for mediation. Perhaps the most complete picture available of the petition and restitution process comes in the case of James and Julia Houghtaling. This couple had a farm in the vicinity of where the modern State Route 9W passes over the Hannacroix Creek. The railroad would bisect their land. While we do not know what the original railroad offer for their property might have been, we do know that the SHRR "had not been able to acquire title thereto, for the reason that the said Company had not been able to agree with the parties who owned or had, or claimed to own or have, estates or interests in the said real estate as to the price or compensation to be paid therefor . . ."

The railroad's attorney, Hudson's John C. Newkirk, presented the requisite petition at a special term of the State Supreme Court at the courthouse in his hometown. The petition also would have been presented to the Houghtalings at least ten days before the action was brought before the court. The court, after hearing from both Newkirk and the Houghtaling's lawyer, John B. Bronk, appointed as required under law, "three disinterested and competent freeholders residing in said County of Greene, or some adjoining County, Commissioners to ascertain and appraise the compensation to be made to the owners . . ." of the land to be taken for the railroad.

In the Houghtaling's case, the three commissioners authorized to decide the value of their land were George H. Power, a steamboat magnate from Hudson, Hugh VanAlstyne, a farmer from Stuyvesant and another Columbia County resident, and New Baltimore's own Baltus Van Slyck, also a farmer. The arbiters decided that $750 was a reasonable sum for the Houghtaling's plot of just over four and a half acres.

The other New Baltimore residents for which there are records of challenging the railroad's offers were Garret and Hannah Houghtaling, Jeremiah and Jane Springstead, Abraham and Sarah Jane Sutherland, Wessel and Maria Van Orden, and George and Clarissa Wolf. Their awards ranged from $725 to $1,337 for up to just over six and a half acres.[4]

The landowners had a variety of reasons to justify higher payments. Some of them were losing swampy muck lands, which could be sold profitably as fertilizer. Others believed in the value of their property for its proximity to the Hudson for shipping purposes. A handful lost access to critical water sources, like a spring, or had farmland split, making parts of it less accessible.

After final settlement of the purchase agreements, construction of the bulk of the line could begin. Under the name of Thomas Hassard, the project's engineer, a classified advertisement appeared in late August issues of the *New York Times* inviting contractors to bid on "grading and masonry on about twenty-one miles of their road in Albany and Greene Counties. The work is of a desirable character, and will be disposed of in contracts of from two to five miles."[5]

Optimistically, the *Recorder and Democrat* newspaper in Catskill was reporting that the Athens line was going into operation around the first of April of 1865. Drew's People's Line steamers then were to run from Athens rather than Albany and "not be subject to any detention on account of low water."[6]

Any dates for starting operations were wishful thinking. Construction was continuing. The 1865 New York State census taken around the first of June shows a nest of largely native-born Irish workers living in makeshift quarters in New Baltimore.

By November that year, the railroad company was holding an auction in Catskill to sell horses, carriages, and other items used in building the line, with operations anticipated in the near future. One wonders, though, if this was because work was near completion or whether excess equipment had to be sold to raise cash to finish the job.

Apparently the only annual report ever recorded with the state engineer by an independent SHRR was dated December 26, 1865. In it, the line's treasurer Henry Keep states that "Owing to the unfinished work and unsettled accounts with contractors the cost of the road cannot be given." Twenty-six miles had been laid so they were a distance from the Schenectady terminus.[7]

It was already January of 1866 when reports came on what may have been the first test train steaming through New Baltimore and the line's other communities. Around then, the *Recorder and Democrat* published that "An engine, with one car attached, was run over the entire length of the Athens and Schenectady Railroad a few days since. Everything worked to perfection, and direct communication from Athens to Saratoga Springs may now be considered complete."[8]

A mid-March *New York Times* article describes in some detail a trek at the beginning of train service. The author gives an account of the Athens facilities, and the route the railroad was taking. After leaving Coxsackie, he or she remarked that "The next station is New Baltimore, which place also contains about 1,000 individuals, and like Coxsackie is situated on the bank of the river, the railroad tapping it two miles in the westward."[9] This article was projecting the line as relying heavily on freight, particularly hay, apples, and other produce from local farms, and transporting of items back and forth from New York City and other eastern points and off to western markets.

By this time, people were starting to doubt the viability of the effort, derisively calling the little railroad the "White Elephant" line. This apt nickname unfortunately stuck for the duration. Blame seemed warranted. The owners were criticized as having spent $2 million into 1866 for essentially no continuing service.

Passenger service in the summer was supposed to be a focus. Operations were hoped to start April 1, a year later than originally thought. By now, a rail bridge at Albany was becoming a reality, which meant that people could travel from New York City directly to Albany by rail or river, making the Athens run more an inconvenience than a preferred route.

An even more ominous sign was on the horizon. At least one bill was wending its way through the state legislature to build a new rail line from Newburgh to Athens, which would complete a Hudson west shore route from the New York City area to Albany. This proposal would not come to fruition for some years but got people talking about the point of having an Athens terminal.

When construction was completed at Athens, the SHRR had quite an impressive facility with freight and passenger buildings, a hotel for railroad travelers and others, and employee housing, all made of brick. The "Brick Row" housing still survives, just north of the village of Athens. The main wharf was over 1,800 feet long. There were freight yards with space for hay, grain, livestock, and other farm products, an oil depot, a gas works, and a store.

Even after the trains starting rolling, the road continued to have problems. A major issue, as noted, was the hassle for people who wanted to get to Albany on a straight shot, rather than layover for even a short period in Athens. Even Daniel Drew apparently had an issue with location since he initially rescheduled the routes of some of his steamboats from Albany to terminate at Athens but soon reversed the decision.

Ebbs and Flows and the End of the Line

Perhaps the inability to drum up adequate business caused management to cajole the New York Central to take over. That momentous event occurred in September 1867 with the much larger entity leasing the Athens run for the long term. The SHRR ceased to exist as an independent company after only about two years of a fitful existence.

Exactly when trains started to operate regularly under the reconfigured organization is unclear. The *Recorder and Democrat* was announcing that "Passenger trains on the Schenectady & Athens Railroad are to commence running on Monday, June 25th." Another article in the same issue references a report from a Schenectady newspaper that the railroad's "Directors have been compelled by the traveling community to attach passenger cars to the freight trains between that place and Athens, notwithstanding the River connections are not yet ready."[10]

It was not long before the freight business through Athens started to blossom a bit. After mid-June, at least two round-trip freight trains a day were rolling through New Baltimore. The *Examiner* of June 30, 1866 reported that 800 tons of mostly flour was shipped from Athens to New York City on a recent Saturday. A little less than a month later, the *Recorder and Democrat* was proclaiming that "The shipment of freight by the new railroad, Schenectady and Athens, are so heavy that the carrying facilities are to be increased."[11]

By mid-November, "The freighting business on the Athens road has been very heavy of late, and it will continue so until the close of navigation." The *Hudson Register* published that, for two weeks, there had been on average ninety to one hundred car loads daily, mostly flour coming from Buffalo. Five barges and two propellers had then transferred the bulk to New York City and Boston. "Something less than one hundred persons" were employed in the venture.[12]

The following year appeared equally busy, with trains carrying both people and cargo. But work in earliest 1868 once again was disrupted. By February, Vanderbilt was pronouncing that the Athens cut-off would carry only freight. He did not want to divert passengers from his railroads on the other side of the river. By spring, he was not going to open the line at all for the season. At the end of May, Vanderbilt had made good on his command. "The long depot is silent." About one hundred men were idled.[13]

In August, citizens at Coxsackie and probably New Baltimore were being urged to sign a petition for the restoration of freight and passenger service. The Central finally relented in the fall and started to make a single round-trip run each day. This movement really may just have been the result of the Vanderbilt interests demonstrating that they had not abandoned the line and its legal rights-of-way. It was a short season. The Athens train ran to mid-December.

In 1869, there was no service. Rumors were rampant. One said that a man who had provided at least part of the right-of-way for the line was going to sue the Central to show cause why the line was not being run for both freight and passengers, as was the original plan for constructing the railroad. Another story spread that the Rensselaer and Saratoga Railroad Company had purchased the line and was planning to put it in operation as a coal hauling road. Neither scenario came to be.

Then the Central took a hard about-face. For the 1870 season, it would divert most heavy freight from the east shore routes to the Athens branch. The key element was securing the services of John Starin to operate a barge service from the Athens railhead to New York City. Starin was a Mohawk Valley native and presumed inventor of the "car float," an oversized barge used to transport loaded freight cars. He had made his fortune providing tug and sloop conveyance of freight to and from railroad yards around New York City.

For the next few years, rail traffic was brisk for New Baltimore and the other trackside communities. On one day, soon after the Starin takeover, there were 111 cars full of grain "at the Athens depot and on the road. . . . This is only a beginning of what will be poured into that channel."[14] Other than watching rail cars frequently roll back and forth, there also was some local excitement in July of 1873. Sparks from a locomotive set grassland aflame on A. G. Hotaling's farm. Ten acres of meadow were burned before the blaze could be doused.[15]

Business really was booming in the spring and summer of 1874. Over two hundred men were working at the Athens depot. About twenty trains a day traversed the tracks through New Baltimore, meeting up to twenty vessels at the southern Hudson terminus to receive or discharge loads. Work gangs were sweating day and night shoveling grain and handling shipments of oil, flour, and other products.

Then, the winning streak ended again. The road had to be closed when a significant portion of track sunk about twenty feet. Rail crews dumped hundreds of loads of fill into the gap, which swallowed the bulk as it was deposited. Trains were backed up or rerouted to other tracks.

This went on for over two months, with the line reopening to great celebration in mid-September. News sources confusingly attributed the site of the cave-in either to a location in Coeymans or a point called Hazard's Fill just north of Athens. But it is interesting to note that a later period map of the line shows a severe c-shaped deviation in the tracks as they passed through the center of New Baltimore. This spot was called Hasset's Dump. Could it have been the gap site?

The restart of rail traffic caused a mini-calamity for New Baltimore farmer Benjamin Houghtaling. On a quiet Saturday, one of his cows was hit by a train. "The locomotive struck the cow with great force, throwing her a considerable distance from the track, hurting and bruising her severely, but she is in a fair way to recover."[16]

The 1875 season was an equally busy one with the terminal handling 80,000 tons of freight in July alone. While there is little documentation of direct service to the farmers and other residents of New Baltimore through the brisker period of road action, there may be a clue in 1875. A late December edition of the *Coeymans Herald* reports in its New Baltimore news column that "We are no longer apprehensive of a dearth in coal since the White Elephant has been brought into requisition."[17]

One assumes that this meant that the railroad was delivering coal to the town, a product that arrived by rail well into the twentieth century.

Disaster struck the final death knell for the Saratoga and Hudson River Railroad on a late spring Sunday night in 1876. The *Catskill Recorder* captured the magnitude of the event: "During the terrific gale of Sunday night last and at about midnight a fire broke out at Athens, which for extent of destruction is unparalleled in the history of this county." The steamboat *John Taylor* was moored at the pier when a blaze of unknown origin broke out in her engine room and rapidly spread throughout the vessel.

Strong winds defeated efforts to cut the boat adrift to prevent the reach of the inferno. Flames and sparks blew over a wide area, causing wholesale damage. The wooden wharf and a nearby line of freight cars loaded with sugar, grain, and other goods caught fire. The brick station and freight house were engulfed, with the fire's glow visible as far as Chatham across the Hudson in Columbia County.

The firemen were applauded for saving the nearby brick row of rail workers' houses, which today stand as the only remnant of the "White Elephant" operation. The fire lasted through the night, causing damage estimated from $800,000 to $1,000,000, an enormous sum in those days. By morning, several vessels were burned to the waterline and sunk. The freight dock was a smoldering ruin along with its contents. More than ninety loaded freight cars were totally destroyed. Along with the housing, only the oil and grain docks and an engine house survived.

William H. Vanderbilt, the Central's vice president, was quoted as assuring that "the fire will not interfere with the business of the road and freight will be received and forwarded as heretofore."[18] But the brief and intermittent periods of success for the former SHRR were largely at an end. The action on the line for the rest of its life generally was to accommodate traffic as it materialized rather than as a regular service.

Besides the damage wrought by the fire, a number of factors worked against any long-term success for the "White Elephant," if any was ever intended. The little line from Athens was becoming superfluous. Both the federal government and the state of New York were making a diligent effort to alleviate the navigation obstructions in the Hudson so the water route was becoming more open to continuing passenger and freight traffic. The east shore Central rail line ran all year, not subject to the vagaries of transport on the unpredictably frozen water course. And, perhaps, most significantly, there was growing momentum to build a rail line on the west shore as a direct link to New York City and southern and western destinations.

For the rest of its life, the SHRR appears to have been primarily an underused avenue of convenience, handling side jobs off the main line and some minor local hauling. The *Coeymans Herald* offers a handful of news reports that the Robb and Carroll paper mill on the Hannacroix Creek in Coeymans just over the New Baltimore border was shipping its products on the "White Elephant" to at least the end of December 1880. Around that same time, New Baltimoreans Jeremiah Dean and Albert Bedell were sending their buckwheat flour and cider off on the rails through the Coeymans depot.

In November of 1881, a proposed New York, West Shore, and Buffalo Railroad was in the works, entering into a $400,000 lease with the Central for the SHRR. In the early 1880s, a large ice house was built on the ashes of the Athens terminal site, eradicating further evidence of the rail yard. By mid-fall 1888, the tracks of the "White Elephant" out to the new main line were being torn up to avoid paying extra taxes on the property.

A West Shore Route

As early as 1865, as the "White Elephant" was starting to putter along, measures were maneuvering the political path through the state legislature to facilitate a rail link between Athens and Newburgh. The goal was to complete a Hudson west shore route from a New Jersey site across from Manhattan up to Albany.

Minimal competition for the quite successful New York Central was a point of interest for many entrepreneurs since the late 1860s. Several sought to mount an assault but most were underfinanced, poorly led, or purely speculative. There was little progress beyond something drawn on a piece of paper or the surveying of proposed routes.

A small web of independent railroads started to spoke its way out of New Jersey into Rockland and Orange counties with an eye toward opening untapped markets. A particularly promising enterprise surfaced in 1866 with the genesis of the New York and Albany Railroad. This was an effort by several stalwarts of the riverboating fraternity to tap into the potential of the rail as a substitute for the steamboat trade.

By the early months of 1867, the company's surveyors were making their way north, mapping out two alternative routes for the line, each of which would have gone through the eastern half of Greene County. The path of the new railroad closely followed that taken by the SHRR through New Baltimore, intersecting the existing tracks near the Coxsackie border.

At least one meeting was held in Athens in March 1868, and others were planned, to discuss possible financing. In those days, if a community wanted to have a rail line run through its jurisdiction, it had to support local bonding to finance construction. Athens leaders successfully approved such a move. The newspapers were silent about the outcome of meetings held elsewhere.

Progress was slowed by financing obstacles and the usual railroad politicking. The state legislature acted on more than one occasion to offer aid for construction but the overwhelming opposing power of the Vanderbilts overrode their efforts. The endeavor stumbled along for several years. The state assembly even passed a bill in 1872 allowing the Delaware and Hudson (D & H) Canal Company to guarantee bonds that the city of Albany might issue to help the New York and Albany. The D & H eventually declined to participate so the campaign fizzled out.[19]

The Wallkill Valley Railway was organized in 1866 by local officials and business people to build a line from Kingston to transport agricultural products to the Orange County village of Montgomery. At that location, it could link with the Erie Railroad and gain access to more major markets. The initial intent of the originators was for tracks through Greene County on to Albany. With construction commencing in 1868, the line was open fully to Kingston by the end of the year in 1872. Carrying the route further was not feasible at that time because the communities to be affected were not interested in financing the extension.

As the decade ended, with construction on a Hudson-side line planned from Albany to Weehawken in northern New Jersey, the Wallkill owners began angling to extend their tracks toward the state's capitol. In early 1880, Wallkill surveyors were mapping a route all the way to Catskill. Rights-of-way were purchased to Albany. Then, in what must have been an interesting sight, crews began working nearly parallel to one another on the competing projects. The Wallkill progressed to grading the roadbed and building bridge piers as far north as Catskill. Whatever the perhaps devious intent of this project may have been, the real West Shore later took the bait and bought out the Wallkill line, which became a rural offshoot of the larger company and never went to Albany.[20]

The southern end of the future West Shore railroad is a litany of lines and more lines. Lots of folks must have been looking to get in on the lottery of railroad ownership with much maneuvering and finagling. The Ridgefield Park Railroad was incorporated in 1867 to run from a main route out of Jersey City to just over the New York state line at Tappan. From there, the Rockland Central Railroad came into being in 1870 to continue the line to Haverstraw, and the Rockland Central Extension Railroad in 1872 proceeded a little further north along the Hudson's west shore.

All three of these routes subsequently merged to form the Jersey City and Albany Railroad in 1873, with the obvious goal of going on up along the Hudson to Albany. Financing still was insufficient to push construction further. Summer travelers had brought a small profit but ridership dropped off as fall came, spelling the end of the campaign.

A bewildering array of organizations and mergers then came. In a further illustration of how confusing all of it was, both the Hudson River West Shore and West Shore Hudson River Railroads were established in 1867 and combined in 1868. The New York, West Shore and Chicago Railroad was incorporated in 1870 and absorbed the West Shore Hudson River in 1877.

The Chicago railroad was to run from a point opposite Manhattan to Athens then along the route of the "White Elephant" to Schenectady then to Buffalo parallel to the New York Central. It slightly deviated from the older line's path in New Baltimore just south of the Hannacroix Creek on lands of Francis Mathews.

By the end of April 1872, the route was surveyed through New Baltimore all the way into the town of Bethlehem. Despite efforts to secure funding from both English and German sources, money ran out by November of the next year. Workers struck over lack of wages, and tools were repossessed through suit by creditors and workmen. After 2.5 miles of track had been laid, the Hoboken Land and Improvement Company foreclosed the West Shore's mortgage on its 28-acre terminal property in Elysian Fields, Hoboken, and the line went into receivership. So, the idea for a complete line along the river lay dormant for a little while longer.

The Chicago company was sold and reorganized as the New York, West Shore and Buffalo Railway in 1880, which six months later merged with the North River Railroad, another set of tracks coming up out of New Jersey. There now was one entity responsible for completing the entire railroad from New Jersey to Buffalo. This organization, finally, was the forerunner of the last and most noted West Shore railroad.

The new road leased the New York Central's Athens Branch and used it as their main line through New Baltimore. New cut-offs were to go from Coeymans Junction (future Ravena) to Albany and, in the south, into a new terminal at Weehawken. The route intersected with the "White Elephant" in Coxsackie near the New Baltimore line. On a planning map for the railroad, the tracks followed the existing road with that slight deviation near "Hasset's Dump" until just past the New Baltimore turnpike where the road took an approximate 45-degree angle to the east near the border of the lands of Benjamin Houghtaling and Albert Bedell (previously Jeremiah Springstead).[21]

Work had commenced in 1881 with construction on the near mile-long tunnel through the lofty cliff bordering the Weehawken flatland where the southern terminal would stand. Nine tunnels in all were needed through the rough terrain on the Hudson's west bank. Laborers also set about upgrading existing trackage.

The local weekly newspapers were a continuing source of updates on the progress of the construction project. In the December 7, 1881 edition, a *Coeymans Herald* reporter called at the West Shore's engineering office on Westerlo Street in Coeymans to get the lowdown on the path of the railroad through the area.

For the New Baltimore section of interest to the writer, the track would diverge from the "White Elephant" on Albert Bedell's property in the vicinity of the New Baltimore turnpike, then angle slightly eastward into the town of Coeymans through the farms of the Ham, Niver, and Gedney families. The laying of the roadbed in New Baltimore and Coeymans was imminent. The overall goal of the workers was to widen the existing road from one to two sets of tracks, straighten the passageway, rebuild bridges, and basically modernize and upgrade the facility. By New Year's Day, representatives were in New Baltimore buying land for the new railroad.

The path was to be straighter and at a more amenable grade than the competing New York Central route on the east of the Hudson. This logistical feature would make the West Shore line attractive to freight carriers into the twenty-first century.

By April of 1882, construction was well into New Baltimore with the *Recorder and Democrat* reporting that "There is a gang of Italians working on the new railroad near Benjamin Hotaling's."[22] News writers and local residents were alternately intrigued and appalled by the multitude of newcomers from southern Europe imported to work the rails.

Two camps for about one hundred workers each had been established near Benjamin Houghtaling's property by Chestnut Lawn Cemetery. The heavy cutting of the landscape through the Houghtaling farm was going slowly with a small work crew. The men with their teams of horses were facing a precarious task with the shifting upper level of sand impeding progress to cutting lower levels of solid rock.

Procurement of land still was an issue even as the workers were at the front door. The *Herald* was reporting on May 17, 1882 that the company had settled with the estate of Albert Bedell. Bedell's heirs were selling four acres to the railroad for $1,000. Property could change hands in process as route plans varied. In early June, West Shore authorities secured more land from the Houghtalings and Nivers for $250 an acre.

The streets of New Baltimore were "thronged Sunday with Italian laborers," probably gaining a brief respite from their hard labors. They were "quiet and orderly." About the same time, however, a crowd of the workers left their jobs in a huff. Their supervisors reportedly were buying bread at 4 cents a loaf and selling it to the men for 8 cents, in addition to taking certain other liberties. Management was criticized for using "every opportunity to beat them out of their hard-earned wages."[23]

As summer approached, considerable tensions grew between the contractor for building the railroad between Coxsackie and New Baltimore and his largely Italian labor gang. It was rumored that he was the culprit who frequently attempted to short the workers' pay. The dissension festered for a while until 300 of the men went on strike. County authorities, including the sheriff, two deputies, and a militia squad, were needed to quell the ensuing riots, arresting the most vociferous offenders. Even the June 23 edition of the faraway *New York Times* reported on the dramatic event that took on the air of the Old Wild West until nerves were calmed:

> At a late hour this afternoon 220 Italian laborers employed on the piece of track, six and a half miles long, between New-Baltimore and Coxsackie, for the New-York, West Shore and Buffalo Railroad, struck for $1.50 a day—the wages being $1.35—which the contractor, Scully, refused to accede to. Led by Frank Cavan, an Italian boarding-house boss, they engaged in a riot, locked the non-strikers up in their shanties, put guards over them, and attempted to throw an engine and 20 flat cars down a 40-foot embankment. Cavan is said to be a desperate character, and to have been a leader of banditti in his own country. He defied Sheriff Churchill and his posse, declaring that he would fight the militia.[24]

The authorities must have succeeded in persuading the ringleaders to mend their ways. No further troubles were reported in the newspapers. In the meantime, grading was progressing with a relatively small crew, near where the new line split from the "White Elephant" on Benjamin Houghtaling's land. The required speed of the project and the lack of a sufficient sturdy work force pushed the company to search vigorously for more laborers.

People in the community already were starting to profit from the railroad even before it opened for business. By summer, a baker from the hamlet, William Burlingham, was supplying bread to railroad employees who now were working above Coeymans. William Sickles had built him a new peddler's wagon that likely carried the freshly baked goods up the hill and out to the laborers' camps. The Bailey firm of Coeymans had done a masterful job in painting the rig. "The entire work reflects great credit on our craftsmen and can not be surpassed by any factory."[25]

Local residents were not immune from the negative impact of the construction work. On one Saturday night in September, horses belonging to the Vanderpools and Nivers wandered onto the tracks where a work train frightened them into flight. The animals sought to run across a narrow trestle but only managed to jostle one another into danger. One horse fell to its death and others were cut badly. Apparently, the rail workers had removed fences in the area to accommodate workers' shanties, a situation that did not sit well with the locals.

One particularly disruptive feature of the construction project had been the removal of the bridge by the Chestnut Lawn Cemetery. It was gone for over six months. As is the case today, this was a main access route out of the hamlet so there was considerable outcry about its absence. New Baltimore highway commissioners had protested fervently over the closure. The newspapers were actively criticizing the inability of local officials to force a resolution.

Little incidents kept occurring because of the detour. One instance involved a near accident suffered by Ephraim T. Van Slyke, a prominent elderly farmer who lived nearby. His horse team was spooked in a cut near the cemetery but reined in without damage, a fortunate result. The whole affair was blamed on the lack of the bridge and the need to travel a dangerous alternative path. By the end of April, a replacement bridge was in place.

Pressure was growing to complete building the roadbed and laying track. The construction supervisors adopted a hectic pace during the spring of 1883. Two hundred new diggers were called to the job. Workers were pushed to the point of toiling nightly under electric lights. Men were putting the finishing touches on the big freight house at Coeymans Junction with completion of the depot next on the list. Other railroad buildings were cropping up along the tracks. In the late fall, a significant number of men became victims of the progress of technology. A group was let go from the project and replaced by two powerful steam shovels that were worked heavily.

As perhaps an indicator of the hurried work needed to get trains moving, danger could turn to disaster at any moment. Alvenus Hurst was coupling cars at New Baltimore when he crushed his thumb and had to have Dr. S. T. Searles amputate the appendage. While maneuvering trains in the vicinity of the Coeymans station, James McGinnis, a New Baltimore boarder at Thomas Haney's house near Dean's mills, was thrown under a car and crushed to death.

Finally, in early June, the New York, West Shore, and Buffalo Railroad was opened for business between Jersey City and Newburgh. The Jersey City site was used awaiting final work on the Weehawken station.

On the afternoon of Monday, July 9, the first official train rolled through New Baltimore, an express freight that arrived in Coeymans at 7:48 a.m. A little later in the morning, the passengers started through town. At this point, someone could board a southbound train from New Baltimore at 9:32 a.m. or 6:18 p.m. or one going north at 9:42 a.m. or 9:22 p.m.

While criticisms were made of the "high" fares, the arrivals of the initial trains were well attended by spectators. The New Baltimore correspondent for the *Coeymans Herald* noted that "Quite a number of our citizens took advantage of the opportunity of boarding the first train up the West Shore RR."[26] While we do not have a New Baltimore count, there were an estimated 2,500 to 3,000 onlookers massed at Catskill.

It is unclear exactly when the New Baltimore station went into service. The *Albany Argus* though reported in mid-July about the embarrassing brief visit of the prospective ticket agent. "He was a young man from Brooklyn. He came up on the train on Sunday, and was left standing in the middle of the track, at the new station, without a human in sight. Taking a survey of the woods and fields, he remarked that 'Brooklyn was good enough for him,' resigned at once, and inquired the way to the river took the first boat for New York."[27]

Despite the outsider's misgivings, the railroad made a difference to small communities like New Baltimore. Travelers previously wedded to river transport now had a new and efficient option. The New Baltimore correspondent for the *Coeymans Herald* was able to exclaim poetically about "all this change, because a little West Shore station cottage marks the spot where the whiz of steam and the ring of bells tarry long enough for the wayfarer to step aboard or dismount"[28]

Additional trains and new timetables were common. New Baltimore, while not a primary stop on the railroad, certainly was caught up with the new enterprise. Six weeks after opening, there were three northbound and four southbound trains stopping at the new station. By the end of August, blacksmith James G. Turner had outfitted a stage line to connect the riverside hamlet with all West Shore trains. This business was the first in a progression of horse-drawn conveyances.

The railroad started to broaden travel horizons beyond the regularly scheduled trips. In the fall, the West Shore, in combination with the New York and New England Railroad, was offering an excursion tour to Boston. People from New Baltimore could board a train at 6:05 a.m., and for a $5 fare, travel to see the New England Institute Fair, take a sail in Boston Harbor, or partake of sundry other virtues of that big city.[29] Later pleasure trips went to New York City, Washington, D.C., and distant locales.

The Weehawken Tunnel finally was finished at a cost of $1 million. The cut under the Palisades at a depth of 140 feet had taken two and half years. Trains now could go to the mammoth and elegant new terminal to take advantage of its six ferry slips to four locations in Manhattan. The main building was 360 feet long by 90 feet wide and had a 40-foot concourse leading to seventeen passenger tracks. There were baggage rooms, ticket and administrative offices, and a dining room, along with abundant stained glass windows and decorative scroll work and a balcony around three sides of the main waiting room. The complex of structures included a two-million bushel grain elevator built on 7,000 piles pounded into the Hudson River and eventually a freight yard with room for 4,300 cars. The new railroad immediately began tapping into the New York Central's business. The lack of a direct link to New York City, however, was a constant drawback, particularly for impatient passengers.

By October, the sight of lumbering passenger and freight cars trailing behind steam locomotives belching clouds of black smoke were increasingly familiar on the tracks through New Baltimore. The mail now was being delivered by train rather than by barge in summer and stagecoach in winter. Turner's stage line won the contract to handle mail deliveries from New Baltimore hamlet to the West Shore depot. By Christmas, three stages were carrying passengers to and from the trains.

The demand must have been there, as the New Baltimore writer for the *Coeymans Herald* generally applauded the new schedule, "which gives us the desired arrivals and departures that we have been patiently waiting for, except a 10:00 down." There were four northbound and three southbound trains spread across a day.[30]

The Modern New York Central

The enemy unfortunately was already at the doorstep. On opening day, the Central cut its passenger and freight rates below those of the West Shore, who responded in kind. By June of 1884, the U.S. Circuit Court appointed Horace Russell and Theodore Houston as receivers as the West Shore slipped into bankruptcy. On October 1, 1885, the New York Supreme Court ordered the sale of the line.

In the meantime, the Pennsylvania Railroad was seeking control of the West Shore to infiltrate the New York Central's coverage area. The Central was making a countermove by initiating its own line down through Pennsylvania. A rate war ensued with both sides suffering financially. Something had to give.

Negotiations ensued between the Central's main banker, J. P. Morgan, Pennsylvania president George Roberts, and his vice president and eventual successor Frank Thomson, leading to an agreement crafted aboard Morgan's yacht *Corsair* sailing up and down the Hudson. The Pennsylvania would sell off its interest in the West Shore. A group headed by Morgan and Central president Chauncey DePew would purchase the stock on the open market and lease the line to the Central. Both sides made concessions to refrain from infringing on one another's territories.

Within two months, the New York Central leased the line, renamed it the West Shore Railroad and continued expansion. By 1889, sleeping and drawing room cars were running on twelve through trains connecting to Chicago, St. Louis, Toronto, and Detroit. Remember, all these trains plus freighters were streaming though New Baltimore at all hours of the day and night.

The Station's World

A number of New Baltimoreans were quick to jump on the bandwagon presented by the new line through town. For the first full travel season of the West Shore in 1884, a company publication provides an extensive list of the hotels, boarding houses, and the like that were available for travelers. Local residents were eager to advertise.

From the New Baltimore station, would-be overnighters could take a stagecoach from any train arrival to the farmhouse of Charles D. Hallock, where accommodations were available for ten guests; the River

Side House of Mrs. W. H. Rowe, the largest facility and able to sleep forty; the hotel of John Colvin; the boarding house of A. L. Wicks; or the farmhouse of J. W. Stover in Coxsackie, which provided its own transportation. The Rowe and Colvin places were well-known hotels down in the riverside hamlet.

From Coxsackie station, you could take a conveyance up the hill into New Baltimore to stay at Warren Smith's farm or J. H. Garrett's boarding house in Grapeville and either a regularly scheduled stage or on-demand carriage or wagon to Medway. There, one could choose a room at the McGee, Carmen, or one of two Bedell farms or move on to the Coonley, another Bedell, or Harden farms at Stanton Hill. These places claimed perhaps generously to offer space for anywhere from fifteen to thirty guests. Rates at any of these establishments ranged from $5 to $10 weekly, with the most common charge listed at $6, children usually half price.[31]

Over the years, stagecoach service to the New Baltimore and other stations remained a regular feature of town life. As the end of the nineteenth century neared, Abram Serls started a route from the New Baltimore hamlet to Coeymans station. He would pick up passengers in the public square at 7:15 a.m. and 4:45 p.m. to connect with the morning train up and the last evening train down. You could take the stage and the train to Albany for a roundtrip fare of 70 cents.

The stage lines of Joseph Turner and Francis Brate were running to the New Baltimore train stop, with Brate having the contract for mail delivery. Emer B. Carman had a four-year deal to carry the mail from the Sylvandale neighborhood in the middle of town to the New Baltimore station. William Muller had a rural free delivery route out through Grapeville.

Political parties, the Epworth League, and other community groups used the station for nominating conventions, meetings, and so on. Other railroad-related structures sprouted, including a freight house across the tracks from the station. Over time, the term "New Baltimore Station" began to be applied to the neighborhood around the railroad building.

Businesses cropped up nearby. The cooper James H. Cary built a large, two-story building to be used as a coal, hay, and feed depot. The Albright family started a barrel factory and branched out into later businesses, including an automobile garage and oil delivery service that remained active into the twenty-first century. The Albrights also ran a successful bus line that became part of the eventual rationale for phasing out New Baltimore train passenger service.

Disaster also could strike the area without warning. In 1894, a building owned by the cooper Lucius Vanaken housed a grocery store run by D. H. Greene and a post office. As was the case with the time's many wooden structures and minimal fire protection, the place went up in flames one night. The Couchman family that lived upstairs barely escaped the inferno.

In 1912, a steam engine was helping to push a separate train with a long string of freight cars up a steep grade near New Baltimore station. The air brakes on the main train failed, causing the auxiliary engine to ram the caboose ahead of it into the next car in line. The caboose derailed and tumbled down an embankment. The tracks were blocked for five hours while debris was cleared. The conductor and brakeman in the wayward car were bruised but luckily not seriously injured.

Two other railroad-related, interesting events came into play during the first decade of the twentieth century. In 1903, a group of investors from as far afield as Newburgh, Connecticut, and Massachusetts proposed to build an electric street trolley stretching from Catskill to Albany. The line would have followed the river road in Coxsackie and New Baltimore then cut up the hill by the Reformed Church. While incorporation papers were filed in Albany, the project never got past the starting gate.

Around 1910, the New York Central was looking for a more convenient way for its east shore line to gain access to western destinations. Their plan was to build a bridge across the Hudson in the Matthews Point area of New Baltimore. Company surveyors were at that location at least twice, in January and February, but keeping their intentions close to the vest. Anticipation was high in the ensuing months.

Engineers came in early July and drilled rock samples on both sides of the river. Apparently, whatever the experts found was not satisfactory. By the end of the month, the men were doing test borings in the northern part of Coeymans. Investigators were back in New Baltimore in the late summer with rumors flying that the bridge would be built there. The hope was for naught as the Central decided that the more effective route was to build to the north. That structure still is used today.

Bad News

New Baltimore went through a period of pretty regular rail service carrying people and products, but the New York Central administration regrettably became increasingly dissatisfied with the dollar return from their investment there. Along with the booming public demand for the freedom of traveling by automobile came vastly deflated patronage for the railroad. As early as 1928–1929, the company was seeking to eliminate service at New Baltimore. The State's Public Service Commission (PSC) declined their initial petition.

As the end of 1932 approached, still facing profit shortcomings, the Central again was seeking PSC permission to curtail service. A step in that direction was to eliminate the station agent job at New Baltimore. In an ironic twist, this was about the same time that the Rip Van Winkle Bridge was in its planning stages.

A hearing was convened at the village hall in Catskill to solicit public input on the agent proposal. The railroad was claiming that financial losses were stirring their ambition. Freight profits were off, and passenger revenue was half that of 1929. Local residents contended that such a move would mean that tickets had to be purchased on board at a premium price and that demand still existed for rail service.

New Baltimore was at a considerable disadvantage at the meeting. Professional counsel represented railroad interests while the New Baltimore defense was left to Town Supervisor Levit C. Powell and the affected agent, Martin M. Clow. While both men undoubtedly provided a sterling effort, Powell demanded and was granted another session so they also could secure counsel.

At the later Albany hearing, Catskill attorney Lester Smith presented the Town's position. One of his main selling points was that the station had a $1,000 increase in earnings over the previous five years. Additionally, the Albright family's gasoline station had run a $5,000 spur line off the main route that would funnel fifty freight cars yearly to their business. Finally, the railroad already was saving money on the operation by paying the agent $300 less yearly than when a previous service discontinuance was turned down.[32]

An array of witnesses provided about two hundred pages of mixed testimony. Station agent Clow had to admit that there was only one regular commuter. On the other hand, the nearby Wardle farm still was shipping significant loads of poultry. Platt Wheat's grocery store received half its goods by rail from Kingston every ten to fourteen days. Levit Powell was getting the bulk of his retail company's coal by train. Most of the discussion though revolved incessantly about how much farther it was to go to Ravena station than to the building in New Baltimore.

While recognizing the increasing money problems, the PSC took a middle ground at this point. The New York Central wanted to eliminate the agent and allow freight to be sent or received from an unlocked and unattended freight house. The sender was to take the risk for theft or damage.

The commission did not find this arrangement to be an attractive option. It authorized the railroad to dispense with the agent but ordered employment of a caretaker who would be on site at scheduled times during the week. Under supervision of the Ravena station, this individual would handle freight during the working hours and also maintain the building in an adequate fashion.[33]

Rail service rapidly was making itself a disadvantageous choice. Potential New Baltimore customers complained bitterly about the lack of overnight train service that could carry perishable goods. They preferred to ship their produce by boat out of Coxsackie where schedules were more amenable. The Central also had reduced the capacity of trains to handle partial carloads of freight. This action severely harmed small places like New Baltimore where a vendor might only have a few boxes or barrels to ship. The problem was exacerbated later when the railroad initiated coordinated rail-truck service to expedite less-than-carload shipments at all stops between New Jersey and Albany. New Baltimore was included among the communities that would have trucks haul items instead of the trains.

The 1931 building of the George Washington Bridge greatly hurt business on the passenger side. Daily ridership went down considerably and was compounded by the Depression, which cut into freight revenue system wide. Track abandonments began in droves, particularly west of Utica.

Starting around World War I and extending into the 1950s and 1960s, government policy and funding promoted use of automobiles, trucks, and buses. At the same time, railroads, probably still being blamed for the long-ago illegal and unethical methods under which many were created, labored under onerous government regulation, having to obtain permission to close even the smallest, least profitable stations. At the same time, for their own fault, the railroads over expanded and overextended their means in the face of meager or no profits. The Central was in constant financial trouble.

Business increased during World War II, perhaps the high point of the West Shore's history. Weehawken became a significant launching point for freight. Passenger traffic was thriving with thousands of troops coming and going. The dawn of the 1950s still saw timetables listing 102 trains carrying people out of the New Jersey terminal. In recognition of modernization, steam engines were phased out for diesel. But that was not enough to breathe life into a dying industry.

In August of 1952, the Central petitioned the PSC to allow the closing of the New Baltimore station. The railroad claimed that there had been neither profitable passenger service for three years nor freight revenue for a year. A hearing was to be held late in the month in Albany. Residents registered little opposition. The unstoppable allure of quick and convenient automobile and truck travel was a much preferred alternative along with the option of taking a bus.

While the commission suggested that it would take six to eight months for a decision on the proposal, it only took until October. With three bus companies serving the area, rail service could be eliminated. The post office, which shared the station building, would have to move and did, into an attachment to a house across the road. Despite the station's closing, two northbound and three southbound trains continued to stop in town daily, with an extra run on Sundays.

The Central was in deep trouble as 1955 arrived. The company went so far as to take out sizable "The end of the line" newspaper advertisements proclaiming their profitability woes and why it "will soon be forced to discontinue its passenger service." The railroad was claiming that 85 percent of its "steady riders" had abandoned riding the trains, costing shareholders $2 million a year.[34]

The resolution for the problem was to file the appropriate paperwork with the PSC to end all passenger travel between Weehawken and Albany. The service just was not a paying proposition. The railroad even posted notices in stations that, effective March 7, only two trains would continue to run.

Opponents were persistent although few in number. The Catskill Chamber of Commerce, for one, wrote a persuasive but seemingly overoptimistic letter to the government protesting the proposal as "very harmful to many thousands of people who patronize the West Shore as the only means of transportation." Particular concerns were the loss of mail and express service and the lack of ferry service to connect people to rail service on the east side of the Hudson.[35]

The PSC was not quick to judge although it surely must have been well aware of the Central's money troubles. The regulatory body ordered service to continue. It would undertake an investigation of the situation and hold public hearings to entertain opinion from all interests on the efficacy of passenger service on the line. Affairs muddled on for a while longer.

Passenger service to Albany ended for good in 1958. About a dozen people watched the last train stop in Catskill. The multiple tracks between

Little Ferry and Dumont and the second track above Dumont began to be torn up in 1958. Only a single track remained by 1961, including at New Baltimore, with passing sidings in some critical places.

Almost all the passenger stations were torn or burned down in the mid-1960s. A tiny item in a 1956 issue of the *Coxsackie Union-News* reported that "L. Ritz and sons are removing the old railroad station from its present spot to their farm nearby. Thus another old landmark passes from view in Hannacroix."[36] Louis Ritz's farm was up the highway a short distance from the station's original location. The impressive Weehawken terminal burned in August 1961.

Even after the decades-ago demise of passenger runs, long freight trains continue to be a daily routine on New Baltimore tracks, particularly into the growing rail centers of New Jersey. Everything from coal to automobiles to wood travels through town today, with containers and truck trailers on flatbeds most prominent.

The financially strapped Central had merged with the Pennsylvania into the Penn-Central that then became the government-run Conrail. As the twentieth century came to a close, the Norfolk Southern and CSX corporations were competing for the prize of taking over the Conrail freight service. The National Surface Transportation Board declared both winners. Norfolk gained control of lines generally west of Cleveland, and CSX got the east.

The number of people who remember the fun and convenience of passenger service is dwindling to nil. A handful of them recall the hook with a dangling mailbag that could be grabbed by a worker on a passing train that had slowed for the pickup. The rest of us just can sit and watch a mix of trains pass across the single railroad crossing on Route 144. The foundation of New Baltimore station still lies in the weeds nearby.

8

War and Modern Times

The first half of the twentieth century was a whirlwind of serious national and international events, the fight against the demon rum, the campaign for women's suffrage, and a depression that may not have affected greatly an already deflated New Baltimore. Most horrific were the battles in the muddy trenches, bloodied woods and fields, and shattered cities of Europe, Africa, and Asia that bookended the period. The new modern conveniences of electric and telephone service also came to town in this time of dynamic change.

War Declared

The clouds of German aggression in the early decades of the century culminated in outright European combat in 1914. America remained neutral as forces battled overseas. After a string of events ranging from a German policy of unrestrained combat against shipping to a series of losses of our vessels at enemy hands, the United States declared its participation.

The *Examiner* published the official war proclamation on its April 7, 1917 front page. The following week's edition announced in its New Baltimore column the animated response of the people as "Old Glory is being displayed throughout the Town." The rival newspaper in Catskill, the *Recorder*, further lauded the patriotic character of the townspeople: "So far New Baltimore leads the way among Greene County's volunteers."[1]

Charles W. Wheat may have been the first New Baltimore man to answer the nation's call, leaving for Fort Ethan Allen in Vermont a week after the war declaration. John Bortle joined him at the New England camp. Earl Mosley had to go all the way to Galveston, Texas for training. Thurston Engel and Fred Freuler were off to Fort Perry, Georgia. Others joined them or went to various preparation sites. Freuler, a laborer in his mid-thirties, was one of the first local soldiers to travel overseas, setting sail from Hoboken, New Jersey on August 7, 1917, landing at St. Nazaire, France to start his tour of duty.[2]

In a remarkable display of national allegiance, the McAuliffe brothers from the southern end of Main Street, Robert, Howard, and Gerald, all ended up in the navy. Robert had been listed in the 1915 New York State census as a pilot on the Hudson while Howard was a steamboat watchman and quartermaster. Gerald was just sixteen at the time.

Some locals already were serving in the military. Levit C. Powell was an active member of the National Guard. Orville Engel had been in the navy for four years but reenlisted for the war. Walter Thorne had been in for about two years. In all, more than fifty young men from New Baltimore went off to fight.

While many people volunteered for service, the federal government worried about a continuing supply of fighters if the conflict worsened. Conscription was their answer. The Congress and president took quick action in enacting a draft program and setting a registration day.

Greene County's Selective Service Board established several registration sites. New Baltimore was sliced into two districts. The eastern half's committee members were Dale S. Baldwin, Platt S. Wheat, P. J. Vanderpoel, Byron Mansfield, and Rufus Bronk while Burton G. Palmer, Arthur Flansburgh, H. A. Travis, K. C. Bedell, and William Travis oversaw the west.

There were two locations for in-person registration, Cornell Hall in the riverside hamlet and the undertaker Ambrose J. Simmons's building near Medway's four-corner crossroads. Screening and drafting of men continued throughout the war.

Around the time of the initial draft rounds, the town had a dose of Germanic excitement from an outspoken visitor. An ice barge skippered by a Captain George Miller docked at the Burns Brothers ice house wharf. The German-descended captain was inexhaustibly critical about Americans and their participation in the budding war, going so far as to volunteer happily to shoot a few patriot soldiers himself.

His disturbing tirade pushed the ice house workers over the tolerance edge. One of them lassoed Miller around the neck. The captain at first thought it all was a joke but fearing for his health and well-being quickly changed his tune. He ended up apologizing and kissing the Stars and Stripes several times.

In September of 1917, a patriotic demonstration and parade were held in ideal weather conditions at Catskill to honor drafted men, an event duplicated on other occasions of leaving for war. Marching bands, veterans from previous actions, firemen, the County Home Defense Committee, Red Cross representatives, and Catskill and Coxsackie Home Defense Corps members all joined the soldiers in a rousing commemoration of their entry into the military. New Baltimore's Peter Vanderpoel led the march of drafted men.

A baseball game and a sumptuous dinner entertained the troops and their supporters. Among other notable speakers lambasting the Germans and lauding American ideals, New Baltimore's Francis Wardle took the forefront, addressing the crowd for the troops and promising their best efforts for the national cause. A few short days later, the men were aboard the 8:07 a.m. West Shore train, a vehicle that took many young, would-be Greene County warriors from Catskill to different training stations.

Some of the New Baltimore troops eventually found themselves moving toward the front lines, sailing the ocean in uncomfortable ships for sometimes a dozen days. Letters from the men were quite common in the weekly newspapers. The troops initially extolled the virtues of the wonders of France, eating snails, admiring French women and scenery, and furloughing in Paris, while anticipating with fearful willingness an opportunity finally to confront the enemy.

The newspapers also mentioned the parts some local boys were playing. Earl Rickard was in France operating a wireless unit. Levit Powell's machine gun unit made it into the thick of the French battlefields by late summer of 1918. Richard Hotaling was helping to coordinate ammunition supplies. Walter Thorne was patrolling the Mexican border.

While a number of letters penned from abroad by New Baltimore soldiers were published in newspapers or are otherwise available, few give hints as to the horror and devastation on the fighting lines or in the infamous trenches. One exception is a communication from Mechanic Henry Mead, somewhere in France, early September 1918:

> Our regiment, the 113th, has been at the front in the trenches twice. We only came out last night, after a stay of two weeks. While the time passed quickly, it seemed an eternity before we got relief, but it came at last, and we are a happy bunch to-day. I spoke in a previous letter about our getting good

> training. We were in the front line then, but it was only for a few days and there wasn't much doing. But this time it was different, we were under shell fire the whole time we occupied the line, and for two days and nights it was pretty hot. They put over some big ones—I ducked several. But while they gave it to us pretty warm we sure did make it more than hot for them. We lost four of our boys, with several other casualties, and this cast a gloom over all of us but we must expect such things. The German casualties were three times ours, and we sure gave them something for the atrocities they have committed in this land. I think they are beginning to know we are here and mean business.
>
> The artillery fire is very bad for us, and we all have learned to get into a dugout pretty fast. We have got some great stories to tell our friends when we get back to the good old U. S. A. We are due for a few weeks' rest now, and we need it—Sherman's saying about war doesn't half express conditions. It is a terrible conflict and I'm praying it will end soon.
>
> The weather has been very good, only two stormy days. We don't like dark, stormy nights. To-day is stormy and cool, very bad for trench life, as we have nowhere to go to get a change of dry clothing. Well, we did get water for shaving. It's a great life. I was a bit nervous at first—I guess the most of them were—but I feel fine to-day.

Henry ends his poignant letter by relaying his appreciation for his loyal friends and the pleasure of getting letters and local newspapers. He asks for everyone's prayers and longingly notes that "I don't know any better place than good old Greene county."[3]

A number of New Baltimore soldiers, including Dale Baldwin, Fred Freuler, Earl Rickard, and Ford Rundell, were present at the Meuse-Argonne offensive. That campaign, known familiarly as the Battle of the Argonne Forest, stretched from the end of September through November 11 of 1918. It was the final big Allied offensive of the war, forcing Germany's defeat and the signing of an armistice.

War Preparedness in New York

Even before war was officially declared, home front protection became a critical concern. New York's governor Charles Whitman called on each county to appoint its own defense committee to act as the state's conduit for any local actions needed to support the war effort. One of the counties' primary initial tasks was to take a statewide inventory of available military, industrial, medical, and agricultural resources.

There also was to be a state military census of all males or females, ages fifteen to fifty, to tap individual talents or characteristics, for example, nursing or telegraphic skills or automobile ownership, which might be useful to the defense campaign. New Baltimore residents had to report either to Cornell Hall or to the Simmons building for registration.

An adjunct operation was to create a home defense corps to supplement police forces and train people to replace the National Guard being mobilized for federal service. New Baltimore's Peter J. Vanderpoel, Dale S. Baldwin, Edward Groben, James Wheat, and Earl J. Rickard answered this call in short order by driving down to Coxsackie to join its Home Defense Guard. The men participated in weekly drilling to achieve a state of readiness to provide any necessary security. Many of these men later entered the military.

The governor took numerous other steps, including declaring an Agricultural Mobilization Day to highlight the need to maximize farming production in case of food shortages and military demands. The mobilization of school boys and adult women as farm labor was just one step taken to ensure full use of the state's human resources. A farm census was ordered to anticipate plantings and determine probable yields. That way, a plan could be developed to target preferred crops and estimate needs for seed, fertilizer, and labor.

New Baltimore's Wyman Kniffen, president of the Greene County Association of the Patrons of Industry, a prominent agricultural cooperative, responded by asking each subordinate association in the county to hold meetings to assess ways for local farmers to increase production, eliminate waste, and efficiently distribute farm products. The town's Echo Association convened at the Rocky Store School. A special meeting of the county association was scheduled for Saturday, April 28 at 8 p.m. at the Medway Odd Fellows hall "to take concerted action on the matter of agricultural mobilization. Greene county farmers must do their share this year, and the Patrons, as the strongest farmers' organization, must take the lead."[4]

Throughout the war, conservation and sacrifice were routine. Shortages were common. At one point in the fall of 1917, the newspapers were reporting that no coal at all was available in New Baltimore. People adhered to designated meatless and wheatless days, had meager sugar supplies, and substituted wood for coal for their cooking and heating. Local fuel administrators were appointed to deal with conservation and supply efforts.

Life went on in many ways in Greene County. The county fair at Cairo was celebrated as scheduled in late August with good weather, large crowds, the usual array of fruit, vegetable, and farm equipment displays, horse racing, and animal exhibits and competitions. The Methodist Church in the village was being renovated. The typical reports of vacationers and visitors dotted the newspapers' gossip columns.

Everything though was happening within the context of a world at war with the obvious worries but also a constant current of patriotic zeal. In the nationalistic bravado of the day, "New Baltimore citizens, without distinction of age or sex, are zealous to do their share towards the overthrow of autocracy and militarism and the maintenance of their international rights on sea and land, and in proportion to population our enlistments are probably not exceeded by those of any other town."[5]

Patriotic rallies, ice cream socials, dinners, and other types of celebrations became a regular feature of daily life. The Ladies Aid Society and Epworth League of the Methodist-Episcopal Church and the Whatsoever Society of the Reformed Church were involved frequently in fairs, drama and variety shows, suppers, and the collection of food and clothes for the troops and those in need at home.

One patriotic demonstration filled to capacity the Grapeville school building. Ford Rundell, from the westernmost reaches of New Baltimore and soon to be off to war, read a paper on "The Army." Other motivational speakers were the Reverend William D. Rockwell from Medway's Congregational Christian Church, Grapeville's Reverend Sidney Aldrich, and regional superintendent of schools Robert M. MacNaught from Windham. The same day, MacNaught attended a similar session at the school near New Baltimore Station with the participation of the Roberts Hill, Stanton Hill, and Bridge districts. Partisan songs and recitations and a flag-raising and salute were orders of the day.[6]

The annual Stanton Hill Farmers Picnic was dedicated in 1918 as a fundraiser for the Red Cross and was by all accounts a big success, fun-wise and financially. Early in the war, the Red Cross chapter gave an evening roast of corn and frankfurters with all the usual picnic trimmings on Charles Mead's lawn overlooking the Hudson. In a modern touch, electric lights illuminated the grounds.

Less than a week after war was declared, there had been an enthusiastic campaign to organize a Red Cross chapter to support the troops and the nation. The group ended up with at least two hundred members, holding frequent meetings in Cornell Hall and other locations to plot contributions to the people in service. Among the leaders were Anna Hotaling, Ida S. Vanderpoel, Ethel Bronk, Elizabeth Baldwin, Dora Bortle, and Ethel Morton.

One typical Red Cross meeting, a large rally with three hundred locals in attendance, was held at Cornell Hall on a June Tuesday evening in 1917. The event featured a number of speakers and a stirring reading of the names of the town's would-be combatants. The New Baltimore Cornet Band provided the musical entertainment with a main address by the Albany lawyer and future congressman William T. Byrne. Surviving members of the Grand Army of the Republic attended. There was a presentation of an American flag by Civil War veteran and former Virginia slave, Charles Lowery. Liberty loan subscriptions were sold, and new Red Cross members recruited. With piano accompaniment, a number of patriotic songs were sung. A stirring rendition of "America" closed the evening's festivities.

The Red Cross participants regularly made and donated clothes, towels and wash cloths, pillows, blankets, and bandages in addition to voicing their fervent moral support to the soldiers. For example, in October of 1917, the New Baltimore chapter sent a variety of necessities to a Catskill distribution center for troop hospitals and the soldiers: twenty-five dozen washcloths, seventeen dozen handkerchiefs, nine dozen substitutes for handkerchiefs, four dozen napkins, two dozen tray-covers, four dozen slings, four dozen fracture pillows, a variable number of head bandages, hot-water bag-covers, Turkish towels, pillowcases, mufflers, denim pillow-slips, sewing kits, and a sweater.

By the end of the year, the Medway neighborhood had its own Red Cross branch. In addition to other functions, the group was to hold socials monthly with dancing, games, and refreshments, all for free-will offerings. The 1918 annual meeting of the now 268-member branch was held to elect or reelect various officers, including the Christian Church minister William Rockwell as chairman, Mrs. Paul S. Palmer as secretary, and Alice Robbins as treasurer.

Over the year, the busy members made and sent to the Greene County Chapter: eighty-one pajamas, ninety-three hospital shirts, 135 pairs of socks, eighty-two sweaters, fifty-eight washcloths, and numerous other sanitary items and articles of clothing for the soldiers and war refugees. The juniors group of the membership contributed twenty-five comfort-bags, eighty joke postcards, eight puzzles, and 1,600 gun wipes.[7]

Frequent pleas from New York governor Alfred E. Smith and other public figures also appeared in the local newspapers urging citizens to purchase war savings bonds, stamps, and certificates. There was a dire need to raise cash to support the war and subsequent retrenchment costs. New Baltimore eagerly joined a campaign that was dominated by an aggressive national Liberty Loan program to sell war bonds.

An early fundraiser was convened at the Rocky Store School in late October 1917 and featured the ubiquitous speaker Dale Baldwin. Several people invested in the savings instruments, and a "pleasant evening" was had by all. On another occasion, the Cornell Hook and Ladder Fire Company graciously lent the use of their large meeting room, which was packed with a patriotic, enthusiastic crowd from all corners of the town.

Uniformed Red Cross members led a march into Cornell Hall to the musical strains of "America." A lead speaker for the evening was Professor Harlan H. Horner, who in 1918 became dean of the New York State College for Teachers. Another lecturer was a Sergeant Muir of the 13th Black Watch Canadian Highlanders, a three-year veteran of the French trenches. Muir regaled the crowd with firsthand tales of "Hun" barbarities. The town more than doubled its original investment subscription quota.[8]

Peace

In the dark, predawn hours of a quiet Monday morning, the glad news came to New Baltimore that the war was done. People flooded the streets in warm embraces, starting impromptu processions as word spread that the Germans had accepted the Allied peace terms. The fire bell in the hamlet began to ring in triumph, joined quickly by the chiming bells at the Reformed and Methodist churches and the one atop the brick school building. From then on, there was music and celebration into the night. A parade of about two dozen patriotically decorated cars drove the town streets in the early afternoon.

At seven in the evening, a couple of hundred joyful citizens gathered at the intersection of Main and Mill streets. Fronted by Uncle Sam, the Cornet Band, and Nickle's Drum Corps, the energetic crowd marched through the streets proudly flying American flags. The party moved to Cornell Hall where a line of speakers engaged the cheering audience. Town Supervisor Edwin Vanderpoel, the Reverends John Anthony and Howard Kanter, and Justice of the Peace Byron Mansfield gave the principal addresses. The celebrators then marched up to Coeymans and back, ending the evening with the burning of a German effigy.

The doughboys started coming back to the states and New York. Corporal Thurston Engel may have been the first man discharged, returning home in January. Corporal Winnie Wheat soon followed. The Home Defense Corps was mustered out in January 1919 with a farewell banquet. Fred Freuler arrived home near the end of August, one of last soldiers back from the French front. While many returnees likely suffered the lingering pains of combat, the town sustained only one war-related fatality, the only apparent female participant from New Baltimore, Carolyn Fay Hallock. She died while preparing to go overseas as a Red Cross nurse.

The end of combat and the troops' homecoming were disrupted by the indescribably shocking Spanish influenza pandemic that killed millions of people and exacerbated the ongoing trauma of the war. The local newspapers reported weekly on the illness. The Red Cross headquarters was closed "owing to the epidemic." The firemen's fair was postponed. The Board of Education heeded the warnings of the town's health officer, Dr. Percy Waller, and declared a week's vacation from school. People strolled on the streets, taking the prescribed sun baths and fresh-air cure. The Grapeville chicken pot pie supper was postponed because of the "grip." The flu remained a problem out in the Staco area well into the next year.

Life gradually went back to normal. The summer of 1919 was a busy time for the little town. Platt Wheat started a long Main Street reign in the grocery and post office business after buying Stephen Whitbeck's store. The Grapeville and Honey Hollow schools were combined, and the State condemned the Staco schoolhouse. Sixty laborers were hard at work modernizing the Coeymans-New Baltimore Road, macadamizing the four-mile-long route. And, quite significantly, a long era of prominence and prosperity came to an end when William Baldwin sold his shipyard to Brooklyn's William Wade.

New Baltimore Dries Up

As the Great War ended, another less violent but emotional battle intensified. Temperance had been a popular pursuit in much of Greene County and New Baltimore over the years. A mid-nineteenth-century law had provided a local option for controlling liquor, allowing towns to license sales.

As early as the end of the Civil War, the New Baltimore Union Temperance Society and fellow campaigners were holding picnics and other events to mobilize opposition to alcohol availability. In an 1874 letter to the editor of the *Coeymans Herald*, a shy writer adopting the pen name of "Yankee" commended "this morning from Medway, where a wave of Temperance has just washed. . . . Let those who lean on the rum interest for support, take notice."[9]

The crusade plunged forward over the next decades as prohibition became a viable option. New Baltimore had its own branches of the Women's Christian Temperance Union (WCTU), the Anti-Saloon League, and the Law and Order League, organizations to combat liquor use and other social ills. Julia Carhart, a milliner, boardinghouse keeper, and official town historian, led the WCTU for years. People by the dozens signed temperance petitions. Churches and other civic groups kept a vigil on the issue with frequent public lectures and fundraisers.

In a last burst of intoxicating commitment, Greene County granted a number of liquor licenses in the earlier fall of 1915, including application approvals for New Baltimore purveyors Griffin J. Kilmer, Herman Schillinger, and Newton Day. These three gentlemen were hotelkeepers, the first two of whom lived in the village and the third on the road to the railroad station.

Right before that year's November elections, anti-liquor rallies at Roberts Hill and Medway set the stage for a vote that saw New Baltimore ban the granting of licenses. This action was replicated in various other locales as the year saw over half the state's towns taking the same step. Not everyone was excited. In the New Baltimore column of the *Recorder*, just after the vote, the writer lamented wryly that "The town went dry by 45 majority. What a good thing we live near the river?"[10]

The coming of World War I provided a particular impetus to prohibition, as a proscription to the now-demonic German beer industry. It also was seen as a protection for our would-be servicemen, saving them from the sins of drunkenness. Whiskey restrictions were justified ostensibly to conserve corn as a valuable food item.

An opening was left for the drinkers. Any interested citizen could initiate a petition to revisit the license issue. As election time approached in 1917, a large group of over one hundred New Baltimore residents did just that, presenting a successful appeal to place licensing once again on the voting agenda. The signers represented a preponderance of the probable drinking contingent, working men in the community—steamboat and shipyard crews, farmers, and laborers.

The temperance gang took up the challenge in various venues, lecturing on the problems of alcohol at the churches, in private homes, and in the Dean's Mills and Rocky Store schools and other public spaces.

The executive committee of the local Law and Order League had decided unanimously:

> that conditions had been very satisfactory under no-license; that the merchants now received money formerly used for intoxicants; that the boys were not exposed to temptations; that intoxicated persons were not seen upon the streets as formerly, and that homes are happier as the result. It is hoped the present condition will continue.[11]

Their hopes were answered as licensing was soundly defeated.

The State was considering liquor restrictions throughout this period. Underscoring the seriousness and local interest of the issue, the New Baltimore Baptist Church minister, George Merry, and the Methodists' John Anthony even traveled up to Albany to hear the assembly debate about the alcohol controversy.

Nationwide action also was coming. The Congress passed the Constitution's Eighteenth Amendment, paving the way for the necessary three-quarters of the states to ratify the measure. The locals were maintaining pressure for approval. In late October 1918, New Baltimore residents were asked to participate in an evening meeting at Cornell Hall "without regard to church, party or particular organization but in the interest of good laws and good government in our great state." The session was designed "to support moral measures in state government, such as prohibition, the defense of the Christian Sunday, the primary law, and the suppression of all forms of vice." The previous Sunday, speakers from the Anti-Saloon League were at the services of the Reformed and Methodist churches.

The local Law and Order League sponsored the event under the leadership of its president, the noted shipbuilder, William H. Baldwin. Despite an audience reduced by the flu epidemic, a dedicated group started the proceedings with a chorus of "America" and a prayer led by the Reverend Merry. Other speakers included the Reformed Church's Howard Kanter, the Reverend Anthony, Justice of the Peace Byron Mansfield, WCTU president Julia Carhart, and Suffrage Club leader Jennie Van Orden. The evening ended with a rousing rendition of the "Star Spangled Banner."[12]

As the decade came to a close, federal authorities enacted legislation, popularly called the Volstead Act, to outlaw the manufacture, sale, and possession of any intoxicating liquor beyond a barely palpable strength beer. Sad days seemed on the horizon for the drinking classes. Bottles and kegs were emptied in public dumping sessions, and saloons closed in droves.

They were not downhearted for long. Prohibition sparked an industry of speakeasies and bootleggers' stills, even in Greene County, and a long period of chaotic lawlessness as enforcement officials attempted to turn off the alcohol tap.

It soon was apparent nationally and statewide that overaggressive attempts at federal containment, organized crime involvement, government-poisoned industrial alcohol and people who drank it, arrests of increasingly prominent imbibers, and overall expense of enforcement turned people against prohibition. Joining other states, New York voted overwhelmingly in late 1926 to memorialize the Congress to amend the Volstead Act to allow states more leeway in determining the relative intoxicating effects of beverages beyond the permitted weak beer.

While not something routinely reported in the New Baltimore, Medway, or other town social columns, you can be sure that bootleg hooch and accompanying legal problems were a feature of life in New Baltimore. The Catskills and surrounding areas were dotted with hotels, boardinghouses, and isolated farms that were an easy spawning ground for the illicit alcohol trade. The notorious Jack "Legs" Diamond had an entire Catskills' compound established up the mountain at Acra and spent quality time at Jerry's Climax roadhouse in Coxsackie.

The May 28, 1928 *Coxsackie Union-News* provided a representative illustration. A handful of federal prohibition agents "swooped" down on a whiskey-making operation in the Honey Hollow neighborhood straddling the New Baltimore-Coxsackie border. Five miscreants were detained, the resident of the target farm, an individual from Catskill, and three men from Albany. The revenuers "smashed" three stills, one a thousand-gallon apparatus, "beyond repair evidently without any compunction."

Around New Year's in 1930, Clarence Parsons was awakened by a blazing cider barn on his expansive farm right in the village. A youthful insomniac later reported hearing through a heating register between the first and second floors the entreaties of a visiting Legs Diamond delegation, demanding that Parsons convert his cider-making operation to a bootlegging one. In an ironic turn of events, his refusal to consent was followed closely by the fire.

Little was said about prohibition in the New Baltimore social columns from the 1920s into the 1930s. Julia Carhart was attending 1929 WCTU conventions in Coxsackie and Binghamton. But the notice of these events may have been more a function of Julia quite possibly authoring those columns. The stock market crash and Great Depression led to the belief that keeping people fed and in jobs was much more important than having the government chase after errant bootleggers and drinkers.

While groups like the WCTU and Anti-Saloon League continued their decades-long efforts to maintain Prohibition, the Eighteenth Amendment was dead. Federal legislation first was authorized in March 1933 with alteration of the Volstead Act to allow production and sale of beer and wine with 3.2 percent alcohol content. Shortly thereafter, New Baltimore got its first taste of real beer (legally!) in many years. Advertisements for Albany's Dobler Brewing Company began appearing regularly in Catskill's weekly newspaper, the *Recorder*.

On May 23, in a generally light vote, New Baltimore followed the county, state, and national example by overwhelmingly supporting the repeal of prohibition. The count was 174 in favor and 97 opposed, with the western district interestingly against repeal, 29 to 18.

In the weeks leading up to the vote and repeal, the New Baltimore gossip column in the *Recorder* gave little indication that impending wetness was of any great concern to town residents. There were no reports of church lectures or local WCTU meetings. Snow-covered roads greeted the Reformed Church's flag- and banner-festooned fall hosting of the thirty-ninth annual convention of the Hudson River Christian Endeavor Union, a prominent Christian youth organization. Their lengthy agenda gave no indication that Prohibition had come and was going.

As a summer of severe drought came, the renewed flow of liquor may have helped soothe the dry weather. There were 187 beer licenses issued in Greene County by mid-July. Whether this had much of an effect on New Baltimore is debatable. Several of the major sources for alcohol purchase and consumption were long gone. The Riverside and Windsor hotels in the village had closed. The 1929 catastrophic fire on the east side of Main Street destroyed the Imperial Hotel and its tavern. The status of alcohol use in boarding houses or places in other parts of town was unreported. On the plus side, an auxiliary effect of the repeal was a small but steady flow of alcohol tax revenue to New Baltimore and other municipalities.

Suffrage

A determined drive to grant women the right to vote in New York began in earnest with a petition presented at the 1846 State Constitutional

Convention. Time was not ripe yet for such a drastic change in the ruling men's thinking nor was it in a subsequent handful of conventions.

Some short-lived progress was made in 1915 with a vote that also featured the Town banning liquor and Dale Baldwin handily defeating William Albright in a Democratic victory for the position of town supervisor. Despite a massive public relations and education campaign from the beginning of the year, the November referendum to amend the New York Constitution to allow women to participate in elections in the state was defeated.

New Baltimore acted definitively in opposition to the women's vote. The final local tally was 125 for and 290 against suffrage. A preelection editorial in the *Recorder* captured the county's majority mood on the topic, criticizing:

> the pernicious proposal to admit all womankind to the ranks of voters already too full of undesirables. Aside from the many valid reasons of sound policy for voting NO, to everyone acquainted even remotely with the seamy side of politics the mere thought of doubling the "float" vote should be sufficient to settle the question.[13]

Activists were not undone by the temporary setback. The New Baltimore suffrage advocates quickly retrenched, meeting the Monday after the election and regularly thereafter. Toward the end of March in 1917, the Echo Association of the Patrons of Industry sponsored a suffrage rally at the Rocky Store School. The assemblage strongly supported a resolution on equal suffrage "with no dissenting voices." It was reported that "a majority of the men present said they would vote for the suffrage amendment in November. A majority of the women expressed themselves in favor of suffrage."[14]

In a remarkable display of the illusory public power of wife over husband versus the anonymity of the voting booth, New Baltimore again refused the measure, 163 yeas and 231 nays. Despite the townsmen's efforts, after winning by a significant margin in New York City and breaking even in the rest of the state, women now could vote in New York.

From May 15 through June 15, 1918, the new electorate had a first opportunity to register in a party of their choice. Only about a quarter of the eligible females accepted the challenge to do so. Of the new enrollees in Greene County, the vast majority went Republican. New Baltimore had a final count of ninety-nine Republicans, sixty-five Democrats, and thirty in the Prohibition Party.

Meanwhile, a series of efforts were occurring in Washington to secure a federal constitutional amendment to achieve a national resolution to the issue. After a handful of failed efforts, the Congress approved suffrage legislation in the late spring of 1918, clearing the way for the state-by-state ratification required for changes in the Constitution. Final approval came in time for the November 1920 elections.

In keeping with the generally more conservative outlooks of Upstate New Yorkers, Greene County and New Baltimore were steadfast in opposition to women's suffrage, voting in the negative whenever presented with the opportunity. A candid commentator from the town's Stanton Hill neighborhood had blithely deflected any culpability after the 1917 victory: "Well, the suffragettes won at last, but I'm sure the men in this neighborhood weren't to blame."[15]

Lights and Phones

As the turn of the twentieth century approached, small-town entrepreneurs began to establish homemade companies to implement up-and-coming modern conveniences. Power providers like the Coxsackie Electric Light Company and Ravena Electric Company and communications enterprises like the Ravena and Medway Telephone Company came into being. Almost immediately, entrepreneurs could smell money and launched a concerted campaign to combine these smaller entities into larger units with wider coverage and superior profit margins.

The Upper Hudson Electric Company, incorporated in 1901, was perhaps the first of these larger local efforts. Formed from the merger of the Athens Electric Light and Power Company and the Coxsackie and Ravena operations, the new enterprise was powering homes and businesses in Athens, Coxsackie, New Baltimore, Coeymans, and Ravena. A rival Atlantic Light and Power Company started to operate early in 1907 and laid claim to overlapping territory, setting off a competitive and litigious struggle with Upper Hudson. Each recurrently disputed the other's payment rates and coverage areas.

Even more overwhelming was the 1900 combination of gas and electric companies in the Newburgh, New York region. This action started a long string of swallowing small, locally run power companies. At the end of 1926, New York State approved a consolidation that brought together many of the remaining operations under the umbrella of the infant Central Hudson Gas and Electric Company, today's power provider.

The same scheme of consolidation was affecting the provision of telephone service to the small villages and rural areas of Greene and southern Albany counties. The State Telephone Company was incorporated on December 31, 1909. Among its initial directors was New Baltimore's Jasper K. Hotaling. State Telephone was an amalgamation of several rural and "farmers" lines, homemade networks of wire strung among farms and denser populated neighborhoods.

The State Telephone territory centered on the villages of Coxsackie and Ravena, extending a little north of Ravena and south of Coxsackie with New Baltimore in between. Users had to turn cranks on their phones to alert operators handling the disposition of local and long-distance calls through offices in Coxsackie and Ravena, with most people on party lines.

One of the smaller companies gobbled up by State was the Ravena and Medway Telephone Company, which had been created in April of 1904. William Harden, the smaller company's president, signed the merger certificate. Harden may have been more familiar as a prominent fruit grower and town supervisor in the middle of the 1890s.

Farming—What Happened?

The peaks of women's suffrage, revived beverage choice, and technological advances was met head on by the valleys of economic downturn and a return to the all-too-frequent bane of human existence—war. First came the stock market crash and a depression that may not have had as much effect in what was already a deflated New Baltimore. The 1929 fire had destroyed much of the business stretch of downtown. The Baldwin shipyard was gone, and ice houses were on their way out. Not a wealthy place to begin with, the town's economy had to be in tatters.

The headlines and New Baltimore gossip columns of the local weekly newspapers reveal little about any depression-created hardships. An occasional legal notice to creditors appeared about some unfortunate person's financial dilemma, but that did not seem excessively different from more normal times or an indicator of larger troubles. There just were the usual array of reports on people coming and going, church dinners, weddings, and Sunday services.

By July of 1931, the Albany banks felt obligated to place ads in Ravena's *News-Herald* regretfully announcing that economic conditions were forcing the raising of interest rates from 4 percent to 4.5 percent. The same paper the previous February editorialized about the federal government unnecessarily planning to tap the taxpayers to provide aid to the poor rather than rely on private helpers.

Otherwise, by the spring of 1931, signs of revival were perceptible. Work was resumed at the Coeymans brickyard. A handful of other editorials were starting to advocate that things were looking up. In New Baltimore hamlet, Henry Fuhrman set up a new Socony gasoline pump in front of his River Road business. The steamboat captain Francis Chapman was building a new house. Charles Stott was erecting a new fueling station and snack bar where his old operation had burned a couple of years earlier. Ravena and New Baltimore authorities were planning how to provide a gravity water system for the little community along the Hudson, a campaign that died out before the following winter.

The bad news really came in the agriculture industry. For decades, New Baltimore had counted on farming as an economic nucleus, especially growing and selling fruit and poultry. By 1875, the town had 248 farms with 33,882 acres under cultivation. Moses Bedell at Stanton Hill was growing apples, plums, peaches, pears, cherries, and quinces. Medway's Roscoe Carman brought in an amazing 20,000 barrels of apples for the fall harvest of 1917.

As World War I ended, William Albright, Charles Lisk, Oscar Youmans, and Levi Bedell all set out new orchards or planted new rows of trees. Wagons and trucks brimming with fruit made their way to cargo boats on the Hudson and the rail stations at New Baltimore, Coxsackie, and Coeymans. Lectures and demonstrations on farming techniques and Echo, Staco, Climax, and Pomona (countywide) Grange meetings were regular occurrences.

As late as 1931, the Wardle farm out near New Baltimore Station hosted the purportedly largest gathering of poultry growers ever held in the region. A last bastion of productivity, the number of chickens reported on farms remained relatively constant at around 26,000 between 1935 and 1950.

Then the bottom dropped. By the time America's involvement in World War II was on the near horizon, New Baltimore was down to 135 farms with 13,722 acres in use. A lethal fusion of negative circumstances started to take their toll.

Many farmers with smaller or more geographically challenged plots could not afford or accommodate the increasing mechanization of the industry or the extra land and effort required for a viable commercial enterprise. Borrowing money and paying higher taxes became inexorable burdens partially as a result of trying to get a bigger, more diverse operation to stay competitive. Extra help became too expensive. You had to have a side job that soon paid a lot better than farming without the long hours and headaches. Many farmers opened rooms in their homes for vacationers for the added income.

Stanton Hill's William Harden, one of the old-timers whose farming exploits were chronicled often in the gossip columns of the local papers, sold his fruit farm to Egbert Blauvelt of Ravena. The hard-working veterans of the fruit-growing industry were aging out of the fields.

A 1932 freeze killed many apple trees. The next summer brought a severe drought and light crops. Some fruit growers faced heavy financial losses. Farmers who depended on wells for irrigation had to cart water long distances at great cost. The end of prohibition cut short the hard cider production that was a small goldmine for an adventurous few.

The number of fruit farms dropped from eighty-eight with 1,227 acres under production in 1939 to forty-seven with 439 acres in 1949. The number of apple trees in bearing age was cut by nearly two-thirds for the same period from almost 35,000 to barely 12,000. Pears dropped by 80 percent.[16] Pretty soon, other places could out-produce and outsell, and then there were no trees in commercial use.

Today, fewer than a dozen farms are active. Most rely on harvesting hay for survival. A couple or so have some cattle. Here and there, you still can see the remnants of once vibrant orchards that had a multitude of different fruit-bearing trees. Agriculture's history in New Baltimore is really the history of the town. In hopes of retrieving a scrap of the great tradition, the Town Board is actively pursuing policies into the twenty-first century to support agriculture, promoting the small farmer and the allure of homegrown products.

World War II

What had been a most unsettled period in American history was slammed closed by more war, ignited by the German army's cutthroat sweep across Western Europe in the spring of 1940. The summer saw a buzz of activity as the average citizens began making preparations for the worst. Army detachments came to guard West Shore Railroad bridges, including the one over the Hannacroix Creek.

The military draft was reinvigorated in the fall of 1940. Local men Raymond Legg, Raymond Powell, and Charles Hohenstein were among the first Greene County names drawn. Clare A. Robbins of Coeymans was appointed as a member of the draft board that covered the towns of Coeymans, Bethlehem, Knox, Berne, New Scotland, and Westerlo. Just after World War II, Robbins and his family would move to New Baltimore where he had a long career of public service, including several years as town supervisor.

The familiar pattern evident in past wars of community spirit and patriotic support surfaced. Around Christmas of 1940, the call went out for machinists, tool and instrument makers, different types of engineers and inspectors, and others whose special talents could lend to national defense.

The Ravena-Coeymans Home Defense Unit was planned to include New Baltimore and Hannacroix residents under its authority. It and similar groups were devised statewide for volunteer men and boys eighteen and up to learn how to be soldiers. Targeted to prospective draftees and men considering enlistment, regular sessions were given over to military drilling, learning to handle and shoot weapons, and instruction in topics like first aid and gas and bomb warfare.

A Greene County War Council was created to handle local logistical support and community activities, intending to help people cope with civic and home life during wartime. Demonstrations in useful tasks, such as canning food and preserving meat, were among their common offerings.

One of the council's first chores was to request the collection of worn silk and rayon stockings for use in making parachutes. Boxes for such purposes were placed in the Medway store and Platt Wheat's hamlet grocery store. The only criterion for a donation was that the stockings be thoroughly washed before being deposited.

Sacrifice and salvage were required. Slowly but surely, many regular household necessities slipped out of the marketplace, placed under the restrictions of rationing—meat, butter, cheese, gasoline. At one point late in the war, the New Baltimore hamlet school was closed because of the fuel shortage. Bans on certain items like raw silk from Japan also popped up.

Calls for scrap metal, tin cans, and paper were routine. It was commonplace for a town truck to motor around and pick up roadside leavings and for regular drop-off points to be designated. There were a couple of more unusual donations—Mrs. Douglas Wheat sent sixteen inches of her hair that she had cut way back in 1927 to the Bendix Aviation Corporation for use in assembling military instruments. In the fall of 1944, folks in Grapeville gathered milkweed pods that would provide the stuffing for life belts. The harvest was stored in buildings at the Chatham fairgrounds to await shipment to a government factory in Michigan.

As in World War I, savings bonds and stamps were put on sale to raise funds for the military campaign. Bond rallies were popular events that could be hours-long affairs. One mid-September 1943 extravaganza at Cornell Hall started with "Pop Wagner's snappy Girls' Drum Corps" bopping out a steady beat after wheeling up from Coxsackie. Boy and Girl Scouts paraded along with them.

The bond campaign co-chairman Orville G. Hotaling led a trail of dignitaries, including the Methodist and Reformed pastors, Luther W. King and William C. Schwab. Church choirs sang a run of patriotic tunes. After an invocation by King, a lengthy list of speakers came to the podium, including Justice of the Peace Henry Fuhrman, Medway area chairman Sherwood Miller, and Echo Grange master Wyman Kniffen. They and others hammered home the audience's duty to support the men and women in service by investing. Many people rose to the occasion and bought $4,000 worth of bonds on the spot before the meeting closed with the singing of more nationalistic anthems.[17]

American Legion posts were registering all members voluntarily for potential national defense service. People were putting together Bundles for Britain, small kits containing a comb, toothbrush, hair pins, razor, notepapers, and pencils that were shipped to New York City and then overseas. The focus of churches, community groups, fire companies, and the like was the war. Any help that could be gotten was given.

Observation posts were being created for volunteers who worked in shifts day and night to alert authorities of any incoming enemy aircraft. William Haas, who made a comfortable living selling Buicks and Chevrolets from his Coxsackie showroom, had a home on the appropriately named Haas Hill in the center of New Baltimore. In a spirit of patriotic fervor, Haas built a surveillance station by his house that was large enough to accommodate bed and board needs for four watchers at a time. Now we might consider such dedication a bit of overreaction but in that world of unknown terror, it was deemed a necessity.

Haas also donated the use of a truck for those manning the post along with gas and oil. The State Telephone Company strung a line to the building for free phone service. A substantial list of avid watchers volunteered their time, and the American Legion and several local businesses provided equipment and supplies.

In the fall of 1941, the federal government ordered a nationwide survey of all farms to estimate the food resources of the country. Greene County's Farm Bureau was undertaking the project locally with the focus on New Baltimore, Coxsackie, and Athens and on the availability of milk, eggs, and poultry. Canvassers were appointed in each of the target towns, with Robert Moore, Paul Palmer, and Albert Hotaling in charge of the counting in New Baltimore. At that point, there were about 650 farms just in those three towns.

Just before Thanksgiving in 1941, disaster struck the riverside hamlet. A neighborhood lady was walking up Main Street when she noticed smoke pouring from the south end of Philip Conrad's house. She promptly alerted the New Baltimore fire department who rushed to the scene. As the flames spread to the Methodist Church next door and several other buildings, units from Ravena, Coeymans, and as far away as Selkirk were called to the scene.

Brave volunteers managed to haul the organ, piano, and church records from the blazing house of worship. Water supplies were limited although over a thousand feet of hose were strung to the Hudson. Firefighters did their best, but the Conrad house and its contents were completely destroyed. The church and homes across the street were severely damaged. Luckily no human injuries were reported even though about 125 people participated in the firefighting and salvage operations.

War is Declared—Again

A little over two weeks later, the treacherous Sunday assault on Pearl Harbor came while Japanese emissaries were in Washington talking peace. The Congress nearly unanimously declared war on the Asian nation. "When the United States Government declared war yesterday afternoon, there was no other alternative. The attack by Japan was a cowardly premeditated one while we were supposed to be at peace with that nation."[18] Germany and Italy quickly declared war on us, and we reciprocated.

As with other, all-too-frequent conflicts, the engines of civilian support motored into action. Men flooded to join local home defense brigades. Women were mobilizing into classes for first aid, home nursing, auto mechanics, and nutrition. Pamphlets were being produced to inform people about defense measures. There were advisories to alert the public on wasting water, avoiding fires, and even minding the danger of lit cigarettes. Information was distributed about extinguishing incendiary bombs. Contingency plans were made to handle the mass of émigrés if New York City residents had to evacuate north.

The Red Cross was on a huge fundraising drive. Mrs. E. H. Thorne was leading the Medway branch in raising their share of $200, and Francis Paul was in charge of the New Baltimore hamlet's efforts to collect $900, numbers that asked to dig deep in the pockets of the relatively poor communities.

Coxsackie High School students, teachers, and staff gathered a total of 780 books in a campaign to collect reading material for the troops. The Knaust brothers mushroom business donated use of a truck to haul the collected works to Albany for subsequent shipment overseas. Schools did a multitude of other fundraising and defense support jobs, including providing first aid, stenography, and machine shop instruction and duplicating numerous safety and defense preparation documents for public consumption. Schools all over the country, including at Coxsackie, sought to raise money to buy 10,000 Jeeps and 100 war planes.

The Town Board stepped in to sponsor the purchase of a service flag to honor New Baltimore's contribution to the fighting forces. An unveiling was scheduled for the village square with special invitations to military families. Supervisor Cecil Hallock was charged with securing a list of the soldiers and sailors and their kin, and board member Henry Fuhrman with buying the flag.[19]

Local life still sought some semblance of order as the social columns and other news items in the *News-Herald* could attest. Its first wartime issue on December 12 tells us that James Baldwin and Henry Wiltsie were elected fire commissioners in a Cornell Hall meeting. The bridge club met as usual on Thursday afternoon. Thick fog forced a number of tugboats with trailing barges to dock at the town wharf. The Reformed Church was planning its December 21 Christmas pageant. The Echo Grange's holiday party was on schedule with neighborhood school children to provide the entertainment. People attending were to exchange 10-cent gifts.

War time went into effect. Clocks were turned ahead an hour. Unscheduled calls for blackouts could come at any time: "keep calm, put out all lights and by no means use the telephone except in case of extreme emergency." Civilian lines could not tie up critical communications. Traffic was to be stopped on Routes 9W and 385. Firemen and defense workers were to report to their assigned stations. Wardens were to patrol local streets to check for visible light. Fred Young was the warden for the River Road under the Coxsackie program. Blasts of the fire alarms warned people about the need to turn lights down.

A *Coxsackie Union-News* correspondent stood at the old Coxsackie ferry landing during one February blackout and reported on the dark stillness, "where not a light could be seen on the skyline in every direction; only the buoy off Coxsackie Island, the airplane beacon above Ravena and a myriad of stars illumined the cold, silent night." Fake aerial bombs could be heard to the north, detonated at Albany to warn citizens and simulate an attack. Practice "victims" were treated by nurses and other emergency staff in downtown Coxsackie.[20]

At the beginning of the year in 1942, the *Union-News* announced that it, "in cooperation with all newspapers in the country, will exercise every discretion in reporting news of war activities, such as troop movements[,] use of planes and other vital information." The media's "sacrifice," in the spirit of national security, to censor strategic news became the rule as the war went on, so much so that later in the conflict, the same newspaper had misgivings and reprinted an editorial from another source criticizing the perceived limitation of a free press.[21]

There was weekly information on the ebbs and flows of war and sundry reports on soldiers' visits home but the news embargo meant that very little detail about men's combat exploits was published. Little hints were rare but increased as time passed. Medway's Gordon Wildey and William Leary were in Africa. Clifford Armstrong flew in the air corps somewhere in England. Other soldiers and sailors were spread across the globe.

Stateside assignments often were mentioned. William Miller was at Camp Sampson in the Finger Lakes region of New York State. Walter Dietz was at Atlantic City. Leroy Curtis, promoted to corporal, was camped at Anderson Field in South Carolina while Raymond Powell and Roger Thorne were stationed at Camp Hood, Texas. Emma Lou Comstock, Edith Pelzer Misur, and Bertha Wade were New Baltimore women in the armed forces and posted at various sites.

Over time, the restraints of wartime censorship loosened a bit for New Baltimoreans. Longer and more detailed soldiers' letters were published almost every week. The WAC corporal Jessie Spence wrote about her posting that was as distant as one might imagine from New Baltimore: "Here I am far away but really happy about the whole thing. We are in the jungles of New Guinea, and believe me, it is really rugged. That is what I asked for. We had a swell trip over here, and now I'm a full fledged seaman." Corporal Spence was a captain's secretary and wrote about her living conditions, work hours, and leisure-time activities—movies three times a week, dancing in a pavilion on the beach, and primitive bathing arrangements.[22]

Heroes

Regrettably, as the lid on the news came off a little, the notices of deaths, injuries, MIAs, and imprisonments became much more common in the columns of the local weekly newspapers, side by side with the lists of new draftees. There also were too brief mentions of awards and commendations for heroic actions.[23]

A short announcement in the January 14, 1944 *Coxsackie Union-News* extended congratulations to Wesley and Mary Hallock Hotaling on the birth of their son the day after Christmas. Wesley had worked on his parents' farm on the River Road before going off to war. The news item noted that Wesley was serving in Italy. A couple of weeks later came a tragic counterbalance. The young military man had been killed in action in Sicily. He had been part of a successful campaign to destabilize Italian participation in the war and open the Mediterranean to Allied ships. Wesley was twenty-one years old.[24]

Technical Sergeant Robert F. Stott was awarded an Air Medal while serving with the Army Air Forces in England. Robert's father, Charles, ran a store and the post office on the hamlet square. The elder Stott also took care of local roads for a while, serving as the town's highway superintendant.

Entering the military in 1942, Robert, a Coeymans High School graduate, had become a bombardier. In the spring of 1944, the War Department notified his parents that he had gone missing over Germany on March 14. Stott had written to his mother just before his misfortune, telling her that he had been on fourteen missions.

The loss was deeply felt in many quarters. L. E. W. Johnson wrote a letter to the paper with an accompanying poem commemorating the heroics of a New Baltimore casualty.[25] The lamentation luckily was premature. Robert had ended up captured and imprisoned. He eventually was liberated and returned home, passing away at age eighty.

In an online request for information about Stott's military career, his daughter reports that her father had weathered fourteen months of the misery of enemy prison camps, including Stalag IV and VI and two weeks at the notorious Buchenwald.[26]

Just a month later, in horrific irony, the sympathetic L. E. W. Johnson and his family got the worst news possible. Their own son was killed in action. David Johnson was a college graduate who had been an employee with the International Harvester Company in Albany. He had entered service and became a second lieutenant. Besides his mother and father, he left behind a wife, three sons, and two sisters.

In New Baltimore, people pushed life forward. A mid-May meeting was scheduled for the Medway Church to organize a fire department. This move had been discussed for years but now was accelerated by a blaze that destroyed the home of community leader Sherwood Miller.

Miller was named the first president of the Medway-Grapeville Fire Company along with Ernest Bartholomew as second-in-command and Frank T. Smith as secretary. The men soon were looking for a site for a fire house and ordering a truck from the Haas garage in Coxsackie.

The dawn of the new year in 1945 saw a pile of snow covering the region. Within just a handful of days, over twenty inches fell, whipped by strong winds that made clearance a major problem. Roads were nearly impassable, and trains were hours off schedule. The Medway church was closed for February and March.

Rationing and restriction still were ordinary facts of life. The Central Hudson Gas and Electric Corporation was clamping down on electricity use, banning virtually all outdoor lighting. As mentioned before, the hamlet school was shuttered for a time in February because of fuel shortages. On the huge plus side, though, battles in Europe, Asia, and Africa were coming to an end.

News trickled in about the town's war victims. Second Lieutenant Arthur Mosley, who had been overseas for twenty-nine months, was wounded at least three times in battles while serving in North Africa, Sicily, France, and Belgium. Walter Labuda whose parents ran the general store near the Baptist Church in Grapeville was wounded at Iwo Jima. Labuda had enlisted in the Marines just after graduating from Greenville High School. Francis Williams was recovering in a Paris hospital from wounds sustained in Germany. We also eventually learned that two other men with New Baltimore connections, John Irving and Ernest Wickham, perished in battle.

Newspapers and post office talk entertained townspeople with the flying exploits of Clifford Armstrong in the European Theater. Armstrong had entered the Air Corps as an Aviation Cadet in January of 1942. He quickly must have shown a particular ability for the task. In his military heyday, the young airman was pilot of a P-47 Thunderbolt fighter plane, the *8-Gun Melody*. He was in the first wave of fighter planes providing air cover for the Normandy invasion troops. His success in dive-bombing Nazi targets prompted a promotion to captain and awards such as the Distinguished Flying Cross and a bundle of oak leaf clusters for his Air Medal. After the war, the much decorated Armstrong came back home to his family farm on the River Road, rising to the rank of major in the Air National Guard, and living to age eighty-six.

As summer started in 1945, Everett Caldwell was in a military hospital in France after being released by British forces in May from a German prison camp. He soon would be on his way home. The young soldier had not yet turned twenty but had been shunted between prisons after his Italy-based plane had been forced down because of mechanical difficulties while on a bombing mission over Rumanian oil fields. He had served for thirteen months in the European theater, including ten of them spent in a German prison camp. Everett had been awarded the Purple Heart, ETO Ribbon with three Battle Stars, and the Good Conduct Medal.

In early May, President Harry Truman announced in a nationwide radio broadcast the glorious news that the war in Europe was over. Schools closed. The New Baltimore Reformed and other churches held commemoration services. The gray, rainy V-E Day brought a sense of quiet gratefulness subdued by the specter of continued fighting in Asia.

The middle of August brought final peace once again. Japan unconditionally surrendered. Soldiers were welcomed home with warm open arms. Things were getting back to normal. New Baltimore candidates were being announced for the fall elections. Among several expected competitive races, the Democrat Sherwood Miller was to oppose Republican Cecil Hallock for supervisor. Hallock would win. Perhaps in recognition of a postwar economic revival, the Albright family's Mountain View Coach Lines was buying a number of new buses and adding runs to their schedules. In December of 1945, construction of the Thruway began. It was the road to the modern era. New Baltimore was entering a long period of quiet domesticity, drifting more into the character of an Albany suburb.

9

Off to School

Schooling may not have been of primary interest for the earliest arrivals to an untamed wilderness like the place that was to become New Baltimore. Friends, family, and skilled neighbors taught newcomers to sew, do rudimentary carpentry, tend livestock, navigate sailing vessels, cure meat, mend fences and tools, and hunt and fish. Life just did not require widespread formal education nor was such a luxury readily available.

There was an early religious seed planted though for more organized schooling. The Dutch came to the new world requiring an educated clergy that could spread the word of God. The ability for parishioners to read and understand the Bible was integral. Under English rule and in later decades, there undoubtedly were private classes and tutoring sessions held, particularly for the children of more well-to-do families.

The river-related industry on which a significant portion of the town's early economy was based meant that at least the area along the Hudson was not isolated and not immune to outside influence. In particular, the close proximity to Albany, from where the pressure to organize schools and later to consolidate them emanated, may have had an impact. It was not surprising that schools came soon after official organization of town government.

A few bits and pieces of historical evidence show the presence of formal schooling in the eighteenth century, probably picking up speed with post-Revolution emigrations. For example, there is record of a man named John Brown teaching in a New Baltimore school from December of 1795 to the middle of March the following year. Brown was paid a fee of six pounds per month. He had a class roster of forty pupils, including Joseph Sherman, Stephen Ayrault, and Andrew and Storm Vanderzee. The school even had its own trustees, James Keeler and Job Pearce.

The Society of Friends members who had come to the Coeymans Patent in the 1780s greatly valued learning, again as a tool for religious study.[1] In September 1795, pressure was brought to bear for the local Quakers to provide financial support for a boarding school at a place called Nine Partners in Dutchess County, an early site of regional meetings for the sect. While initial prospects apparently were dim for such aid, minutes kept for the local Quaker meeting note that the Field, Hoag, Bedell, and Powell families all sought to send children to the school from 1797 on. Starting in 1802, the local people were being assessed for part of the school's expenses.

Right before the Town's organization of its first common schools, the Quakers appointed a group of members to oversee schools and teachers within their community. A second small assemblage was chosen to raise money for a permanent education fund but this seems to have been an illfated venture. By 1826, the minutes say that no schools were being maintained that met the group's requirements. Whether this meant that they were now participating in the now active town-wide education scheme or just did not operate schools of their own is unclear.

The earliest schools often depended on the generosity of well-to-do neighbors and community supporters. An 1819 indenture between the local entrepreneur Paul Sherman and the trustees of the hamlet's District 10, David Dinsmore, Thomas Houghtaling, and James Haight, is illustrative. For the sum of one dollar, Sherman made available sufficient land to build a school house that was to be at least twenty-eight feet deep and twenty-four feet wide. The building was to stand where a previous one had recently burned down.[2]

This may have been the same building described in an 1876 handwritten commentary by a fifteen-year-old student, Benjamin I. Carhart. He tells us that:

> It is a large two story frame building 30 x 40 ft. It contains about 140 seats 2 morning glory stoves 4 or 5 brooms 4 Black boards a library & books a water pail 2 dippers 2 teachers & 2 teachers desks and about 100 scholars, 13 windows a coal bin in the hall and nails to hang up hats coats shawls etc.

> Window curtains at each window, an old map and dictionary. Its condition is very bad the floors are worn very near through the desks are cut very bad and the chimney is falling to pieces.[3]

New Baltimore's Public Schools

Meanwhile, pressure had been growing in New York to provide some form of government-supported schooling that would formalize the scattershot approach used until then. The state's first governor, George Clinton, was one of many leaders who believed that education of the masses was key to survival of the nation.

Laws started to be passed to establish a public school program for children of all ages. A small success came in 1795 when legislation was approved to set aside 20,000 pounds for each of the next five years to promote common schools. This was a wholly inadequate amount, and the law was not extended. Discussions on the topic continued.

A big move forward came in 1812 with landmark legislation that started a surge for organizing public schools. The legislature approved "An Act for the establishment of Common Schools." The new law created a superintendent with statewide authority to "prepare plans for the improvement and management of the common school fund, and for the better organization of common schools." The bill authorized localities to establish school districts according to their self-perceived needs. The number of districts quadrupled statewide after the education law was passed.[4]

The law's funding provisions also opened a hornet's nest that persists up to today. The State was to provide financial aid to the new districts based on the number of residents ages five to fifteen. The districts had to open school at least three months a year and match the amount of state aid with local tax revenues, the ubiquitous and long-lived school taxes. If any more money was needed for operations, the districts could require people to pay "rates," or tuition, for students to attend classes.

In later years, the rates proved to be difficult for some poorer people to accommodate with their meager finances. The State abolished the payments and instead installed a system of property taxation that still poses a dilemma for many citizens and school administrators. The tinkering with funding formulas and the degree of local versus state administration of the schools was a constant feature of legislation and rulemaking over many decades.

New Baltimore was an early subscriber to the new structure of schooling. A town meeting was held Tuesday, April 6, 1813 at house of farmer Jonathan Miller, out in the center of town, to certify local election results. Tunis A. Van Slyke, Anthony Van Bergen, and Noah Wheeler were elected as commissioners of schools and Elmor Chase, Conradt Houghtaling, Anthony Van Bergen, Peter Bronk, and Jeremiah Bedell as inspectors of schools.

The men must have taken a good look over the next few months at how many children lived where and how far they would have to walk to a school. Toward the end of the year, after what must have been a general analysis and survey of population densities and locations and debate about placement down to the individual household, the officials met once again at Miller's farm to mark out a series of school districts along geographical lines.

With an eye toward limiting travel time for the children, the nine districts in number order ran from the southeastern corner of town across to the southwest then from the far northwest back across to the Hudson:

> District No 1 Beginning at the South East bounds of the Town and running North to the house of Ephrm Bronck including West to include Baltus Van Slyck to Nathan Burns included South to include Thomas Houghtaling to the South Bounds of the Town East to the place of Beginning
>
> No 2 Beginning at Peter Houghtalings along the South Bounds of the Town to Caleb Gages North to include Thomas Hallocks to Caleb Griffens East by the Wilsons to Samuel Wilson included South to the bounds of the Town to the place of Beginning
>
> No 3 Beginning to include Nehemiah Mead thence North to include Jonathan Miller Junr to include Anson Roots thence West to include Joseph Calder thence to Michael Turpins from to the South Bounds of the Town thence East to the Place of Beginning
>
> No 4 Beginning at Nathaniel Smiths north East to John Saltus included to Slaiks from thence West to Nathaniel Palmers

from thence to the South Bounds of the Town East to the place of Beginning

No 5 Beginning at Thomas Powells Running to the north west Bounds of the Town East on the Town line to Jason Wins Widow thence South to Slaiks West to the place of Beginning

No 6 Beginning at the Widow Wins East on the Town line to Abner Hoags then South to John Osborn included west by Caleb Griffen to Schuler North to the place of Beginning

No 7 Beginning at Abner Hoags by Simeon Garretts to John Osborn East by John Wolfs Lisks Youngs & from Youngs by Tompkins & Trumans to John Armstrongs from thence to John Coonleys included West to the place of Beginning

No 8 Beginning at John Garretts running the north Bounds of the Town to Garret Houghtalings South including Henry C Houghtaling John Gays & from John Gays to Henry Bogardus thence including Tunis Wolf & Barent Houghtalings to John Garrets

No 9 Beginning at Garrets Houghtalings to include running to the north Bounds of the Town thence East to the River thence South along the River to include Derrick Van Slyck from Derrick Van Slyck including Tunis P. Van Slyke Garret T Houghtaling & David Dinsmore & from Dinsmore to include Conradt T Houghtaling to include Thomas C Houghtaling & Garret A Houghtaling[5]

In subsequent years, the Town altered the boundaries of districts on numerous occasions and created new districts as need arose, either as a result of citizen petition or to remedy perceived needs. Convenience of travel was a primary motivator for parcels of land to be moved from one district to another. Population growth also played a role, prompting new districts to handle increasing class sizes.

As early as March of 1814, several households were moved from their previous assignments into District 2. Later that same year, the commissioners of schools agreed to alter Districts 6, 7, 8, and 9 and create a new District 10. A long-standing trend was set as a portion of District 10 was annexed to the Coeymans school system.[6] It was not unusual even then for a town's children to attend school in another municipality, a precursor to future mass consolidations. By the end of September in 1866, New Baltimore had a high-water mark of seventeen districts spread across the town.

While the number of common schools grew throughout this period, there was little state-level supervision of their activities in New York. The local districts elected trustees who hired teachers, built and maintained school houses, and selected and bought textbooks and supplies. An 1814 follow-up law made the creation of common schools mandatory but administration remained the province of groups of local authorities in various configurations.

The majority of students in the state and probably all of them in New Baltimore went to one-room, ungraded schools that were in session often for only twenty-eight weeks, just enough time to meet requirements for receiving State support. The basics were stressed with drills as a common instructional technique often reinforced by strict discipline ("taught to the tune of a hickory stick"). Attendance was not compulsory for many years.

An assortment of minute books and other documentary sources remain from these common schools and provide a brief look into the responsibilities of school boards and teachers and the learning experiences of students. A good example is referenced in the Rocky Store School discussion later in this narrative. Another is from the Elmendorf School or common school district (CSD) 12. (A school often was nicknamed for benefactors, prominent citizens who lived nearby, or the popular name for its home neighborhood.) This district was created by the New Baltimore government in 1824 in the central part of the town.

In 1832, the school received $15.52 in public money from the Town of New Baltimore and $3.22 from the Town of Coeymans (another example of a district crossing borders to accommodate children who lived close by). One of the major business transactions at the early trustees' meetings was to arrange for the purchase of firewood for the stove. That one chore could cost $5 or $6 dollars a year, a good percentage of the funding from the Towns. The trustees voted in 1839 to raise $15 in taxes to establish a school library and buy a bookcase. Six years later, money from the library account helped obtain a globe.

Finances always were an issue, particularly for upkeep of the school building and outhouses. The 1850 proposed Elmendorf budget had to go through two roll call votes to raise $60. The first balloting ended in a 15 to 15 deadlock. One citizen appears to have saved the day for education in the district. The second vote was 16 to 14. Wood still was an expensive and critical item by 1907, its $113 cost second to the teacher's wages of $140.

There were attempts to make instruction more consistent, efficient, and, perhaps, cost effective through combined efforts. In 1877, a meeting of delegates from thirteen school districts in town came together at the Medway building. Their task was to select the textbooks that would guide teachers in the various subjects taught to the children.

Reading was first on the agenda. The group decided to keep the lessons already being used plus the "Independent Sixth Reader." The attendees then proceeded to select a daunting pile of volumes of learning: "Quackenbos's History, Robinson's Mathematics, Swinton's Geography, Brown's Grammar, Steel's Fourteen Weeks in the Sciences, Patterson's Speller, Swinton's Word Analyzer, Quackenbos's Language Lessons, Spencerian Penmanship, Krusic's Drawing."[7]

Education still could be somewhat of a catch-as-catch-can affair. There is a ninety-second birthday reminiscence by Jennie Trego Wickes whose family moved in 1852 to a house in the middle of New Baltimore hamlet. She talks about attending the Coeymans Academy and three elementary schools apparently in private homes or, in one case, a building sponsored by Theodore Cornell, a dentist and brother of the Reverend James Cornell.[8]

"Higher" Education

If a student wanted to pursue more advanced studies, perhaps with an eye toward going to college, he or she had to travel to Greenville or Coxsackie or another location. New Baltimore itself never had a high school.

In what seems like a modernistic and businesslike approach for the times, the Greenville Academy advertised in the *Catskill Recorder* in the spring of 1820 for prospective students. The announcement informed the public that the school would be open under the administration of Andrew Huntington, A.B., and "that the various branches will be taught in said academy that are required for admission into any of the classes of the various colleges." In anticipation of the strain of extensive studies or to attract young people from afar: "Board can be procured in respectable families, at from twelve to sixteen shillings per week; including washing, lodging, candles, etc."[9]

One can only guess at the advertisement's effectiveness in attracting New Baltimore learners. They had a way to go from previous years. In an 1817–1818 student roster, only two local boys, Andrew A. and Baltus T. Van Slyke, were listed among ninety-two total "Gentlemen" students. There were no lady attendees from New Baltimore.[10]

Perhaps it was the cost or course offerings that were prohibitive or unattractive. A late October edition of the *Catskill Recorder* announced that school was continuing for the new term. Tuition for the languages and higher branches of mathematics would be five dollars for the quarter. Three and a half dollars would be the charge for each reading, writing, common arithmetic, English grammar, geography, and composition course. Interestingly, room and board had gone down from the 1820 rates to a new range of nine to fourteen shillings a week, washing still included.[11]

An Idea Gone Bad

The flaw in the whole affair was that common schools basically were uncontrollable. There was no standardized curriculum or consistency in instruction or in teacher preparation from neighborhood to neighborhood let alone across the state. New York authorities made a multitude of moves to arrange and rearrange statewide and local administrative structures, always tending toward coordinated operating efficiencies. Solely local authority for education began to flow away almost from the start of the common school campaign.

As time passed, the pool of school-age children grew abundantly. School buildings were overused, poorly maintained, and deteriorating. Dollars were short to support a level of education suitable for a modernizing society and economy. Plus the State was pushing persistently for more efficient school operations. Longer periods of teaching targeted more to age groupings was deemed a necessity. People also were clamoring even then for tax relief.

Funding seemed to always be short for the trustees who ran the tiny, one-room common school districts. The buildings were crowded with bulging populations and aging rapidly, worn out from decades of tramping feet. There was no modern equipment. One teacher could be responsible for tailoring coursework for a sizable class that could have a range in student ages from barely out of the crib to the late teens.

New York's answer to all these issues and demands was, and would be, for many years, the consolidation of the little and generally inadequate common districts under expanding state administrative authority. New York passed a law in 1853 that started to modernize the local education bureaucracy, allowing one or more smaller districts to establish union-free school districts. The hope was that these units would offer a broader, more efficient, and professional program of studies and also could operate high schools if they so chose.

It took until 1900 for the trustees of New Baltimore hamlet's District 10 to adopt a union-free format. This was the only local district that ever broke the mold of the unitary common school. In August, voters in the hamlet were called to a special session to decide if they were to convert to the new set-up. Thirty-five people voted in favor of the move with one blank vote. A new school board was elected at the same time.

As early as 1856, the diversion of authority away from towns was accelerated. The town superintendent position, which had replaced the old system of commissioners and inspectors, was abolished. For a while, there was an intervening level of supervision by counties. That soon disappeared, replaced by district superintendents of schools who reported to the State and became the local coordinators for the consolidations that occurred throughout the middle of the twentieth century.

Dire financial circumstances during and after World War I, particularly in agricultural communities, exacerbated the tensions of the existing system of school funding. While it is not clear whether such moves related to finance, New Baltimore's CSD 13 merged into 4 in 1919, and 6 into 12 the next year. CSD 14 had disappeared into 11 in 1899.

The State answered the problem in 1925, shaking the education system mightily with passage of the Cole-Rice Law. Along with changes in per pupil aid, the new legislation instituted transportation and building aid incentives for the creation of centralized rural school districts. Local trustees saw dollar signs, and combinations of schools began to gain momentum.

Coupled with the advent of the Great Depression and strong state promotion, it is easy to see the attraction of centralization for the residents of the rural area in western New Baltimore and the neighboring town of Greenville.

Greenville Central School

In late November of 1929, the campaign for consolidation in the Greenville area picked up considerable steam. A capacity audience gathered at that town's Presbyterian Church. The group represented the interests of all the communities that would have their schools included in a joint district, including New Baltimore's Grapeville and Medway students. An array of speakers praised the benefits of centralization. The ability to provide a wider breadth of courses relevant to preparing students for agricultural or industrial careers would be a keystone of any new arrangement.

A featured orator was C. J. Mousaw, the superintendent of schools from the integrated Schroon Lake system up in the Adirondacks. Mousaw gave a summary of the applicable state statutes and provided an overview of effects of the conversion in his jurisdiction. He emphasized, perhaps most importantly for the locals, that the tax rates had remained unchanged. The Greenville correspondent to the *Recorder* newspaper was moved enough to report that "The outlook for the establishment of a centralized school is very promising."

A series of meetings began to be held for residents, generally to inform them about the perceived benefits of combining antiquated common school houses into what were then being called central rural school districts. One well-received event was convened at the Grapeville school house where Medway residents also were present. No details are available about any public comments made at those sessions.[12]

A number of men from the proposed district even had the opportunity to visit a handful of operating central districts at Treadwell, Laurens, and Milford to view their advantages firsthand. Several themes predominated at these places: stable or lower taxes, efficiencies in operations, a wide range of courses, coordinated transportation, better facilities and equipment, lower class sizes with less broad age groupings, and more professional and better trained teachers.

Little opposition formed. A man named Charles Newman appears to have been one of the few people voicing any dissent. This probably is the same Newman who shows up in the 1920 federal census as a rural delivery mail carrier living in Greenville with wife Nettie.

Charles published his opinions on more than one occasion in the local media. His comments ranged over a multitude of issues from uncertainty about the true costs of the venture and potential tax increases to questions about the validity of petition signatures and the loss of education home rule. He even comments on the undue influence of outsiders: "we residents of Greenville have been asked to accept the consolidated rural school on the mere 'say so' of those persons who are more interested in the perpetuation of their jobs than in the farm boy or girl—namely the bureaucrats in Albany and others closely connected with them."[13]

By the end of January in 1930, the regional superintendent of schools Robert M. MacNaught signed the application for a Greenville-based central rural school district that was to include four shared districts that served New Baltimore. Almost exactly two months later, this action was confirmed by New York State's commissioner of education Frank P. Graves. He issued the official order to lay out the new jurisdiction.

The wheels of centralization were set in motion for New Baltimore. The new amalgamation was to encompass twenty-three small districts in several towns. The only wholly New Baltimore district involved at that point was the Staco school in the far northwestern part of town. However, New Baltimore children joined Coxsackie and Greenville students in attending Greenville CSD 7 (Kings Hill) and CSD 10 (Surprise) and Greenville, Westerlo, and Coeymans pupils at CSD 6 (East Greenville), all included in the combined package.

During April, the clerks of the towns affected by the proposed consolidation made the requisite legal postings for publicizing the commissioner's order and noting the scheduled meeting for those allowed to vote. New Baltimore's Lyles Nelson did his part of the chore, hanging notices in central locations.

Eligible residents met in the village hall in Greenville on April 29, 1930 and elected to form the ungainly named Central School District No. 1 of the Towns of Greenville, Durham, Coxsackie, New Baltimore, Cairo, Greene County; Coeymans, Westerlo, Rensselaerville, New Scotland, Albany County. An accompanying board of education also was chosen. The vote in favor was very substantial, 351 for and 23 against, and was said to be the largest plurality at that time given the size of the population. It was the first centralized district in Greene County. The *Examiner* newspaper positively noted that "There is a general sentiment that Greenville and vicinity have taken a great step forward in insuring to their children all possible advantages of modern education in the public schools."[14]

The incentive to unite districts remained powerful. The Grapeville CSD 4 and Medway CSD 6 joined Greenville in 1946 and 1948, respectively. The former inclusion seems to have been relatively uneventful. There had been a contract in place for some time to transport children from the Grapeville Baptist Church to Greenville.

Medway was a little more complex. State authorities had proposed that it be included in the Coxsackie-Athens central district, which was just in the process of being established and lay south of New Baltimore. However, concerns about the quality of the Coxsackie-Athens facilities led Medway residents into a two-year battle to merge with Greenville. One internal State Education Department (SED) memo went so far as to say that Coxsackie had "wretched buildings."[15] It was so serious an issue that district trustee Paul S. Palmer and a committee of residents were scheduled to visit Barry V. Gilson, an SED associate commissioner, for a personal appeal.[16]

Despite continuing opposition from some of his own staff, Education Commissioner Francis T. Spaulding issued the order for Medway to become part of Greenville. In light of an internal SED memo from Assistant Commissioner for Rural Instruction Edwin R. Van Kleeck, it would seem that common sense and local support won out in the end: "I have never agreed with the Rapp recommendation in this respect for the people are rural people like those in Greenville; they have closed their school entirely and contract with Greenville; the Greenville school bus serves them by contract; they are so eager to be annexed to Greenville that they are doubling or tripling their school tax in order to do so."[17]

In 1952, many voting-age residents of the Upper Stanton Hill area may have been inspired by their Medway and Grapeville neighbors. A sizable group of signers petitioned to dissolve their district and annex it to one of the three contiguous central districts. This action resulted from about two years of discussion generated by a change in transportation and tuition funding that would have doubled local tax rates.

Franklin B. Clark, district superintendent of schools, surveyed the situation and recommended that the district be added to Greenville. After some SED formalities, CSD 10 of the towns of New Baltimore and Coeymans became the last independent district in New Baltimore, effective October 22, 1952. There apparently was little commemoration. The *Examiner-Recorder* quietly announced in a small but front-page article that District 10 was officially annexed, adding about eighteen students to the Greenville rolls. No mention was made of the Stanton Hill school being the last of its kind.[18]

Coxsackie-Athens Central School

Throughout this period, State pressure for consolidation continued unabated. The Regents Inquiry into the Character and Cost of Public Education (1935–1938) criticized the State's tentative approach to centralization and the creation of too many small central districts. By 1941, a Temporary State Commission on the State Education System was convened to examine the situation and offer recommendations. This so-called Rapp-Coudert Commission produced a master plan for school consolidation in 1947 that was to provide the impetus for dissolution of the remaining New Baltimore schools. The bottom line was that bigger was better.

The path to uniting schools for the southern part of New Baltimore began as early as the late-1930s. A number of people in Athens sought to organize a coordinated approach. The State quickly short-circuited the campaign because the town's schools did not meet minimum state requirements for numbers of pupils and assessed valuation. A consolidation, though, was in the air and took a while to ferment. Factions in Athens would remain pretty much unhappy all along the way.[19]

In 1944, a petition was submitted for a central district originally consisting of twenty smaller units in Athens, Coxsackie, New Baltimore, and Cairo. The components were to include the aforementioned Medway and Grapeville and five other districts, either wholly serving New Baltimore children or shared with neighboring towns. Not all the New Baltimore districts still had students but existed legally and contracted with other schools to offer instruction and transportation.[20]

This was just the start of a rather lengthy period of negotiation and review. One major delay for the proposal was the insistence by Athens residents that they retain a school with elementary through middle school grades, sending only youth in their later years of study to the centralized high school. This demand was not acceptable to state authorities.[21]

Children started to drain out of the New Baltimore schools well before any large-scale consolidation. It became standard fare for one location to enter a contractual relationship with a larger district to provide instruction. Generally, certain grade levels, usually older people first, would transfer to be followed later by additional years.

In the summer of 1945, the *Coxsackie-Union News* reported that there were plans for seventh and eighth graders from New Baltimore's Rocky Store school (CSD 2) to go to Coxsackie for the start of the next school year. An August 17 special election finalized the move. High school–age students were already there. About twenty more children were scheduled to be bused southward. The probable primary goal was to free time for the one district teacher to attend more to the curriculum needs of the younger children.[22] Ten students from the Otter Hook school on the River Road had been going to Coxsackie for several years.

In mid-May 1947, the centralization issue was coming to a head. The SED had developed a proposal that initially would have combined six New Baltimore districts, four from Athens, and nine from Coxsackie. William Sickles, head of the board of trustees for the hamlet's four-room brick school, contacted the SED about their desire for uniting with Coxsackie and Athens rather than with any Ravena district.[23] Despite Sickles's inclusion of a petition proclaiming near unanimous local support for linking to the south, the SED declined to include District 1 in the new combination. Also, by the time the proposal was due to be implemented, Grapeville and Medway were aligned with Greenville.

By mid-June, the required number of petitions had been collected and filed with the SED, and the road to centralization was paved. A special meeting of the qualified voters of the proposed district was convened for June 30 at 10:00 a.m. with balloting to continue to 8:00 p.m. Haas Hall in Coxsackie was a beehive of activity that day as a steady stream of voters invaded the premises.

It must have been a long night. After the balloting was closed, a crew of people counted the votes and reported the findings. The result was a resounding 458 to 203 in favor of centralizing sixteen smaller districts in the towns of New Baltimore, Coxsackie, Athens, and Cairo.

After the accounting was completed, the remaining throng approved appointment of a nominating committee to select candidates for a nine-person school board. Robert Moore of New Baltimore and John Satterlee of Medway were chosen to run for one- and three-year terms, respectively. In the end, the new Central School District No. 1 of the Towns of Coxsackie, Athens, New Baltimore, Cairo, Greene County included New Baltimore's District 2 (Rocky Store), 3 (Roberts Hill), 7 (Lower Stanton Hill), and 11 (Otter Hook). A year later, the official name became the Coxsackie-Athens Central School District.[24]

Any satisfaction was short lived if there was any to begin with. A vocal group in Athens was never happy with the union. Almost as soon as the consolidation was approved, they wanted to dissolve it, believing that the tax rate was $6 above what was advertised in the State's pre-election promotional materials.[25] The dispute continued on some level or another well into the 1950s with assorted litigation. The state and local authorities could not be persuaded to move backward, and the centralization prevailed.

Ravena-Coeymans-Selkirk Central

School centralization came last to the northeastern part of town. As with the Athens dissension, disagreement on inclusion in the new district raged from a Selkirk contingent of concerned citizens. As indicated by the 1947 Sickles's petition noted earlier, New Baltimore people had mixed reactions about aligning with the Coeymans community.

New Baltimore children had been sharing schools with Coeymans students or attending school over the border in certain grades for a number of years, particularly for high school studies. However, the next big step toward consolidation came in 1949 with the circulation of petitions for and against merger incorporating schools in New Baltimore more formally and inclusively with those neighbors to the north.

There was a pocket of resistance in the Hannacroix area as twenty-seven people registered in favor and thirty-eight against the combination but the rest of the affected districts were strongly in support. As a result, Commissioner of Education Francis T. Spaulding ordered that a Central School District No. 1 of the Towns of Coeymans and New Scotland, Albany County, and New Baltimore, Greene County be established from:

> Union Free School District (UFSD) No. 1 of the Town of Coeymans;
>
> UFSD No. 3 of Coeymans and New Baltimore (Ravena);
>
> UFSD No. 1 of New Baltimore (Hamlet Grades 1-6—children in other grades were going to UFSD No. 3 in Ravena); and
>
> 10 Common School Districts, including New Baltimore's 8 and 9 (Dean's Mills and Hannacroix or Sandbank— both inactive but still existing on paper) and 12 (Aquetuck—active) of Coeymans and New Baltimore.[26]

The proposal was to go for a vote of qualified residents of the districts in mid-June. The anticipated benefits supporting consolidation included a more equitable spread of the tax burden, additional state aid under a state-favored centralized structure, and availability of certain courses (e.g., physical education, remedial reading instruction, home economics, art, and agriculture studies) and services (e.g., guidance counseling, nursing and dental hygiene services, kindergarten) not previously offered in all schools.

Alternatively, much concern surrounded the perceived need to build new schools, provide more expensive services, and incur more debt and overall cost to do so, resulting in higher taxes for low-tax rural areas. New Baltimore storekeeper Orville Hotaling was forthright in his opinion that "I'm not in favor of it. I think we're all right the way we are." Another hamlet resident, A. L. Wheat, summarized his opposition to the union:

> I'm against it, because they never put it up to us straight. They (Coeymans and Ravena) put a bus on us last year and paid only about $400 of the $1,400 cost after saying they'd pay half. Better to leave our schools alone. We had a school

> here and if they hadn't cut our school aid we'd be all right. I was on the school board 26 years. But if they can show me something good in this on Tuesday, I'll vote for it.[27]

There was considerable legal upheaval from another front about the consolidation, with the election in the balance up to the last moment. The UFSD No. 1 of Coeymans, New Scotland, and Bethlehem (the so-called Selkirk district) laid claim to North Coeymans CSD 2 under a previous consolidation vote in 1947. It now was slated to be included in the new combination. The Selkirk residents generally wanted to have their own school district and their own high school. The powers-that-be maintained that there were an insufficient number of students in the area to do so.

The furor and legal entanglements were sufficient enough for Supreme Court Justice Roscoe V. Elsworth of Kingston to rule that the election could not proceed. State education officials traveled to Monticello the Monday night before the Tuesday vote and persuaded Appellate Justice Sydney Foster to overrule. The basis for the decision was that a judge was not authorized to restrain a state official from performance of duty without due notice. The contention was that Commissioner Spaulding was not given notice.

In the final analysis, the election was held, and the outcome was not close. A special election at Ravena High School resulted in a vote of 1,017 in favor of a single school district, 317 against, and 6 voided votes. It was a relatively low turnout. The North Coeymans district was included in the consolidation that was to be effective July 1, 1949. A tense lull ensued as the next chapter was awaited.

In May 1955, the final piece in the unification puzzle was put into place when Education Commissioner Lewis A. Wilson laid out what we know today as the Ravena-Coeymans-Selkirk (RCS) district. On June 22, 1,134 people voted for the combination, 927 against, with 2 blank votes and 69 voids. The Selkirk residents were still fighting their inclusion through the courts, claiming that their votes should not have been lumped with the other areas. They voted overwhelmingly against the merger but were folded into the RCS district anyway.[28]

Rocky Store: The Last One-Room School

Into the 1880s, what some believe was the original Rocky Store school was in use near the corner of today's Route 51 and Dean's Mill Road.

We do not know whether the number of students outgrew that building or if it was just deemed unsuitable but, in 1892, the motivation toward having a new structure reached full strength. A new school was to be built.

The accounts journal for the district for the post-1892 period has several interesting entries that convey a flavor of the construction and initial development of the second Rocky Store school. In the summer of 1892, $100 was entered as a payment to Catherine Vincent for the site for the new building; $50 to Frank Albright for laying a foundation; and miscellaneous outlays for putting up a fence on the north side of the school grounds. W. K. Church was to get $35.86 for a stove, locks and knobs, pipe, elbows, and wire. A. G. Powell was to receive $20 for miscellaneous construction work and grading and $50.47 for a bell. Actual construction costs appear to have been $900 to $1,000.

As the fall came and the students must have begun classes, we get some clues about the beginning of the life of the building. On October 22, 1892, $22 was registered in the journal for Barney Gardinier to paint the school house and clean the inside. Other entries noted the costs of $24 for twelve seats at $2 each, $3 for two rear seats at $1.50, $6 for a teacher's desk, and $40 for a blackboard. Various payments also were approved for coal, oil, paint, and insurance.[29]

The facility was modern for its day, with a double outhouse, screwed-down desks, and a new bell. There were individual cloakrooms for boys and girls—one on either side of the entrance we know today. Children in grades one through eight (the number of grades served was reduced as time passed) were educated at the start in the building, and the attendance rosters contained such familiar names as Albright, Meyer, Hallock, and Dietz.

Over the years, the revolving classes of Rocky Store students and their teachers settled into a routine of learning ABCs and sums and about history and geography. Students would obtain textbooks from graduates in their grade or from the teacher's catalog. They would walk to school in the harsh winter's ice and snow to be warmed by the coal stove that stood in the room. Trips to the outhouse in the back yard could be similarly adventurous in colder months.

The students participated in ball games in the school's front yard where long hits were chased down the hill toward where the town garage is now. Competitions with other schools also were common. A 1946 *Coxsackie Union-News* article reported on five schools—Rocky Store, Roberts Hill, Medway, Grapeville, and New Baltimore hamlet—having a Friday field day at Medway. Events for boys and girls included a bag race, hundred-yard dash, baseball throw, relay race, and two kinds of broad jump. The day was capped by a softball game won by "New Baltimore," undoubtedly students from the brick school in the hamlet by the Hudson River.[30]

As was the case with other common schools in town, Rocky Store was a center of community activities. Temperance meetings, wartime bond drive sessions, church services, sing-a-longs, 4-H Club meetings, and numerous other events would be held at the schools. Rocky Store even entertained weightlifting classes for a short time.

In the 1940s, as we have noted, local school mergers occurred continuously. A wider age range of Rocky Store students were transferred off to Coxsackie. Then the big consolidation came. From 1947, Rocky Store was an active part of the Coxsackie-Athens district.

As the 1960s dawned, the move to centralize schools was at a peak. The 1960–1961 school year saw Rocky Store with only five pupils in grades one through three, down from eight the previous year. The enrollment in 1900 had been fifty. Anna Johnson who had taught at the school for fifteen years oversaw the activities of the last students. An article in the *Coxsackie Union-News* captures some aspects of life in the school at the end of its active days:

> With centralization in 1947, Rocky Store lost some local control but retained the power to keep the school open if the taxpayers wish. Mrs. Cecil Hallock and Edward O. Bedell were the last trustees of the school district. Rock [*sic*] Store children bring their lunch to school. Milk is provided by the government milk program. Water is obtained from a deep well on the school property and is served from a glass cooler. A large space heater keeps the one room school comfortably heated. Mr. and Mrs. Wilbur Albright, who reside across the road from the school, are the janitors.[31]

The families of the remaining students made the fateful decision that too little was left. They would send their children to Coxsackie-Athens. The little district voted to consolidate wholly with its larger neighbor and close its doors. The last active one-room school in New Baltimore, and in fact Greene County, was gone.

Pieter B. Coeymans and the Last of the Last

The final death knell for New Baltimore's schools came in February 1962 when the construction of two new elementary school buildings was approved for the RCS district. One of them, the Pieter B. Coeymans Elementary School, was completed in Ravena and was convenient for New Baltimore students. The new facilities opened for business in the fall of 1963.

By the early 1960s, the RCS district was in a bind. Elementary school children were spread among several locations for their studies. Administrators were planning fall 1962 classes for schools at New Baltimore, Ravena, Coeymans, Selkirk, South Bethlehem, Feura Bush, and Jericho. The district also was renting space in four other buildings with at least one more place on emergency hold. Many of the youngsters were being educated in space that was not designed for classroom use.

The appropriate consultants were hired to plan two new elementary buildings on land the RCS leaders had purchased in the Selkirk area and near the intersection of Westerlo and Main streets in Ravena. The project had to proceed quickly though. The giant Atlantic Cement Company was being constructed out on Route 9W. If that business went on the tax rolls before the schools project got rolling, the district might have been subject to a prohibitive reduction in their share of the significant state aid that was spawning a wave of education-related construction across New York.

As a result, RCS speedily got an architectural review underway and scheduled a vote on the elementary school building program for February 3, 1962. In the next couple of weeks, the school board met with an Albany architectural firm to discuss initial specifications for what were proposed to be two identical buildings. The two elementary structures were just one part of a major building program for the district that featured a new junior-senior high school across the state highway from the Atlantic Cement complex.

As plans were being formulated, at least one New Baltimore resident found fault with the whole proposal. Raymond Johnson took the floor at a Board of Education meeting. He offered support for the Selkirk building but felt that the one in Coeymans was unnecessary. One particular concern was his feeling that the New Baltimore school actually was in good shape and could be preserved. In essence, Mr. Johnson believed that the elementary students could be housed in the buildings being vacated by students moving into the new junior-senior high school.

Johnson's position was reinforced through his letters to the editor in the *News-Herald*, the Ravena weekly paper. These missives enlarged the scope of his complaints, dealing with what the writer felt were inadequate and misleading financial data supporting the construction proposal and disregard of 1958 promises to renovate the New Baltimore, Ravena, and Coeymans buildings when the new junior-senior school was completed.[32]

The vote, though, went off as scheduled at the Ravena High School. Two resolutions were on the ballot, one for each school. The result was not close. Both measures were approved by a nearly two-to-one margin, with the plurality a bit larger for the Selkirk resolution than the Ravena complement.

Just as the election was coming off, the hamlet of New Baltimore was well on its way to losing another of its local institutions. On the Sunday afternoon following the schools vote, a joint meeting was scheduled of the New Baltimore, Ravena, and Coeymans Methodist Church congregations for preliminary discussions on merging into one unit in Ravena. A committee subsequently was formed with four representatives from each church to draft a merger resolution. That plan was carried out, and the New Baltimore congregation dissolved.

The Board of Education was hoping to get solicitations for construction bids out as soon as possible so the work could begin around the start of July. When the new buildings were all completed, New Baltimore, Coeymans, Cedar Hill, and Jericho schools were planned to be closed along with the handful of rented quarters that the district had been using. Obviously, New Baltimore students were to be transferred to the Ravena building.

It took until the end of May for the architects to complete their work in preparing the required plans for the buildings. At that point, the Board of Education was able to entertain bids for the construction work. Contractors quickly were retained, and work begun. Groundbreakings at the Ravena and Selkirk sites were held on the evening of June 29.

In the meantime, the new school year began in the fall of 1962 with students going to class in the old brick, two-story building. The *News-Herald* reported in late November that a new fire escape was considered for the structure. Fire and insurance inspectors found that current safety features were sufficient, and no action was taken.[33]

Steel and masonry work progressed nicely throughout the fall eventually to be finished off with a clean surfacing from the Powell and Minnock brick company in Coeymans. A November meeting saw the board take up the naming of the new buildings. It was decided that a commemoration of the two earliest settlers in the Selkirk and Coeymans regions was appropriate. Albertus W. Becker was chosen for the northern sector. The south was named for Pieter B. Coeymans when the intent actually may have been to memorialize his father, Barent Pieterse Coeymans.

In February, the RCS Board of Education convened meetings in Selkirk and New Baltimore to explain plans for closing their schools. Only three people other than board members or teachers showed up for the latter session. This could have been from a lack of interest or an understanding that the New Baltimore Fire District was proposing to take over the building.

The construction of the new schools was proceeding as planned in the summer of 1963 as the board started to consider the contingencies of the fall opening. In the southern part of the district, eleven classes in kindergarten through grade two were to go to the old Ravena school while fourteen classes in grade three through six would attend the new school. It had been hot and humid when New Baltimore's youngsters streamed out of the old brick school house for the last time. A tradition was lost. There were no more schools in the town of New Baltimore.

Over the years, the school buildings were sold off, converted to other uses, or destroyed. The Otter Hook school was auctioned off in 1954 to a local citizen for $1,200, a price that included the contents and land. It has been converted to a home. The Stanton Hill school was moved across the road to become part of the barn complex on the Court family farm. The Dean's Mill school is a utility shed in a backyard. One of the oldest buildings, the stone Staco school, was enlarged and became a private home. The Medway school was the home of the fire company out in that part of town before its conversion into a small house.

As for the last two active buildings, the Rocky Store building had been relegated to a variety of occasional uses during its handful of dormant years. After a few other possibilities were discussed, including use as a firehouse, some enlightened individuals saw its potential as a good place to locate the previously roaming town offices.[34]

The first town meeting had been held in 1811 when New Baltimore was formed from the town of Coxsackie. With most of the population centered away from the river, the initial governance session likely was in a tavern at the intersection of Route 51 and Roberts Hill Road and the second near Medway Four Corners. Over the years, town business was conducted in various locations, including the Imperial Hotel and the Wheat store on Main Street in the hamlet, both long gone.

For many years, municipal affairs were conducted in rented space in Cornell Hall, the home of the Cornell Hook and Ladder Fire Company, with the odd session being held in other locations such as Town Clerk Clifton Baldwin's flower shop on Route 9W. Generally, town business was done where it was done. If you were town tax assessor, your office and the tax records were at your home. It was not the most efficient way to govern. A centralized location was considered necessary.

The Town Board minutes for the period mention the process of taking over and renovating the building. At an August 4, 1964 meeting, it was decided that the board would inspect the "Town Building & Property" at Rocky Store. However, the object of attention at first was not the school. A subsequent special meeting was held at the town garage to discuss expanding that facility to include office and meeting space with a secondary purpose of investigating the possibility of using the now-empty Rocky Store school house just up the road.[35]

From late August on, the decision to transfer attention to the school was made, and conveyance of the building arranged. At an August 25 special meeting, the Coxsackie-Athens Board of Education unanimously approved a resolution for the qualified voters of the former Common School District 2 to hold a special meeting on September 19 at 12:00 p.m. at the former school. Voters would submit ballots on the following resolution:

> Shall the Board of Education of Central School District No. 1 of the Towns of Coxsackie, Athens, New Baltimore, and Cairo, Greene County, be authorized to convey the real property of former Common School District No. 2 to the Town of New Baltimore, Greene County, without consideration, for the purposes of such town or for a public use.[36]

On the appointed day, a handful of local residents met at the school to determine the building's destiny. Temporary Chairman Frank Smith called the session to order. The group proceeded to the formalities of electing officers for the special meeting and reading the meeting notice that had been posted for public consumption. At 1:00 p.m., Chairman Betsy Hallock declared that the polls were now open. From then until 4:00 p.m., thirty-seven people registered and voted, with thirty-three in favor of transferring the school to the Town. With a final, formal acceptance of the decision by the attending officials, the session came to a close at 4:05 p.m.[37]

In its regular October monthly meeting, the Coxsackie-Athens Board of Education unanimously accepted the result of the balloting and charged itself with ensuring that a quit claim deed was sent to the Town.[38] By then, a letter had arrived in the hands of Town officials announcing that Coxsackie-Athens had voted to dispose of the building. There also was a letter from the Greene County Historical Society requesting that certain unspecified items from the school go to the Bronck Museum for preservation. By November 10, the key and deed had been delivered, and a meeting was scheduled for the Town Board to inspect the premises.

Now it was up to New Baltimore to prepare the building for its next life. The process started with a discussion at the beginning of December about what procedure to follow for renovations. The board authorized Town Supervisor Clare Robbins to draw up specifications and send them out for bid. By late spring, the renovation was done.

It seemed as though the Town officials themselves could not believe that they really had a place of their own now. The first meeting held in the renovated building on May 25, 1965 was noted as being at the "Town meeting rooms at Hannacroix, New York." It was not until June 1, 1965 that the board was convening at "Town Hall." At that session, the board also considered a resolution that the Town Hall could be used by public and civic organizations, making it truly a public building. An open house was held on June 20 to celebrate the occasion.[39]

Many people have traveled in and out of the building in its second life. A large addition was constructed in the 1990s for office space, with the original schoolroom now serving as the main meeting place for the Town. With historic buildings being razed every day, it is commendable that at least one town has managed to retain a viable use for a locally important edifice.

The last town school, the two-story hamlet building, originally constructed for less than $10,000 and opened in September of 1895 under Principal Byron Mansfield, took a different turn. After closing, the structure also was proposed to be a new, larger fire house. The New Baltimore Fire District purchased the property but decided that the location was not adequate for its purposes. A site on Gill Road was preferable, and a new facility was built there.

The firemen put the school up for sale, and it eventually ended up in private hands. Part of the building served for many years as an art studio and sometime gallery. It is a centerpiece of the hamlet along with its across-the-street neighbor, the New Baltimore Reformed Church.

Today, the words "New Baltimore" do not appear in the names of any of the public school districts or school buildings that educate local children. Some students are home-schooled. The Grapeville Baptist Church in the western part of town operates its own K-12 private educational institution, but New Baltimore's public schools are a lost heritage.

10

The Road to New Baltimore

The earliest emigrant farmers, millers, and tradespeople had two ways to get up and down the Hudson valley, the river that could be frozen in winter and too shallow in a few spots or rudimentary Indian trails that went through hill, dale, swamp, and overgrowing brush. First choice obviously was by boat. It was easier and efficient to settle along navigable water. The pioneer homesteaders could ship and receive goods and set off on voyages virtually from their front doorsteps.

As more settlers came and younger generations needed land, people started to push away from the river a bit for their homes and farms. Short pathways from one's house to the field or mill or the son's place gradually were transformed into longer and more public roads that still led to the main highway, the Hudson and its tributaries.

Long-standing Indian trails probably served as the basis for an expanded travel system. Settlers recognized and used them. The native populations often needed to head inland for good hunting grounds and viable spots for mining stone for weapons and tools and for safer wartime travel. The history of these trails is meager beyond clues offered by archeological investigations and occasional mentions in European deeds and later briefly in recorded histories.

An undated but probable eighteenth-century Coeymans Patent map shows a "Catskill Indian Foot Path" while a 1784 John Lansing drawing of the Coxsackie Patent portrays a "Mohican foot path." This trail is believed to have been a prime travel avenue from Fort Orange down to Catskill. There, it would link with a variety of other trails out to Leeds and Cairo, through the Catskills west, and also to southbound routes. Early deeds and patents for land of Gerritse (Van Bergen), Bronck, and Houghtaling all mention the path as an important landmark or boundary.

King's Highway

It took wartime to push toward more dependable north-south land routes. Effective strategic travel had been a problem in King William's War (1689–1697), the first of the French and Indian Wars. While the bulk of the fighting took place outside the Hudson Valley, troops, supplies, and equipment often had to follow the river to those battlefronts. Soldiers and horses got stuck in the muddy paths, had to push or pull heavy wagons and cannons up steep hills and control them on the downside, and could be stopped dead by deep forest and brush or flooded streams. The other option, the Hudson, could freeze in winter and was prone to shallowness and shoaling in some places. None of this helped the military cause.

With threat of further French intrusion, alarmed colonial administrators decided to take action to organize a little these adventurous forays into the hinterlands. The governor and colonial council moved to enact laws that pushed towns and their residents to build and maintain highways and fences. None of this helped. People were more interested in keeping their homes and farms going than in working on the roads.

A big push forward came in 1703 with passage of "An Act for the Laying out Regulateing Clearing and preserving Publick Comon highways thro'out this Colony." All these roads became known as King's Highways because of the royal authority under which they were devised. The law allowed a small set of strategic pathways to "be laid out preserved and kept for ever in good and Sufficient Repair." Authorized roads were to come up out of New York City through Westchester and Dutchess counties and over toward New Jersey. Most importantly for our purposes, there was to be "one other Publick Comon General Highway to extend from the Southerly Bounds of the County of Orange, thro' the Same County of Orange to the County of Ulster & County of Albany of the breadth of four Rod English Measure at the least to be Continue and remain for ever the Publick Comon General Road and highway from the Southerly bounds of the County of Orange aforesaid to the City of Albany & from thence to the Town of Schanectady in the County of Albany aforesaid."

When fully functional, this King's Highway ran from the New Jersey border near Ramapo through Monroe, Goshen, Shawangunk, New Paltz, Rosendale, Kingston, to a ford across the Esopus Creek at the mouth of the Saw Kill near Kingston, then north to Albany. In New Baltimore, the route followed the foot of the Kalkberg ridge or basically within half a mile from or on the path of Route 9W.

Given the need to connect farms, mills, and other outposts of settlement and in hopes of creating some measure of consistency and order to the networking of roads, the 1703 law further authorized the establishment of four-rod wide "Comon Highways" that would link "the Several Towns and Villages within this Collony to their next Contiguous Towns and Villages and from one Town or Village to another as to the seyerall and respective publick Comon and General Roads and Highways before mentioned and to Such Convenient Landing places in each respective Town & Village . . ." The powers-that-be recognized the commercial and passenger promise that a proper linking of highways "for the better & easier Transportacon of goods and the Commodious passing of Travellers as Direct and Convenient as the Circumstances of place will admit . . ."[1]

The colonial council acknowledged that such a momentous task was an ongoing process and not easily achievable. As early as 1705, they needed to extend the older act for another three years because "the Service by that Act intended will in all probability remaine undone and Imperfect and it being necessary and requisite the same should be performed and fully accomplish'd."[2]

By 1723, the Albany County road situation still was difficult, prompting more legislative action. The highways were "mightily out of Repair and in Some places not yet well or Sufficiently laid out to the great Inconveniency of the Inhabitants" causing "great Complaints."[3]

Subsequent renewals and revisions of the highways law over the next decades tried diligently to fine tune supervisory structures and functions and require improvements and useful new features like sturdier, modern bridges.

Over the year, highway commissioners for the Catskill-Coxsackie-Coeymans segments in Albany County included Peter and Casperus Bronk; Peter Coeymans; William Van Allen; Samuel Van Vechten; David Verplanck; Peter, Martin, and Anthony Van Bergen; Henry Houghtaling; and John Barclay. It seems apparent that New Baltimoreans were keenly interested in a proper road system, likely to further their own laudable commercial and land speculative motives.

New Baltimore's First Official Roads

The King's Highway was the first official public highway through the future New Baltimore. Land transfer records throughout the post-Revolution period of accelerated settlement frequently refer to the road as a key geographical marker, characterizing it at times as the "Public Road," "Along the highway," and even "the great Road commonly called the State Road."

The influential 1802 New York State maps of Surveyor General Simeon DeWitt show two roads in New Baltimore although there probably were more informal byways. The riverside hamlet certainly had streets planned or built around the Revolution. One route depicted on DeWitt's map, in a north-south road direction, was the approximately hundred-year-old more modern version of the King's Highway from the Coeymans-Albany County line to the south through West Coxsackie.

The other east-west pathway traveled from the Hudson shoreline out across the Hannacroix Creek, following the route about where New Baltimore Road now goes. This route was called quite aptly the "Main Road to New Baltimore Landing." Whether this second road was a result of the King's Highway law's effort to promote linking roads or just a local start at looking west is unknown.

A representative 1791 indenture detailing a land transaction between Albert and Teunis Vanderzee on one hand and Paul Sherman on the other recognized the two highways. The involved property included "all that Certain Parcell or tract of Land and Improvements in New Baltimore So Called Beginning at the Corner of the Roads that Pasfe North and South and East and West through the Said New Baltimore . . ."[4]

The handicaps of traveling on these early roads are apparent. They essentially were dirt paths, some wider than others. Larger trees were girdled and left to rot in place. Riders and wagons had to go around them. Stumps were left at a level so as not to entangle axles but still could easily trip horses or snare inattentive wagon drivers. Ridges and valleys were not graded and had to be negotiated. Steeper hills were a challenge for keeping control of a wagon going up or down.

Shallower creeks and streams were forded, with heavy rains and spring thaws raising dangerous havoc. More expansive bodies of water were impassable totally and had to be detoured. Bridges were rare, expensive, and difficult to maintain. Often just a row of logs lashed together from bank to bank would serve as an overpass. Swamps and bogs might be crossed by a corduroy pattern of logs. All were easily rotted or dislodged.

The Turnpike Era

In the few years before the town of New Baltimore was created, a new trend in road building came to be. People had to go places, and goods had to get to markets. Something had to be done to modernize transportation. A few enterprising entrepreneurs saw dollar signs in private companies that would sell shares to raise money to build and maintain highways in strategic locations. Stopping points or toll houses would be established along the routes to collect fees from passersby. This was the birth of the turnpike era.

The first such business that covered New Baltimore was the Coxsackie Turnpike Company, incorporated by the State in March of 1805. The principals in the venture included Robert Vanden Bergh, Leonard Bronck, Peter Adams, Dorrance Kirtland, Roswell Reed, and Archibald McVickar. The road went from Coxsackie village, out across the flats, up the hill to Medway, and eventually toward the Susquehanna Turnpike in the town of Freehold (now Greenville). Today's Route 26 roughly approximates the direction taken by the turnpike.

The New Baltimore and Rensselaer Turnpike came into being in April of the next year. Albert Vanderzee, Pelatiah Whitmore, Paul Sherman, John K. Brown, Joseph Platt, Stephen Parsons, Henry C. Houghtaling, Samuel Skinner, Tunis A. Van Slyke, John Van Dyck, David Densmore, and Joseph Requa were the officers. Little record of any of these roads is available but the following advertisement appeared in the *Recorder* newspaper of Catskill in 1807:

> Wanted at New Baltimore, 20 miles above Catskill, by the subscriber, 10 or 15 sworn turnpikers to work on the Baltimore and Renssellaer Turnpike, to whom good wages will be given. No Dutchman need apply unless he is pretty well Yankeyfied; and no Irishman unless he can demolish a quart of Rum per day.

The road traveled from New Baltimore northeasterly to meet the Albany and Delaware Turnpike in the Albany County town of Rensselaerville. By 1812, the turnpike had been completed, but with significant public dissatisfaction about its western gate. It never managed to gain momentum. As a result, the state legislature decided on May 26 of that year to make it a public highway to the hamlet of New Baltimore. A short course of the road was layered with wooden planks near Chestnut

Lawn Cemetery during the brief period of popularity for that type of construction.

Probably the most pivotal turnpike action came in April of 1806 with creation of the Albany and Greene Turnpike Company. The highway's administrators were John Rensselaer, Francis Nichol, David McCarty, Levi Blaisdell, Benjamin Baker, Abraham Van Dyke, Thomas Lawrence, and Samuel Haight. The road was an extension of the Albany and Bethlehem Turnpike, which came from the north to Coeymans Landing. The route then continued on to the drawbridge in the center of Catskill. The turnpike had several toll gates, including one in New Baltimore just north of the junction of the Sickles Creek and the Coxsackie Creek. The section of the turnpike running through New Baltimore was abandoned in 1852 but converted into a public highway. The Albany and Greene Turnpike today would be Route 144 south into Main Street into County Route 61, diverting from that modern road just south of the two-creek confluence. It then traveled on a now-abandoned bed over a bridge at the former Van Bergen mill site and became Riverside Avenue in Coxsackie.

In the nineteenth century, public roadways were basically the domain of local government. One of the first actions taken by the administering board of the infant New Baltimore was to divide the wide territory of its jurisdiction into a series of twenty-nine road districts crisscrossing the town.

Overseers were elected to ensure whatever construction and maintenance was needed for their stretch of road. Nonelderly adult male residents in rural areas like New Baltimore then would perform an assigned amount of work on the road as a form of taxation. One could choose to pay a fee in lieu of the work but most chose to labor. Regrettably, in many places, people may not have felt incredibly obligated to fulfill the task so the quality of highways could vary greatly from town to town or even neighborhood to neighborhood.

Over the years, improvements were made to systematize and professionalize operations. Highway departments were created with paid employees overseen by highway superintendents who were elected officials and, at least in theory, had applicable experience and/or education.

Medway Road

As spring neared in 1873, an alliance of farmers and millers in the inland parts of town and traders and businesspeople along the Hudson began to see the value of having a more direct route to the port at New Baltimore hamlet and the railroad junction. The ancient circuitous and hilly road from Medway to the river had deteriorated over the years, making passage east a very questionable proposition. It had reached the point where it was not uncommon for travelers to sink in muddy bogs in wet weather, making travel by horse and carriage impossible.

The stockholders of the road company met to elect a host of well-known businessmen as officers and directors, including Benjamin B. Hotaling (farmer) as president, George W. Smith (merchant), secretary, Thomas D. Tallmadge (merchant), treasurer, and Amos Hotaling (farmer), general superintendent. The men commissioned a survey of the proposed path of the new road. By the Fourth of July, the New Baltimore and Medway Turnpike Company was advertising for the "forming, grading, and entire construction of the said Turnpike Road to be built from New Baltimore to the Coxsackie and Greenville Turnpike at or near Medway Four Corners."[5] Little did they know that the rest of the task was not going to run quite so smoothly.

In mid-September, the road company principals met at John Colvin's hotel by the Hudson, convening a group of twenty-four men who then traveled the entire surveyed route. The party ended up at the J. W. Reynolds' hotel at the west end to vote a final determination on whether the road should be built. While the result was a clear-cut decision to proceed with construction, dissent was growing, as evidenced by a subsequent letter in the *Coeymans Herald*, which started a trend of similar back-and-forth criticisms:

> Your correspondent thinks it strange there should be any opposition to the enterprise. I can say, speaking for the minority, that it arose entirely from our belief that the road would cost the town about twenty thousand dollars, and not two or three thousand as part of the road company tried to convince us. They had also two lawyers there whose main object it seemed to be to convince us we had no right to consider the cost, but should swear to its necessity, regardless of cost. Perhaps they convinced the majority—they did not the minority.[6]

This argument sets out the Medway road political, logistical, and economic issues that would inflame the town for the next few years. No matter how optimistic the principals might be, it would not be easy to surmount the problems of the variable terrain between the Hudson and the Four Corners, making the actual cost of the project difficult to gauge. The question of who was to build and finance the road, the turnpike company or the town, had to be addressed first and foremost.

There was considerable buzz about the identity of the writer of the continuing flow of anti-road letters to the editor. The likely author was Jeremiah Dean, the prominent Hannacroix Creek miller. Dean's operation had a clear, straight pathway to the river's steamboats and barges and the railroad through Coeymans, a well-worn route for his goods-laden wagons. Any other highway that might allow millers from the outer parts of town and beyond similar access could pose a serious threat to Dean's economic well-being.

This assault did not sway the would-be road builders. Toward the end of the year, the directors and stockholders of the turnpike company convened a session to discuss a resolution regarding their position on the road. A unanimous vote held that since the New Baltimore Commissioners of Highways had laid out a route very similar to the company's planned path, it made much of their private enterprise's efforts unnecessary. The intent was for the town commissioners to obtain the rights-of-way, fence the proposed route, and then turn the whole package over to the company, which would build and maintain the highway.

The project then took a backstage. Warren Smith took over as supervisor from Benjamin Hotaling. Smith generally had been portrayed as holding an anti-road position but perhaps it was an anti–turnpike company orientation. So there was little action on the project for the summer and well into the fall.

The fact of the matter was that Highway Superintendent Albert Wheeler and his able crew of men and horses had broken ground on the road and were making rapid progress. In a remarkable complication, the Town had contracted in October to pay J. R. Baldwin and A. G. Hotaling $6,000 to build the new road from New Baltimore to Medway. It turned out that the turnpike company was not a legal entity under existing state law and could not undertake the project. The Town had to build the road anyway.

At the November 1874 annual meeting of the Greene County Board of Supervisors, Supervisor Warren Smith submitted a resolution to finance the New Baltimore-Medway road. It was that higher level of government's responsibility to approve such expenditures. The County would let the Town assess and collect $3,406 from local taxation, which then would be provided to the commissioners of highways to pay landowners for damages done to their property from the laying of the road.

In total, twenty men and women would receive sums ranging from $15 for Peter Vanderpool to $600 to Jane Colburn for their troubles.

Another item on the agenda was to pay Baldwin and Hotaling $2,000 as partial satisfaction of their contract. There were legal problems about that too. The board determined that the bill would be paid but not until the following fiscal year.[7]

Right before Christmas, a meeting of interesting parties, reportedly representing all spectrums and parts of New Baltimore, was held at the Christian Church at Medway. The agenda was to discuss the road project and the legality of all related actions that occurred to date. After a lengthy debate, a vote of the participants was reported as unanimous in opposition to the road and in favor of further investigation of the process. A study committee was formed to report back at a subsequent meeting.

The pro-roaders were quick to respond with their criticisms of the Medway group's actions. They obviously took measure of the magnitude of the attendance and the objectives of the people at the church meeting:

> Perhaps a baker's dozen that took part in the exercises to consider whether our Commissioners are men capable of performing their duties as required by the statutes, styling themselves as a sort of detectives to look into matters not at all within their jurisdiction. Who elected these men to take such an active part in the drama of building roads? . . . they concluded to appoint a committee of such men as they thought were technically wise and arbitrary, to see if an explosion could not be effected.[8]

The bitter, malicious debate continued in the *Coeymans Herald* with almost every new issue as the old year went and the new year dawned. The language was getting even more colorful with effectiveness of the reproach undetermined:

> Tis said "variety is the spice of life," admitting this to be true, 'tis apparent the good people of this Town are deprived of many luxuries, as they cling as tenaciously to THAT road as "a flea to a pigs caudal appendage" . . . we are actuated by no prejudicial motive, yet we venture the assertion knowing that future developments will demonstrate the truth of our assertion, that if the road commissioners regard the anti-roaders as a battalion of barn yard cadets, and flatter themselves on

> a speedy completion of the road, at their expense. They will find that these anti-roaders are as stubborn as a western mule.[9]

The anti-roaders managed to hold sway once again in April of 1875. Despite an apparent feeling that a great majority of the town's residents wanted to see the highway completed, election results told a vastly different story. Supervisor Smith and his compatriots retained their political power and offices. Some folks thought that made the continuation of the project a moot point. The key issue though was that the rights-of-way were in place, so considerable resources already had been invested in the effort.

Continued financing was a roadblock. At their fall meeting in 1875, the County Board again was faced with a New Baltimore proposition on the Medway highway. First, there were smaller dealings with unpaid property damages to Benjamin Lisk and John Marshall, plus an additional payment for attorneys' services.

More importantly, Supervisor Smith presented a proposal that he neither was endorsing nor drawing any conclusions as to its legality or propriety. In it, the New Baltimore government, following a late September meeting, requested that the County Board approve that Smith, in his official capacity, be permitted to borrow $3,000 in three separate bonds to defray the indebtedness on the Medway road. The bonding was to be done according to authority granted under a new state law. After consideration was delayed twice, a vote came on the afternoon of the eighteenth. It was a resounding defeat as all twelve voting supervisors, including Warren Smith, nixed the bonding.[10]

The key argument was that the town's commissioners of highways had no authority to hire Baldwin and Hotaling. No funds had been provided by law to build the road, and neither the Town nor County Boards could authorize borrowing of money to build a road under current law.

Following the November County Board session, the *Coeymans Herald* published a vibrant exchange of articles that enlivened the 1875–1876 holiday season. One commentary described a meeting that apparently featured Supervisor Smith accusing Town Clerk Jacob Bedell of traitorous behavior for selling out the pro-road contingent, a charge Bedell promptly denied. Mr. Bedell, in turn, accused Smith of double-dealing since the latter seemingly had reneged on an election campaign promise that if the road proposal were approved by the Town Board, the supervisor would guide it through the County Board. Where Smith really stood remained a puzzler.

The April elections of 1876 pushed the political tide back the other direction. All the pro-road candidates but one were victorious. The basic question by this time appeared answered. The road was well on its way to conclusion. In late August of 1876, the big day finally came at least as far as the fate of the traveler was concerned. The new road from New Baltimore hamlet to the Medway Four Corners was completed, cutting the distance between the two points by about three miles.

New supervisor Henry Harden brought up the funding issue again at the 1876 County Board annual meeting. He hoped to secure the members' permission to borrow $4,000 in 1877 to pay for the Medway road. The measure passed unanimously.

State Highways

As the nineteenth century ebbed, a number of groups began a concerted effort to promote road building, including one unlikely source, bicycle riders. These people criticized the labor tax system as inefficient and more a matter of political patronage than an effective way to manage transportation. This was the process that made local residents responsible for the upkeep of assigned portions of roads for specific periods.

Better highways also would allow speedier trips for getting products to markets and people to town and back. The number of vehicle registrations also was booming. On the other hand, more conservative rural dwellers saw the spending of added money on roads as equating to more property taxes out of their pockets.

The concisely named Good Roads Movement advocates were not to be denied. The primary initial result of the campaign was the Higbie-Armstrong Act signed into state law in 1898. This statute allowed a county board of supervisors upon petition by the majority of residents on a public highway to request the State to rehabilitate part or all of a road. The state engineer then would determine whether the highway was important enough to be considered for improvement. More importantly, New York was to underwrite half the cost of any project. That same year, the Fuller-Plank Act authorized state funding to towns that abandoned the labor tax system in favor of a dollar taxation of residents.

The Good Roads campaign was long lasting and widespread. The March 21, 1913 edition of the *Recorder* reported on a Good Roads meeting held earlier that week at the Greene County Courthouse. The participants were State Highway Commission representatives, and county and town officials interested in making and maintaining roads. They discussed a number of issues, including something as simple as the need to dissuade people from creating ruts by driving repeatedly in the same track. New Baltimore's representatives were Supervisor Henry J. Miller, Town Clerk Platt Wheat, Highway Superintendent Barney Gardinier, and Justice of the Peace Byron Mansfield.[11]

The statutory improvements prescribed under the new laws could include sufficient resurfacing for local conditions and widening where necessary. Roads also might be straightened or redirected to avoid grades. From this period on, the State used subsequent legislation to strengthen its authority over what it considered to be the major roads within its borders.

On November 7, 1899, New Baltimore voted in favor of changing to the money system by a good majority. The Town Board, however, had some undefined issue with the legality of the process, and no change was authorized. A petition two years later from a collection of prominent citizens again called to alter the arrangement but no result was published. Eventually, the change was made.[12]

Over the next few years, the Greene County Board of Supervisors and ad hoc unions of residents took occasional advantage of the opportunity to get state-supported road improvements for a handful of thoroughfares. In a December 1906 meeting of the supervisors, New Baltimore first was mentioned for cashing in on the State's new largesse. The primary highway that was a successor to the old King's Highway and ran north and south near the Kalkberg was designated for state aid along with the Coxsackie Turnpike from Climax out through Medway and Grapeville and the less than half mile of the Coxsackie-Greenville highway lying in town. For the most part, these designated roads were the curvy pathways in the vicinity of the modern Routes 9W, 26, and 81.[13] It was quite a while, though, before any significant work was started in the town.

A further state law passed in 1908 was another major step in modernizing highways. It contained a long litany of responsibilities for roads categorized under state, county, or town authority. It also provided for certain highways that had received a favored designation under the 1898 legislation "shall be state highways and shall be constructed or improved at the sole expense of the state."

One of them, to be called Route 3, ran from the New Jersey–New York state line in Rockland County "thence northerly through the eastern portion of Greene county to points at or near Catskill, Athens and Coxsackie, to a point to be determined by the commission, on the dividing line between Albany and Greene counties, running thence northerly to the city of Albany."[14]

The provision that the actual path of the road was to be decided by a "commission" is interesting. The State set out essentially two choices for where the road would go, inland along the trail of the King's Highway or generally following existing roads near the Hudson through the villages of Catskills, Athens, and Coxsackie (today's Route 385), and then out to the King's Highway, shadowed by the Kalkberg up through New Baltimore. State authorities held a series of hearings where local residents could voice their preferences. The river route won for the time being.

In the meantime, a whole network of improved highways was outlined across the state. Reconstruction started and crept northward on the west side of the Hudson. By this time, New Baltimore had a not inconsiderable ninety-six miles of highways within its borders.

The year 1912 turned out to be critical for road building. It did not start out on a very high note. In the first week in May, Highway Superintendent Barney Gardinier had a work crew near New Baltimore Station. He had "landed the steam roller in this part of town, but it did not work any better than was expected of it. It slid into the ditch too often, and the superintendent and everybody was disgusted. The town did not want any such medicine."[15]

The Town Board had called its annual meeting a little over a year before. Right after lunch, Supervisor Henry Miller and the rest of the board had reconvened to hear Buffalo Steam Roller Company representatives extol the virtues of one of their machines. After thirty minutes with some discussion, the board agreed to lease a roller for four years to be used seventy-five days a year at $10 a day. The decision apparently did not work as they had hoped.[16]

A few days after the roller mishap, the State published contract solicitations for rebuilding highway 5198, the 4.62-mile section that ran south of the New Baltimore Station–Medway road to the Coxsackie town line. By this time, the State had created a system of dividing up these main lines into numbered segments for administrative purposes. New Baltimore's roads that had been selected for repair included Route 3's local components, highway 5198, Coxsackie-Ravena Part 1 and highway 5370, Coxsackie-Ravena Part 2.

The county had begun to fulfill its mandated responsibility to secure rights-of-way for the new roads. It usually was bits and pieces of people's property that were purchased. For the northern end of the Coxsackie-Ravena highway, for example, few plots larger than a half acre were required. All along the route, though, were valuable orchards that pushed the prices up a bit more than the usual. Harry Vanderzee was in a particular bind. Not only did he lose a number of fruit trees, but the new road cut was so steep that he could not get across from one field to another.[17]

Counties generally did not want the often difficult task of road bed purchasing. Many people, of course, wanted much more for their land than the government wanted to pay. It was common for some transactions to end up in court, and the whole purchase process for a given fraction of an acre could drag on for years. Eventually, the State took over the task to the local's sure relief.

The winning bid from several proposals submitted for highway 5198 was $48,853.60 tendered by Criswell and Mallery of Mechanicville, New York. The road was to receive an application of "water-bound macadam with surface application of hot oil." This was a combination of smallish stones, stone dust, and water, a mixture that resulted in a sturdy and well-draining pavement, with oil spread atop for further binding and to limit dusting.[18]

The men were hard at work with their stone crusher, shovels, rakes, and rollers by the end of June. Several laborers chose to board with local families. The *Recorder* newspaper reported that one group of Coxsackie lads of Italian extraction pitched tents "in the shade of a maple tree" near Thomas Albright's farm. In the somewhat raw language of the 1900s, they called their compound "Camp Wopo."[19]

Work had progressed as planned toward New Baltimore Station. Toward the end of August, State Superintendent of Highways C. Gordon Reel published notices for bid solicitation for several more roads. The list included highway 5370, the 2.7-mile stretch from the Medway road north to the Albany County line. This time, D. H. Craw of Ravena was awarded the contract at a projected cost of $27,950.95, beating out several other firms, including Criswell and Mallery.

A month later, the latter company had nearly finished its end of state road, spreading on its last coats of stone and oil. The State's stone crusher was moved north from Captain Hawley Miller's quarry, and contractor Craw had begun laboring on his portion of the route to Ravena. The locals also were busy. Highway Superintendent Gardinier was completing work on reconditioning Main Street and was planning to move his own crusher down the River Road.

Demand grew both from state authorities and the locals that important side roads not be forgotten while the main lines were up for improvement. There was tremendous pressure from local interests and even from inside the State's political and bureaucratic structures that secondary roads also had to come under the great improvement umbrella. After all, if you could not get your crops to market, people to work, and tourists to their destinations, the point of rebuilding the main roads was lost.

In June of 1911, the county supervisors initially had considered another resolution to support upgrading of the secondary road that came from the Coeymans town line near the Hudson through New Baltimore hamlet up to the New Baltimore Station neighborhood. This eventually turned into the modern Route 144. It is interesting to note that the original extent of the highway targeted for improvement started at the intersection of the Stanton Hill and Medway roads, today's Y meeting of County Routes 51 and 54. It was several years, though, before substantive work began on the Coeymans road.

When the State finally moved ahead with advertising for a contractor in the spring of 1916, New Baltimore's own Edward S. Sickles ended up as low bidder. There was some debate about the path the highway was to take, with at least two petitions circulated proposing people's positions on the subject. The hamlet-Medway road was well established by now, leading from the state highway, past the rail station, and down into the riverside community. The former Albany and Greene Turnpike was Main Street, leading north and south.

In 1868, John B. Marshall had sold Francis Parsons and several family members a narrow piece of property. This land appears to have provided the Parsons a straighter, less severely graded path from their farm a little northeast to the turnpike. Wagons, horses, and walkers could avoid the street near the Reformed Church that was steep and had right-angle turns at its bottom, right before a runaway would propel headlong into the Hudson. The Parsons bypass was an obviously direct way to connect the Medway Road and Main Street. Construction was started but there were news reports about the slowness of the whole affair.

War, financial quibbling, and perhaps less than satisfactory stewardship of the initial project delayed the work. Shortly after the World War I armistice, the company of Albany contractor Joseph Walker found itself in charge of the project. The new contract was for an estimated price of $62,347 and still was to entail installation of a water-based macadam surface.[20]

It was a slow start as Walker prepared for the job, including securing housing for many workers who came from outside the town. The men finally buckled down to the job through the summer of 1919. In one noteworthy aside, a local highway worker, William Quinn, was relieved of the very sizable amount of $144 from clothes hung aside while he worked. Unnamed "Italians" were blamed.

Money remained an issue as winter approached. State highway authorities asked the County Board of Supervisors to provide a larger cut of the action. The board responded affirmatively with additional borrowing of $9,500, which supplemented a 1916 bond of $12,500. Favorable winter weather helped the project through to the end, taking the road on the path we know today.

With completion of the work on the New Baltimore Station highway, the meshing of the old Medway road and the Albany and Greene Turnpike became whole except for one major improvement. Town Board minutes from 1927 discuss a petition by a group of concerned taxpayers to remedy the deficiencies of the Hannacroix Creek bridge and its approaches. The petitioners were criticizing the one-lane nature of the structure and the steep, angled roads that came down to the crossing on either side.

The bridge, of course, lies in the town of Coeymans, which probably complicated matters a bit. It took a couple of years but, in 1930, the Albany County Board of Supervisors passed a resolution authorizing the purchase of rights-of-way for rebuilding the structure, a busy link for hamlet residents to the north, to Ravena and Albany.

The Riteway Construction Company of New York won the bidding for the project. By the end of the month, laborers were hard at work, repositioning the bridge to the east. The iron structure ended up being eighty-two feet long with a three-lane concrete road bed. It opened January 24, 1931, remedying what had been considered a serious menace to traffic.

After the war, road building boomed nationally. The Federal Aid Highway Act of 1925 created a system that essentially set a national standard for roads. The law responded to the haphazard development of numerous important highways without any guidelines for names, locations, construction, or maintenance. Roads now would be numbered and exhibit standardized signage.

The end result locally for this program was the assignment in 1926 of United States Highway 9E from Jersey City, New Jersey to Albany, and 9W from Albany to Glens Falls. The 9E designation was removed in 1930. Thereafter, 9W started at the intersection of Clinton Avenue and Lark Street in Albany, wending its way south through the city and down through New Baltimore where it subsumed the aforementioned roads 5198 and 5370.

When New York's governor Alfred E. Smith had begun his second stint in the state's highest office in 1922, he fervently believed that highways either were insufficient in number and quality or rapidly deteriorating. Smith had great hopes of making New York's roads a standard for transportation systems. The whole system, though, was in need of rehabilitation.

The governor appointed a former commander of a combat engineer battalion, Colonel Frederick Stuart Greene, as superintendent of public works. Greene became a whirlwind transformer of the state's road system into a uniform, professionally run operation, limiting political influence to the good of transportation. The governor and Greene instigated a massive effort to rebuild the so-called mainline highways across the state. The object was to make the roads smoother, wider, and more appropriate for the greatly increasing truck and car traffic. The main routes along both sides of the Hudson were a particular focus.

The new road on the west was to follow the general path of the King's Highway, straightening bad curves and moderating grades. Widened up to thirty feet and surfaced with concrete, the new route 9W was to avoid the more settled areas of Catskill and the villages of Coxsackie and Athens, seeking to limit mounting congestion in those places. The State was not intending to abandon the old path of the road but believed that two primary, well-maintained roads on both sides of the Hudson were a commercial, personal, and strategic necessity.

The piece of the project to come through New Baltimore, though, still was on the horizon. Heavy equipment and laborers were hard at work between Catskill and Coxsackie in 1931 after having completed the Ravena-Albany stretch the year before. A connection between these two sections was on the planning boards. With the Depression a major concern, the state legislature was hesitant or unable to provide money for much road-building in the early thirties.

Despite taking that position, by the end of 1933, the Catskill–West Coxsackie section was finished, cutting over three miles of the trip over the old way. The old road now was Route 385 with the new road officially designated as 9W.

Over the next couple of years, there was considerable dissent by the Greene County Board of Supervisors over the requirement that the County was responsible for purchasing or condemning local properties to secure rights-of-way for both state and county highways. This was not a palatable task in many peoples' opinions. In the late winter of 1935, the board approved and sent a resolution to the state senate and assembly supporting a pending assembly bill that would have transferred that authority solely to the State. Shortly thereafter, they acceded to the state requirement and started to process the paperwork and undertake any necessary litigation for the New Baltimore land that would be used for the Coxsackie-Ravena part of the 9W reconstruction.

Their hesitance in undertaking such responsibility is understandable given the lengthy list of individual property owners with whom they had to deal. But rebuilding this stretch of road was critical to completion of the important link between Catskill and Albany. The County was still processing related land acquisitions at least into the 1940s and paying off the debt for previous settlements for many years. The State eventually took over the rights-of-way task.

It was not until September that the state commissioner of highways, Captain Arthur W. Brandt, announced that the Coxsackie-Ravena project was among the nearly 109 miles of road scheduled for construction. A great incentive was $23 million now available in federal money to underwrite the whole program, with an estimated $636,000 for the 9W component.

Bids were requested, and the M. F. Dollard Company came in lowest at $511,978.77 to construct a 7.88 stretch of concrete, three-lane-wide road bed from West Coxsackie to Ravena, along with a few patches uncompleted near Catskill. Problems arose in a cloud of smoke shortly after midnight on a dark Wednesday night in mid-December of 1935.

The Dollard Company had leased the West Shore Railroad freight house at New Baltimore Station as a headquarters for its work. Making his rounds on the construction route, a watchman discovered a fire that burst into full force as he arrived.

He quickly alerted fire authorities, the railroad, and his supervisor. Trains were stopped because of the closeness of the blaze to the tracks. The Cornell Hook and Ladder Fire Company was called in due haste but it was too late. The building was destroyed. Various explosions exacerbated the situation and terrified nearby residents. Burned electric lines caused the railroad crossing bell to ring continuously for half an hour. About $25,000 in Dollard machinery, parts, and supplies were lost. Quick work by firemen saved other buildings used by workmen, draftspeople, and other company officials.

Work crews stepped on the gas in the spring of 1936. Men were working double shifts, eliminating curves and getting ready to pour concrete by June. Fourteen dump trucks were hauling gravel for the road base. Locals like Ralph Albright were laboring on the job. Harlen

Walker was a night watchman, and Henry Wiltse drove a steamroller. The Wade Sand Company was hauling road material from river barges.

There were some problems as progress was being made. One of Dollard's large iron hoppers used to load trucks collapsed, dropping forty to fifty tons of sand. No one was hurt, and the equipment was replaced within a week. A weighty sand truck broke through a culvert by the Reformed Church. Over the Memorial Day holiday in 1937, the road at the Ravena five corners was down to a single lane, causing considerable traffic backup for both the north- and southbound travelers. Concreting of the three lanes was proceeding as planned.

As summer came, work drew to a close to the delight of would-be travelers. Several minutes now were cut from the journey to Albany or Catskill. In August, the State sent a small crew down to the Ravena corners to count cars. Over 12,000 vehicles passed through the intersection between seven in the morning and seven in the evening.

The Thruway

The 1950s brought a major national push to improve the country's highway system through a network of interstate roads. New York State authorities took the lead in this effort by promoting as early as 1942 construction of a superhighway that would connect the state's major cities. In July 1946, Governor Thomas Dewey broke ground in the Syracuse suburb of Liverpool for the first section of work. The State created an independent public corporation—the New York State Thruway Authority—that would manage the road. The project was supposed to be self-liquidating as tolls and other income would pay the bonds down over the years.

Given the complexity, scope, and sheer magnitude of such a gigantic project, it took until the winter of 1951–1952 for the State to start serious acquisitions of land from owners in the New Baltimore area. The wheels of government turned slowly, and it was fall of 1952 before contractors were solicited for the highway's section from Coxsackie to Ravena.

From five bids, the Savin Construction Corporation of East Hartford, Connecticut took the prize with a low estimate of just over $4.6 million. The road was to be two concrete paths, each twenty-five feet wide and nine inches thick, with a intervening grass mall at least forty-four feet wide and include applicable access roads. There also was to be room for an additional twelve-foot lane on both sides of the highway.

Five bridges had to be built in New Baltimore alone, overpasses for Routes 9W and 144 and underpasses for the Hannacroix Creek, the New Baltimore-Aquetuck road, and the West Shore line of the New York Central Railroad.

The Savin operation quickly set up shop. The company established an operations base in Hannacroix about a quarter mile east of the railroad tracks on Route 144, building an office and maintenance garage 65 by 140 feet in size. They began actual grading of the right-of-way in late November of 1952 with thirty employees to be active over the winter. About 145 more workers were to be added in the spring, with hopes that most would be local hires.

While there were not an inordinate number of landowners disadvantaged by the project, there were some problems. Properties had been transferred in ownership only for a couple of weeks when the earthmovers arrived. One person was concerned because he was still living on his land but seemed unaware of his exact status. He had not been paid yet and was not sure how to handle impending local tax bills or even when he was supposed to vacate his property.

A neighboring farmer's barn was to be razed, and wells were to be taken over. Given the quick turnaround on the land sales, he had yet to arrange for movement of items from the structure. It seemed in general that Thruway authorities had not been too enthusiastic or detailed in relating their plans to the locals.[21]

In general, the bidding and initial construction phases of the project appear to have proceeded relatively quietly in New Baltimore and Coxsackie. The construction of the 9W overpass though was to be a somewhat complicated affair. There had to be a ten-foot deep cut below the existing travel lanes to accommodate the path of the new highway. As a result, Roberts Hill Road had to be rerouted around a stone house owned by Fred Baxter and more commonly known to contemporary readers as the Van Bergen-Warren House. Instead of the road meeting 9W south of the house, a new spur was cut through, renamed Scheller Park Road, and entered the state highway just north of the big house.

Contractors also had to deal with the Sinay residence. It was in the way. In a minor marvel of engineering, the owner decided to move the structure, which is believed to be a Houghtaling house dating from the late eighteenth or early nineteenth century. In the late spring of 1953, the haulers arrived to jack up the place and insert wheels underneath to start the journey to the corner of King's Road and Mansion Street in Coxsackie. Crowds of onlookers watched the operation in amazement. It took a day to get the 42- by-62-foot building movable, and less than an hour to roll it to the new location where it still stands at this writing.

Another obstacle to the bridge work brought an unforeseen surprise that provoked considerable anguish and anger. A Houghtaling family cemetery also was in the way of the construction crews. The burial ground was about a quarter acre in size and lay about one hundred feet south of the modern Scheller Park Road and 425 feet west of 9W. It would have been just in from the corner of the old end of Roberts Hill Road and 9W. Familiar names dotted the tombstones, Armstrong, Houghtaling, Roberts, Clough, and Van Bergen. Recorded burial dates ranged from 1831 to 1891.

The State Department of Public Works published a somber warning in local newspapers in the late winter of 1953 in an effort to locate interested parties who could register opposition to the removal and reburying of remains. Shortly thereafter, state authorities were soliciting bids for the grisly project.

Two different funeral businesses successfully met the State's requirements, Albany's Sorrentino Funeral Home was the successful bidder for removal of unmarked graves and the Niagara Falls' Spellano Funeral Home for marked sites. For its part, the State had purchased three large cemetery plots measuring one hundred by twenty feet at the Riverside Cemetery in Coxsackie, a space that could accommodate as many as eighty-five sets of remains.

Once the bulldozers started scraping away, the Sorrentino laborers had a big and unpleasant surprise. They kept uncovering more and more unmarked graves, 118 in all, or about triple what the State had originally estimated. Once the project started, other troubles quickly arose. The Riverside Cemetery space might not be sufficient to handle the greater number of reburials. Headstones were cracked, smashed, or scratched. Whether a result of the unexpected graves or other reasons, visitors were banned from the site, causing further upset.

The State Department of Public Works representatives who were supervising the work became the subject of considerable criticism from attentive newspaper editors and the thwarted onlookers. The reburials in Coxsackie were made in what ended up being a mass grave with salvageable tombstones arranged neatly but randomly nearby, a sad but unavoidable conclusion to the story.

In June of 1954, a strike of cement company workers in the Hudson Valley brought work on the highway to a halt. That issue swiftly was resolved, and the project was completed. Finally, on Tuesday, October

26, 1954, Governor Dewey came to the Thruway interchange at Leeds to celebrate. Serenaded by the Coxsackie-Athens High School band's rendition of the "Star-Spangled Banner," the state's chief executive was on a leg of his journey to formally open the Thruway. Traffic has flowed for ever after.

New Baltimore Service Area

Usually, if someone has heard of New Baltimore, it is because of the rest stop by exit 21-B between Albany and Catskill. In July of 1953, the Thruway Authority named one of three bidders, Hot Shoppes, Inc. of Washington, D.C., to operate the Thruway dining areas scheduled for Greene County. This firm evolved into the Marriott Corporation. Lunch counter and snack bars were planned for the Leeds intersection and the Coxsackie area. There also were to be gasoline stations in the service areas.

On April 9, 1957, the New Baltimore Service Area at Milepost 127 on the eastbound side of the road was opened to customers. Four years later, the State Department of Public Works announced their intention to buy 1.85 acres from Clifford Armstrong whose farm abutted the Thruway.

The slice of land at first was publicized to accommodate a restaurant and rest area for northbound travelers. Instead, state administrators decided to use the acquisition to provide access to the already existing complex. Just before Christmas in 1964, the New Baltimore Service Area was opened to northbound motorists when a new two-lane vehicular bridge over the Thruway was completed. The restaurant facilities were enlarged to handle the increased volume. The New Baltimore stop is one of only two service areas on the entire road accessible to both directions of traffic. Angola, out in the far western part of New York, is the other.

Since then, of course, there have been renovations and a complete rebuilding of the facility in the early 1990s. While a variety of businesses have filled the retail space in the intervening years, some residents with long memories still call the place the "Hot Shoppes."

Exit 21-B: The Entrance to New Baltimore

Thruway planners left the New Baltimore and Coxsackie motorists and business people in the lurch almost from the start of planning for the highway. There was not going to be an interchange between Catskill and

Selkirk. Some New Baltimore people could gain a bit of an advantage going north by using the Selkirk exit but its placement on Route 144 was out of the way for many travelers.

Local residents obviously felt slighted since most interested people considered the Thruway to be the avenue to economic progress. If the foreseen traffic could not get off the road and visit the stores and restaurants that existed or might come because of the new visitors, all was lost. The local American Legion had spearheaded a committee seeking an interchange as early as 1951 but to no avail. An engineering report at that time had concluded that a Coxsackie exit would not be economically feasible until 1960 but the issue would be revisited after the road was completed.

So, after the Dewey October ceremony, the advocacy group was expanded and energized at a meeting at Red's Restaurant that included a number of people from Coxsackie, New Baltimore, and Greenville, places that could benefit from the exit. The committee's plan was to launch an even stronger and broader-based appeal to convince the Thruway administrators of their shortsightedness. This campaign was to last nearly the next fifteen years.

After the first of the year, the committee managed to schedule a meeting with Bertram Tallamy, Thruway Authority chairman. By all public appearances, Tallamy was politely supportive. He promised to have engineers examine the situation and provide recommendations on the cost and location of a Coxsackie interchange. A decision would be based on two qualifying determinants: traffic projected counts and the degree of potential benefit to the motorists and the involved communities. The chairman needed time to accomplish this and asked that the committee not expect results until close to the fall.[22]

The committee went home and set to work on gathering data that would support their request. A first step was to convince local businesses to send letters, describing in particular the trucking services they needed—number of trucks and trips, freight tonnage, destinations, and so forth. All their efforts came to naught—an exit was not self-supportive. The years of surveys, persuasion, and frustration mounted up.

Then, a banner headline in the January 18, 1968 *Greene County News* proclaimed a Coxsackie interchange was on the near horizon. Assemblyman Larry Lane personally had informed Nelson Rockefeller during the governor's visit to Catskill that an exit was needed. The project was placed on the construction calendar but lengthy consideration was given to an exact location. The State decided that the most convenient spot would be about 4,000 feet north of the 9W overpass. An interesting aside was that Lane also announced that a connecting road was to be built between the exit and Route 81. That idea was discarded when final plans were published.

The same newspaper issue also publicized the dedication of the dam for a new Coxsackie Reservoir that would provide a much needed water source for the village of Coxsackie. That body of water, of course, lies in the Medway neighborhood of New Baltimore.

The State Department of Transportation was projecting a fall 1969 date for letting bids on the interchange. Preliminary plans were accepted and progress was being made by the department in securing rights-of-way and taking further preparatory steps. In January, a brief span of warmer weather in an otherwise frigid winter allowed a crew of about twenty hardy workers to pour fourteen truckloads of concrete for the integral bridge footings. Work sped along.

On October 29, 1971, the so-called Coxsackie Interchange 21-B was opened at Milepost 124.5. New Baltimore got the short end of the stick. The exit is in New Baltimore, not Coxsackie. There was no evidence at the site that the place even existed. Annoyance was so great that town officials were threatening to boycott the opening ceremonies. Supervisor William Finke and the Town Board were quoted that the omission was "flagrant carelessness."[23] In the end, the Thruway Authority promised a supplemental sign that would alert motorists that you get off at 21-B for New Baltimore.

The Thruway has become a prominent part of local life for the town, even if most outsiders and some neighbors still think the exit 21-B is in Coxsackie. Commuters and tourists find it a useful avenue to other places. Law enforcement ticketing and arrests occurring on the Greene County stretch of the road find the offenders going to court in the New Baltimore Town Hall for disposition of their cases. This means dollars in coffers of the town, which shares in a small portion of levied fines. Some businesses sprung up around the entrance ramp. Perhaps most significantly, the accessible major highway often is mentioned in framing the potential for commercial development in the vicinity of the exit. This, of course, has its pros and cons. Some see development as progress and lower taxation. Others see an intrusion into the attractive rural nature of New Baltimore.

Commercial New Baltimore faded away after the 1929 and 1936 fires. The Riverside Hotel had been torn down in the 1920s. The Windsor Hotel starting falling down, and local authorities determined that it too had to be demolished. The burned Imperial Hotel was rebuilt as a hotel for a short while then evolved into a nursing home that disappeared into a private residence. An ill-fated attempt to promote an art/antiques colony led to a series of tax foreclosures. The county ended up owning the two little, side-by-side general stores on Main Street and eventually removed them. Runoff drainage plagued the narrow buildings. Coupled with lack of demand, they were closed. One local tale had the owners addressing high waters by opening the front and back doors and letting the stream flow through.

The Grapeville general stores that served many a man, woman, and child closed their doors. Albright's café, tourist cabins, and bus line went out of business. The Medway general store also disappeared. Most of the once plentiful farms put away their plows and tractors, leaving overgrown fields, ghosts of fruit orchards, and collapsing barns. Joe Dimino's bar and grill and neighboring turn-of-the-nineteenth-century house that had been an early hotel and later the Blarr Health Farm went under the bulldozer.

People still made New Baltimore their home, commuting to state jobs in Albany, to the Powell and Minnock brickyard, and to the Atlantic Cement plant. A few rays of economic sunshine burned through. The Boat and RV Warehouse; the Fox Run gas station, motel, and restaurant; the Best Western New Baltimore Inn; a Holiday Inn Express; and the hamlet marina are a few of the current enterprises operating under new or old names. Many local residents are working out of their homes, some making good use of the Internet.

In the 1970s, the Town was called on the carpet by government authorities for the running of sewer lines into the Hudson. Pressure was brought to bear for someone to take action to remedy the situation. Supervisor Nils Backlund had a resident expel sewage from their home into the river in front of potential government funders, and the hamlet got a sewer system. An ill-fated attempt to install a public water system was voted down twice.

More recently, the Greene County Industrial Development Agency (IDA), a "public benefit corporation" formed by the Greene County legislature in 1972, has begun to generate projects to grow jobs. The agency fostered development of two shovel-ready business parks on the Route 9W corridor. A hallmark attraction for potential commercial interests is proximity to Thruway exit 21-B. So the efforts of the 1950s interchange committee and Larry Lane may pay off after all for New Baltimore, if you are on the pro-development side.

A good portion of the northern component of the property, the Kalkberg Commerce Park, sits in New Baltimore. It has become a combination of industrial development and nature preserve with a healthy piece of open space maintained for wildlife and hiking. The IDA, county, and town officials convinced corporate managers to build a mattress manufacturing plant at the site.

During 2007, the IDA proposed a gigantic mixed-use retail and entertainment park on lands north of the Kalkberg Park, in a space between County Route 61 to the east, Route 9W to the west, open fields to the north, and the New Baltimore/Coxsackie town line to the south. Several designs were outlined with different combinations of a destination retail store, smaller retail outlets, restaurants, hotels, and housing. Other options included an indoor-outdoor water park and entertainment facilities. All proposals professed an attempt to balance development with environmental concerns.

Much publicity was given to the proposal with decidedly mixed public responses. Some people saw lower taxes and new jobs. Others saw the loss of environmentally sensitive space. The irony for some was not lost on building a water park while a water supply for the hamlet was voted down. Many observers envisioned a drastic change in town life with such a significant development and its possible benefits and consequences. The economic downturn probably was the greatest momentum changer as the whole project was put on the back burner. As of this writing, the water park is back in the news with a new proposal.

In the final analysis, it was a transportation link, the Hudson, which brought people to New Baltimore. And it may be a transportation route, the Thruway, which takes New Baltimore to the future.

Notes

Chapter 1. Prehistoric Times: Our Landscape and First People

1. An updated and concise exposition on the geology of New York is provided in Y. W. Isachsen et al., eds., *Geology of New York: A Simplified Account* (Albany, New York: New York State Museum, 2000).

2. Two fundamental sources are William A. Ritchie's *An Introduction to Hudson Valley Prehistory* (Albany, New York: New York State Museum and Science Service, 1969) and *The Archaeology of New York State* (Garden City, New York: The Natural History Press, 1969). Other individual reports are listed later.

3. Arthur C. Parker, "The Great Algonkin Flint Mines at Coxsackie," *Researches and Transactions of the New York State Archeological Association* 4, no. 4 (1924): 109.

4. Hetty Jo Brumbach and Judith Weinstein, "Material Selection, Rejection, and Failure at Flint Mine Hill: An Eastern State New York Chert Quarry," *Northeast Anthropology* 58 (1999): 1–25.

5. Lucianne Lavin et al., "Stage III Archaeological Investigations: The Goldkrest Site, CNG TL–470, East Greenbush, New York" (Submitted to Consolidated Natural Gas Transmission Corporation, Clarksburg, West Virginia, January, 1997): i–2, 121–127.

6. Arthur C. Parker, *The Archeological History of New York, Part 2, Bulletin 237–238* (Albany, New York: New York State Museum, 1922): 567.

7. E-mail exchange with Beth Wellman of the New York State Museum, January–March, 2005.

8. Mary Ivey, Gary Berg, and Susan Halpern, "Final Archaeological Impact Evaluation, State One Survey, Town of New Baltimore: Sewer Facilities" (Report to Morrell Vrooman Engineers, August, 1977).

9. Robert E. Funk, *Recent Contributions to Hudson Valley Prehistory, Memoir 22, New York State Museum* (Albany, New York: University of the State of New York, State Education Department, 1976): 46–58, 256–257.

10. Paul L. Weinman and Thomas P. Weinman, "The Fred Young Site, A River Phase Component," *The Bulletin: The New York State Archeological Association Bulletin* 43 (July 1968): 1–6.

11. Robert E. Funk, "The Middle Archaic in New York," *Journal of Middle Atlantic Archaeology* 7 (1991): 7–18.

12. Edward V. Curtin, "Phase 2 Archaeological Survey, Proposed Kalkberg Commerce Park, Towns of New Baltimore and Coxsackie, Greene County, New York" (Prepared for Greene County Industrial Development Agency, September, 2004): 1–15.

13. Shirley W. Dunn in her *The Mohicans and Their Land, 1609–1730* (Fleischmanns, New York: Purple Mountain Press, 1994) and *The Mohican World, 1680–1750* (Fleischmanns, New York: Purple Mountain Press, 2000) provides a valuable overview of the Mohicans and the many property transactions to which they were a party in early colonial days. T. J. Brasser's essay "Mahican," volume 15 in the *Handbook of North American Indians* (William C. Sturtevant, general editor, and Bruce G. Trigger, volume editor, Washington, D.C.: Smithsonian Institution, 1978) has been considered a fundamental piece on this native group. See especially Shirley W. Dunn, ed., *The Continuance: An Algonquian Peoples Seminar, Selected Research Papers, 2000* (Albany, New York: University of the State of New York, New York State Museum, 2004). These sources offer numerous other citations for further research. The 2004 Dunn compilation cites many of the latest research findings on the Mohicans.

14. Edward V. Curtin, "The Ancient Mohicans in Time, Space and Prehistory," in *The Continuance: An Algonquian Peoples Seminar, Selected Research Papers, 2000*, ed. Shirley W. Dunn (Albany, New York: The University of the State of New York, New York State Museum, 2004): 5–18.

15. Dunn, *The Mohicans and Their Land*, 280. The spelling of names and places was unreliable in many old documents. We will try to use either the spelling as in a document or modern versions but hope it will be understood who or where we are talking about.

16. Hendrick Aupaumut, "Extract from an Indian History," *Collections of the Massachusetts Historical Society* 9 (1804): 99–102.

17. Robert Juet, *Juet's Journal: The Voyages of the Half Moon from 4 April to 7 November 1609* (Newark, New Jersey: New Jersey Historical Society, 1959): 31, 33.

18. Charles T. Gehring, ed., *Fort Orange Court Minutes, 1652–1660* (Syracuse, New York: Syracuse University Press, 1990): 57, 59, 61–62, 127.

19. Edmund Bailey O'Callaghan, ed., *Documents Relative to the Colonial History of the State of New-York, Volume IV* (Albany, New York: Weed, Parsons, and Company, 1854): 902.

20. Edmund Bailey O'Callaghan, ed., *Documents Relative to the Colonial History of the State of New-York, Volume V* (Albany, New York: Weed, Parsons, and Company, 1855): 562–563.

21. O'Callaghan, *Documents Relative to the Colonial History of the State of New-York, V*, 662–664.

22. Jonathan Pearson, trans., *Early Records of the City and County of Albany, and the Colony of Rensselaerswyck, 1656–1675* (Albany, New York: J. Munsell, 1869): 334–335.

23. Edmund Bailey O'Callaghan, *The Documentary History of the State of New York, Volume II* (Albany, New York: Weed, Parsons, and Company, 1849): 162.

24. Dunn, *The Mohicans and Their Land*, 214.

25. Harry Andrew Wright, ed., *Indian Deeds of Hampden County* (Springfield, Massachusetts: n.p., 1905): 136.

26. Samuel Hopkins, ed., *Historical Memoirs, Related to the Housatunnuk Indians* (Boston, Massachusetts: S. Kneeland, 1753): 74–75.

27. Alexander Hamilton, *Gentleman's Progress: The Itinerarium of Dr. Alexander Hamilton, 1744* (Chapel Hill, North Carolina: University of North Carolina Press, 1948): 60.

Chapter 2. Europeans Settle in Greene County

1. Cornelis Van Tienhoven, "Information Relative to Taking Up Land in New Netherland," in *The Documentary History of the State of New-York, Volume IV*, Edmund Bailey O'Callaghan, ed. (Albany, New York: Charles Van Benthuysen, 1851): 30–31.

2. Shirley W. Dunn, *The Mohicans and Their Land, 1609–1730* (Fleischmanns, New York: Purple Mountain Press, 1994): 280.

3. Arnold Johan Ferdinand Van Laer, ed., *Minutes of the Court of Rensselaerswyck, 1648–1652* (Albany, New York: University of the State of New York, 1922): 183.

4. Arnold Johan Ferdinand Van Laer, ed., *Van Rensselaer Bowier Manuscripts* (Albany, New York: University of the State of New York, 1908): 739.

5. Charles Gehring, trans. and ed., *Fort Orange Court Minutes 1652–1660* (Syracuse, New York: Syracuse University Press, 1990): 186–187.

6. Gehring, *Fort Orange Court Minutes*, 110. A schepel was a wooden tool a little less than a cubic foot in size used to scoop grain, beans, and other items.

7. Gehring, *Fort Orange Court Minutes*, 148.

8. Gehring, *Fort Orange Court Minutes*, 248–249.

9. Gehring, *Fort Orange Court Minutes*, 286–287.

10. Gehring, *Fort Orange Court Minutes*, 350.

11. Gehring, *Fort Orange Court Minutes*, 394–395.

12. Gehring, *Fort Orange Court Minutes*, 415.

13. Janne Venema, trans. and ed., *Deacons' Accounts, 1652–1674, First Dutch Reformed Church of Beverwyck/Albany, New York* (Rockport, Maine: Picton Press, 1998): 63, 65.

14. Gehring, *Fort Orange Court Minutes*, 190.

15. Gehring, *Fort Orange Court Minutes*, 290–291, 386.

16. Jonathan Pearson, trans., *Early Records of the City and County of Albany, and the Colony of Resselaerswyck, 1656–1675* (Albany, New York: J. Munsell, 1869): 298.

17. Berthold Fernow, trans. and ed., *Documents Relating to the Colonial History of the State of New York, Volume XIII* (Albany, New York: Weed, Parsons, and Company, 1881): 309–310.

18. Charles Gehring, trans. and ed., *Fort Orange Records, 1656–1678* (Syracuse, New York: Syracuse University Press, 2000): 113.

19. Land Patents, New York State Archives, Book 2, 237.

20. Arnold Johan Ferdinand Van Laer, trans. and ed., *Minutes of the Court of Albany, Rensselaerswyck and Schenectady, 1668–1673, Volume* I (Albany, New York: University of the State of New York, 1926): 174–175.

21. Arnold Johan Ferdinand Van Laer, trans. and ed., *Minutes of the Court of Albany, Rensselaerswyck and Schenectady, 1675–1680, Volume II* (Albany, New York: University of the State of New York, 1928): 300; Arnold Johan Ferdinand Van Laer, trans. and ed., *Minutes of the Court of Albany, Rensselaerswyck and Schenectady, 1680–1685, Volume III* (Albany, New York: University of the State of New York, 1932): 43–44.

22. Jonathan Pearson, trans., and Arnold Johan Ferdinand Van Laer, ed., *Early Records of the City and County of Albany and Colony of Rensselaerswyck, Volume III* (Albany, New York: University of the State of New York, 1918): 377.

23. Van Laer, Minutes *of the Court of Albany, Rensselaerswyck and Schenectady, 1680–1685, III*, 467–469.

24. Land Patents, New York State Archives, Book 6, 203–207.

25. Gehring, *Fort Orange Records*, 165–166.

26. Bronck Manuscripts Collection, Vedder Research Library, Greene County Historical Society, Coxsackie, New York.

27. Arnold Johan Ferdinand Van Laer, trans. and ed., *Minutes of the Court of Fort Orange and Beverwyck, 1652–1656, Volume I* (Albany, New York: University of the State of New York, 1920): 299.

28. Van Laer, *Minutes of the Court of Rensselaerswyck, 1648–1652*, 103–104.

29. Shirley W. Dunn, *The Mohican World, 1680–1750* (Fleischmanns, New York: Purple Mountain Press, 2000): 318.

30. Francis Lovelace Coeymans patent confirmation dated 1673, titled "Coeymans Old Pat.—Copy," Bronck Manuscripts Collection, Vedder Research Library.

31. Land Patents, New York State Archives, Book 8, 60.

32. Berthold Fernow, trans. and ed., *Documents Relating to the Colonial History of the State of New York, Volume XIV* (Albany, New York: Weed, Parsons, and Company, 1883): 325–326.

33. Peter R. Christoph, Kenneth Scott, and Kenn Stryker-Rodda, Kenn, eds., *New York Historical Manuscripts: Dutch, Kingston Papers, Translated by Dingman Versteeg, Volume II* (Baltimore, Maryland: Genealogical Publishing Company, 1976): 385.

34. Land Patents, New York State Archives, Book 7, 127–128.

35. J. B. Beers and Company, *History of Greene County, New York* (New York, New York: J. B. Beers and Company, 1884): 369.

36. Land Patents, New York State Archives, Book 8, 333.

37. New York (State) Historian, *Second Annual Report of the State Historian of the State of New York* (Albany, New York: Wynkoop Hallenbeck Crawford Company, 1897): 471–472.

38. Edmund Bailey O'Callaghan, *The Documentary History of the State of New-York, Volume I* (Albany, New York: Weed, Parsons, and Company, 1849): 372–373.

39. Fernow, *Documents Relating to the Colonial History of the State of New York, XIII*, 26.

40. O'Callaghan, *The Documentary History, I*, 364.

41. Beers, *History of Greene County, New York*, 237.

42. New York (State) Historian, *Second Annual Report*, 454–455.

43. New York (State) Historian, *Second Annual Report*, 461–478.

44. Edmund Bailey O'Callaghan, ed., *Documents Relative to the Colonial History of the State of New-York, Volume VI* (Albany, New York: Weed, Parsons, and Company, 1853): 391–392.

45. T. W. Egly Jr., *Goose Van Schaick of Albany, 1736–1789: The Continental Army's Senior Colonel* (N.p.: T. W. Egly, 1992).

46. New York (State) Historian, *Third Annual Report of the State Historian of the State of New York, 1897* (Albany, New York: Wynkoop Hallenbeck Crawford Company, 1898): 763, 789, 830–831.

Chapter 3. Revolution Opens the Door

1. Bronck Manuscripts Collection, Vedder Research Library, May 19, 1776. Leonard may have been the first of his family to drop the "c" in his last name.

2. Bronck Manuscripts Collection, Vedder Research Library, April 11, 1775.

3. James Sullivan, ed., *Minutes of the Albany Committee of Correspondence 1775–1778, Volume I* (Albany, New York: University of the State of New York, 1923): 27–28.

4. Sullivan, *Minutes of the Albany Committee of Correspondence 1775–1778, I*, 113, 448.

5. Albany Institute of History and Art collections.

6. Bronck Manuscripts Collection, Vedder Research Library, May 28, 1776.

7. Sullivan, *Minutes of the Albany Committee of Correspondence 1775–1778, I*, 464–465.

8. Bronck Manuscripts Collection, Vedder Research Library, September 23, 1776.

9. Sullivan, *Minutes of the Albany Committee of Correspondence 1775–1778, I*, 551–552.

10. Sullivan, *Minutes of the Albany Committee of Correspondence 1775–1778, I*, 564.

11. Sullivan, *Minutes of the Albany Committee of Correspondence 1775–1778, I*, 582, 585.

12. Bronck Manuscripts Collection, Vedder Research Library, June 27, 1777.

13. Bronck Manuscripts Collection, Vedder Research Library, July 26, 1777.

14. Bronck Manuscripts Collection, Vedder Research Library, September 16, 1777.

15. Sullivan, *Minutes of the Albany Committee of Correspondence 1775–1778, I*, 853.

16. Hugh Hastings, ed., *Public Papers of George Clinton, First Governor of New York, 1777–1795–1801–1804, Volume III* (Albany: James B. Lyon, 1900): 514–515.

17. Victor Hugo Paltsis, ed., *Minutes of the Commissioners for Detecting and Defeating Conspiracies in the State of New York, Volume I, 1778–1779* (Albany, New York: James B. Lyon Company, 1909): 144.

18. Paltsis, *Minutes of the Commissioners*, I, 492.

19. Bronck Manuscripts Collection, Vedder Research Library, September 1, 1778.

20. Hugh Hastings, ed., *Public Papers of George Clinton, First Governor of New York, 1777–1795–1801–1804, Volume V* (Albany: James B. Lyon, 1901): 796–797.

21. Hugh Hastings, ed., *Public Papers of George Clinton, First Governor of New York, 1777–1795–1801–1804, Volume VI* (Albany: James B. Lyon, 1902): 93–94.

22. Paltsis, *Minutes of the Commissioners*, I, 492.

23. Hastings, *Public Papers of George Clinton, VI*, 305.

24. Hastings, *Public Papers of George Clinton, VI*, 893–897.

25. Bronck Manuscripts Collection, Vedder Research Library, May 24, 1781.

26. Bronck Manuscripts Collection, Vedder Research Library, November 4, 1781.

27. *Manuscript Collection, Pension, Military: Revolutionary War Folder*, Vedder Research Library, Greene County Historical Society, Coxsackie, New York.

28. *Manuscript Collection, Pension, Military: Revolutionary War Folder*, Vedder Research Library.

29. *Manuscript Collection, Pension, Military: Revolutionary War Folder*, Vedder Research Library.

30. Bronck Manuscripts Collection, Vedder Research Library, December 30, 1780.

31. Sullivan, *Minutes of the Albany Committee of Correspondence 1775–1778, I*, 306, 518.

32. Hugh Hastings, ed., *Public Papers of George Clinton, First Governor of New York, 1777–1795–1801–1804, Volume I* (New York, New York: Wynkoop Hallenbeck Crawford Company, 1899): 640–641.

33. Paltsis, *Minutes of the Commissioner, I*, 171–172, 174, 177.

34. Victor Hugo Paltsis, ed., *Minutes of the Commissioners for detecting and defeating Conspiracies in the State of New York, Volume II, 1780–1781* (Albany, New York: State of New York, 1909): 834–835.

35. Bronck Manuscripts Collection, Vedder Research Library, 1785.

36. Paltsis, *Minutes of the Commissioners, II*, 567–568, 578–579, 585, 617, 731–732.

37. Paltsis, *Minutes of the Commissioners, II*, 742–749.

38. Sullivan, Minutes *of the Albany Committee of Correspondence 1775–1778, I*, 428.

39. Bronck Manuscripts Collection, Vedder Research Library, April 5, 1779.

40. Bronck Manuscripts Collection, Vedder Research Library, July 14, 1779.

41. Bronck Manuscripts Collection, Vedder Research Library, May 21, 1778; October 8, 1778; June 8, 1779; June 14, 1779.

42. Bronck Manuscripts Collection, Vedder Research Library, August 7, 1780.

43. Bronck Manuscripts Collection, Vedder Research Library, August 15, 1781.

44. Bronck Manuscripts Collection, Vedder Research Library, October 25, 1782.

45. Bronck Manuscripts Collection, Vedder Research Library, June 7, 1783.

Chapter 4. New Baltimore is Born

1. Edmund Bailey O'Callaghan, *The Documentary History of the State of New-York, Volume I* (Albany, New York: Weed, Parsons, and Company, 1849): 370–373.

2. Edward Ely Sherman Memorial Collection, Vedder Research Library, Greene County Historical Society, Coxsackie, New York; *Albany Gazette*, August 18, 1791.

3. Frances Dietz, longtime New Baltimore town historian, produced an informative, unpublished 1984 monograph, "Under the Care of Friends: New Baltimore's Eighteenth- and Nineteenth-Century Quaker Meetings," which provides an overview of the Quaker experience in New Baltimore.

4. Elias Hicks, *Journal of the Life and Labours of Elias Hicks* (New York, New York: Isaac T. Hooper, 1832): 21.

5. Coeymans Preparative Meeting (Society of Friends), Friends Meeting of Coeymans Manuscript Records, New York State Library.

6. Raymond Beecher, *Out to Greenville and Beyond: Historical Sketches of Greene County* (Cornwallville, New York: Hope Farm Press, 1977): 15–26.

7. A Tax Roll for the District of Coxsackie . . . , New York State Library, 1786.

8. Albany County Clerk, Deed Book 16, 94.

9. Titus-Bedell Family Papers, New York State Archives.

10. Town of New Baltimore, 1837 Assessment Roll, 1837.

11. A Tax Roll for the District of Coxsackie . . . , New York State Library, 1786.

12. John Maude, *Visit to the Falls of Niagara in 1800* (London, UK: Longman, Hurst, Rees, Orme, Brown, and Green, 1826): 16.

13. Anthony J. Gambino, *By the Shores of New Baltimore: Its Shipyards and Nautical History* (Westerlo, New York, A. J. Gambino, 2009): 7.

14. Sherman Memorial Collection, Vedder Research Library.

15. Sherman Memorial Collection, Vedder Research Library.

16. *Journal of the Senate of the State of New York at Their Thirty-Fourth Session* (Albany, New York: S. Southwick, 1811): 6, 22–23, 29–30.

17. *Journal of the Assembly of the State of New York at Their Thirty-Fourth Session* (Albany, New York: S. Southwick, 1811): 241–242.

18. *Catskill Recorder*, April 10, 1811.

19. Town of New Baltimore, Minutes, 1811.

20. Chapter 64, Laws of New York, 1788.

21. New York (State), Governor, *Public Papers of Daniel D. Tompkins, Governor of New York, 1807–1817, Military, Volume I* (New York and Albany, New York: Wynkoop Hallenbeck Crawford Company, 1898): 258–259.

22. New York (State), Governor, *Public Papers of Daniel D. Tompkins, Governor of New York, 1807–1817, Military, Volume II* (Albany, New York: James B. Lyons Company, 1902): 384.

23. New York (State), Governor, *Public Papers of Daniel D. Tompkins, Governor of New York, II*, 471.

24. New York (State), Governor, *Public Papers of Daniel D. Tompkins, Governor of New York, I*, 648.

25. *Catskill Recorder*, June 24, 1812.

26. Unless otherwise noted, details about the military service of individual soldiers come from two sources: claim applications for service in the War of 1812, New York State Archives and Compiled Service Records and Pension Applications and Pension Payment Records, National Archives and Records Administration.

27. New York (State), Governor, *Public Papers of Daniel D. Tompkins, I*, 377–379; New York (State), Governor, *Public Papers of Daniel D. Tompkins, Governor of New York, 1807–1817, Military, Volume III* (Albany, New York: James B. Lyons Company, 1902): 108–112.

28. New York (State), Governor, *Public Papers of Daniel D. Tompkins, Governor of New York, III*, 140.

29. New York (State), *Governor, Public Papers of Daniel D. Tompkins, Governor of New York, III*, 153.

30. New York (State), *Governor, Public Papers of Daniel D. Tompkins, I*, 409–410.

31. Greene County Court of Common Pleas Papers, Vedder Research Library, Greene County Historical Society, Coxsackie, New York.

32. New York (State), Governor, *Public Papers of Daniel D. Tompkins, III*, 250–251.

33. New York (State), Governor, *Public Papers of Daniel D. Tompkins, III*, 223–226.

34. Horatio Gates Spafford, *A Gazetteer of the State of New-York* (Albany, New York: H. C. Southwick, 1813): 243.

35. Greene County 1813 Assessment Roll, Vedder Research Library, Greene County Historical Society, Coxsackie, New York.

36. New York (State), Governor, *Public Papers of Daniel D. Tompkins, I*, 445–449.

37. New York (State), Governor, *Public Papers of Daniel D. Tompkins, I*, 457–461.

Chapter 5. Town Growth and Another War

1. Horatio Gates Spafford, *A Gazetteer of the State of New-York* (Albany, New York: B. D. Packard, 1824): 338.

2. Patrick Shirreff, *A Tour Through North America; Together with a Comprehensive View of the Canadas and the United States, As Adapted for Agricultural Emigration* (Edinburgh, Scotland: Oliver and Boyd, 1835): 33.

3. Thomas F. Gordon, *Gazetteer of the State of New York: Comprehending Its Colonial History* (New York, New York: Printed for the Author, 1836): 473.

4. John Disturnell, *Gazetteer of the State of New-York* (Albany, New York: J. Disturnell, 1842): 261.

5. New York State Assembly, Report No. 100, February 27, 1844.

6. The spellings of names are as given in the census rolls.

7. *Recorder and Democrat*, April 18, 1861.

8. Unless otherwise noted, the information on Civil War soldiers and units is drawn from Military Service and Pension Applications and Payment Records, National Archives and Records Administration; J. R. Baldwin, "Complete Record Relating to Officers, Soldiers, and Seamen Composing the Quotas of Troops Furnished to the United States . . . in the War of Rebellion," December 2, 1865; New York (State), *Adjutant General's Office, Annual Report of the Adjutant-General . . . Registers of New York Regiments in the War of the Rebellion, 1893–1905* (the forty-three volumes of which now are available online through the New York State Library Digital Collections at www.nysl.nysed.gov); 1865 New York and 1860, 1870, and 1880 federal censuses; Frederick H. Dyer, *A Compendium of the War of the Rebellion* (Des Moines, Iowa: The Dyer Publishing Company, 1908); Frederick Phisterer, *New York in the War of the Rebellion, 1861 to 1865* (Albany: James B. Lyon, 1912). The accounts of soldiers' activities in this chapter should not be treated as an all-inclusive listing of New Baltimore's Civil War veterans.

9. Theodore Burr Gates, *The "Ulster Guard" (20th N.Y. State Militia) and the War of the Rebellion* (New York, New York: Benjamin H. Tyrrel, 1879); Will Plank, *Banners and Bugles* (Marlborough, New York: Centennial Press, 1963) talks about the role of Ulster County men in the Civil War, discussing several of the units that also included New Baltimore soldiers.

10. *Recorder and Democrat*, May 23, 1861.

11. Charles A. Burns, "General Affidavit," Military Pension File, National Archives and Records Administration.

12. *Recorder and Democrat*, July 17, 1862.

13. Cornelius Van Sandvoort, *The One Hundred and Twentieth Regiment, New York State Volunteers: A Narrative of Its Services in the War for the Union* (Rondout, New York: Press of the Kingston Freemen, 1894).

14. *Recorder and Democrat*, August 14, 1862.

15. *Examiner*, August 30, 1862.

16. *Recorder and Democrat*, September 10, 1863.

17. http://www.civilwarhome.com/brewstergettysburgor.htm.

18. *Recorder and Democrat*, July 9, 1863.

19. Robert H. Kellogg, *Life and Death in Rebel Prisons* (Hartford, Connecticut: L. Stebbins, 1865): 56–58.

20. Andrew T. Hotaling, Military Pension File, National Archives and Records Administration.

21. Van Sandvoort, *The One Hundred and Twentieth Regiment*, 156–157.

Chapter 6. Life on the River

1. Robert Juet, *Juet's Journal: The Voyages of the Half Moon from 4 April to 7 November 1609* (Newark, New Jersey: New Jersey Historical Society, 1959): 31.

2. John Maude, *Visit to the Falls of Niagara in 1800* (London, UK: Longman, Hurst, Rees, Orme, Brown, and Green, 1826): 268–270.

3. The *New Baltimore Globe* was the other paper. A few editions of the *Sun* are available at the Vedder Research Library of the Greene County Historical Society, Coxsackie, New York.

4. Edmund Charles Genet, *Memorial on the Alluvions or Obstructions, at the Head of the Navigation of the River Hudson; The Impossibility of Removing Them Effectually; the Practicability of a Lateral Canal along Those Impediments for Vessels of all Descriptions, as the Only Lasting Remedy; with a View of the Political Advantages of that Contemplated Improvement, and of the Accession of Albany to Maritime Commerce* (Albany, NY: I. W. Clark, 1818): 4, 15.

5. Chapter 152, Laws of New York, 1819.

6. New York (State) Commissioners to report a plan for improving the navigation of the Hudson River, "Plans for Improving the Navigation of Hudson's River," 1820.

7. Charles V. Lincoln, *State of New York, Messages from the Governors, Volume III, 1823–1842* (Albany, New York: James B. Lyon Company, 1909): 26–29, 48–50.

8. William J. McAlpine, et al., *Reports and Estimates for a Ship Canal and Basin from Albany to New-Baltimore* (Albany, New York: Weed, Parsons, and Company, 1853): 3.

9. McAlpine, *Reports and Estimates for a Ship Canal and Basin from Albany to New-Baltimore*, 11.

10. Chapter 190, Laws of New York, 1853.

11. Charles V. Lincoln, *State of New York, Messages from the Governors, Volume IV, 1843–1856* (Albany, New York: James B. Lyon Company, 1909): 732–744.

12. *Coeymans Herald*, September 29, 1897.

13. Hugh Hastings, ed., *Public Papers of George Clinton, First Governor of New York, 1777–1795–1801–1804, Volume III* (Albany: James B. Lyon, 1900): 117.

14. Anthony J. Gambino, *By the Shores of New Baltimore: Its Shipyards and Nautical History* (Westerlo, New York: Anthony J. Gambino, 2009).

15. Gambino, *By the Shores of New Baltimore*, 152.

16. *News-Herald*, May 17, 1929; May 24, 1929; *Recorder*, May 17, 1929; May 24, 1929.

17. *Recorder*, April 24, 1936.

18. *Recorder*, December 2, 1898.

19. *Recorder*, May 22, 1903.

20. *News-Herald*, March 3, 1911.

21. *Examiner*, June 23, 1927; *Recorder*, June 24, 1927.

22. *News-Herald*, January 17, 1930.

23. *Examiner*, January 24, 1883.

24. Greene County Clerk, Deed Books, Liber 74, 465.

25. *New York Times*, March 21, 1870.

26. *Coeymans Herald*, October 25, 1899.

27. *Coeymans Herald*, January 17, 1883.

28. *Coxsackie Union-News*, February 17, 1961.

Chapter 7. The Train Arrives in New Baltimore

1. Town of New Baltimore, Minutes, April 5, 1864.

2. Saratoga and Hudson River Rail-Road (map), Greene County Clerk, Catskill, New York, June 15, 1864.

3. Clifford Browder, *The Money Game in Old New York: Daniel Drew and His Times* (Lexington, Kentucky: University Press of Kentucky, 1986).

4. New York (State), Supreme Court, Greene County Supreme Court Records, Vedder Research Library, Greene County Historical Society, Coxsackie, New York, 1864–1865. Spellings are as in records.

5. *New York Times*, August 23, 1864, 7.

6. *Recorder and Democrat*, February 9, 1865.

7. New York (State), State Engineer, *Annual Report of the State Engineer & Surveyor of the State of New York and of the Tabulations and Deductions from the Reports of the Railroad Corporations for the Year Ending September 30th, 1865* (Albany, New York: Weed, Parsons, and Company, 1866): 486–487.

8. *Recorder and Democrat*, January 19, 1866.

9. *New York Times*, March 19, 1866.
10. *Recorder and Democrat*, June 22, 1866.
11. *Recorder and Democrat*, July 20, 1866.
12. *Examiner*, November 17, 1866.
13. *Examiner*, May 30, 1868.
14. *Coxsackie News*, April 23, 1870.
15. *Coeymans Herald*, July 31, 1873.
16. *Coeymans Herald*, October 29, 1874.
17. *Coeymans Herald*, December 29, 1875.
18. *Catskill Recorder*, June 23, 1876.
19. "New York and Albany Railroad," *American Railroad Journal* (May 4, 1872).
20. Carlton Mabee, *Listen to the Whistle: An Anecdotal History of the Wallkill Valley Railroad in Ulster and Orange Counties, New York* (Fleischmanns, New York: Purple Mountain Press, 1995).
21. Map and Profile of the Alteration and Change of the Route of the Road of the New York West Shore & Buffalo Railway Company (map), Greene County Clerk, Catskill, New York, December 18, 1881.
22. *Recorder and Democrat*, April 12, 1882.
23. *Coeymans Herald*, May 17, 1882; May 24, 1882.
24. *New York Times*, June 23, 1882.
25. *Coeymans Herald*, June 28, 1882.
26. *Coeymans Herald*, July 11, 1883.
27. Cited in *Catskill Recorder*, July 13, 1883.
28. *Coeymans Herald*, October 3, 1883.
29. *Coeymans Herald*, September 5, 1883.
30. *Coeymans Herald*, January 2, 1884.
31. New York, West Shore & Buffalo Railway Company, *Summer Resorts along the West Shore of the Hudson River and in the Catskill Mountains*, 1884.
32. New York (State), Public Service Commission. Minutes of Proceedings, New York State Archives, 1932.
33. *Recorder*, November 11, 18; December 16, 1932; January 6, 1933.
34. *Examiner-Recorder*, December 16, 1954.
35. *Examiner-Recorder*, January 20, 1955.
36. *Coxsackie Union-News*, April 18, 1956.

Chapter 8. War and Modern Times

1. *Examiner*, April 7, 14, 1917; *Recorder*, April 20, 1917.
2. Shortly after the war's end, local authorities were asked to coordinate the completion of questionnaires by veterans. Julia Carhart, the town historian, was in charge of this effort in New Baltimore. Regrettably, the response was not strong. However, those collected records are available at the New York State

Archives and provide some interesting details about a handful of local soldiers, including Fred Freuler.

3. *Recorder*, October 4, 1918.
4. *Recorder*, April 20, 1917.
5. *Recorder*, June 8, 1917; *Examiner*, June 9, 1917.
6. *Recorder*, April 27, 1917.
7. *Recorder*, June 15, 1917; October 12, 1917; September 20, 1918.
8. *Examiner*, November 3, 1917; *Examiner*, May 11, 1918.
9. *Coeymans Herald*, February 19, 1874.
10. *Recorder*, November 5, 1915.
11. *Recorder*, September 21, 1917.
12. *Recorder*, November 8, 1918; *News-Herald*, November 8, 1918.
13. *Recorder*, October 29, 1915.
14. *Examiner*, March 31, 1917; *Recorder*, March 30, 1917.
15. *Recorder*, November 16, 1917.
16. Maurice Chester Bond, *New York Census Data by Counties, 1950 Census of Agriculture and Long-Time Changes* (Ithaca, New York: New York State College of Agriculture, Cornell University, 1953).
17. *Coxsackie Union-News*, September 17, 1943.
18. *News-Herald*, December 12, 1941.
19. Town of New Baltimore, Minutes, August 3, 1942.
20. *Coxsackie Union-News*, February 6, 13, 1942.
21. *Coxsackie Union-News*, January 23, 1942.
22. *Coxsackie Union-News*, October 13, 1944.
23. As with discussions of other wars in this narrative, I apologize for not being able to personally recognize each individual hero.
24. U.S. World War II Army Enlistment Records, 1938–1946; Records of World War II Prisoners of War, 1938–1946, National Archives and Records Administration, Washington, D.C. (databases online: aad.archives.gov/aad).
25. *Coxsackie Union-News*, March 31, 1944.
26. www.com-web.com/wwboard/ARCHIVE/PRE-2009-09/messages/70206.html

Chapter 9. Off to School

1. Coeymans Preparative Meeting (Society of Friends), Friends Meeting of Coeymans Manuscript Records, n.d.; Frances Dietz, "Under the Care of Friends: New Baltimore's Eighteenth- and Nineteenth-Century Quaker Meetings," 1984.
2. Sherman Memorial Collection, Vedder Research Library.
3. Benjamin I. Carhart, "Our School House," New Baltimore Collection, Vedder Research Library, Greene County Historical Society, Coxsackie, New York, 1876.
4. Chapter 242, Laws of New York, 1812.

5. Town of New Baltimore, Minutes, 1813.

6. Town of New Baltimore, Minutes, 1814, 1819.

7. *Catskill Recorder*, November 9, 1877, 3.

8. Town of New Baltimore, Historian's Collections, New Baltimore, New York.

9. *Catskill Recorder*, May 3, 1820.

10. Greenville Schools Collection, Vedder Research Library, Greene County Historical Society, Coxsackie, New York.

11. *Catskill Recorder*, October 24, 1823.

12. *Recorder*, November 29, 1929; January 10, 1930.

13. *Recorder*, February 14, 1930.

14. *Examiner*, May 1, 1930.

15. Memo from E. R. Van Kleeck to Dr. Briand, February 20, 1948, New York State Archives, Albany, New York.

16. Letter from Francis E. Griffin to Paul S. Palmer, September 26, 1947, New York State Archives.

17. E. R. Van Kleeck to Dr. Briand, February 20, 1948, New York State Archives.

18. *Examiner-Recorder*, September 4, 1952.

19. Letter from Burton H. Belknap to E. E. Brady Jr., July 22, 1938, New York State Archives.

20. Application for Laying Out Central Rural School District, January 25, 1944, New York State Archives.

21. Letter from John B. Severance to Francis E. Griffin, March 5, 1945.

22. *Coxsackie Union-News*, August 10, 1945, August 31, 1945.

23. Letter from William H. Sickles Jr. to Francis T. Spaulding, May 19, 1947, New York State Archives.

24. *Coxsackie Union-News*, July 4, 1947.

25. Memo from E. R. Van Kleeck to Mr. Griffin, January 30, 1948, New York State Archives.

26. Order of Commissioner Francis T. Spaulding, May 25, 1949, New York State Archives.

27. *Knickerbocker News*, June 17, 1949.

28. *Times Union*, September 9, 1956.

29. Rocky Store accounts ledger, Hallock Family Collection, Vedder Research Library, Greene County Historical Society, Coxsackie, New York.

30. *Coxsackie Union-News*, June 7, 1946.

31. *Coxsackie Union-News*, February 26, 1960.

32. *News-Herald*, December 8, 1961; February 2, 1962.

33. *News-Herald*, November 23, 1962.

34. Portions of the Rocky Store discussion first appeared in the *Greene County Historical Journal*, Greene County Historical Society, 1999–2000.

35. Town of New Baltimore, Minutes, August 4 and 18, 1964.

36. *News-Herald*, September 11, 1964.

37. Common School District No. 2, Town of New Baltimore, New York, Minutes, Special Meeting, September 19, 1964.

38. Board of Education, Coxsackie-Athens Central School District, Minutes, October 6, 1964.

39.Town of New Baltimore, Minutes, November 10 and December 4, 1964; May 4, May 25, and June 1, 1965.

Chapter 10. The Road to New Baltimore

1. *The Colonial Laws of New York from the Year 1664 to the Revolution, Volume I* (Albany, New York: James B. Lyon, 1894): 532–533.

2. *The Colonial Laws of New York from the Year 1664 to the Revolution, I*, 587.

3. *The Colonial Laws of New York from the Year 1664 to the Revolution, Volume II* (Albany, New York: James B. Lyon, 1894): 156.

4. Sherman Memorial Collection, Vedder Research Library.

5. *Coeymans Herald*, June 26, 1873.

6. *Coeymans Herald*, September 18, 1873.

7. Proceedings of the Board of Supervisors of Greene County at Their Annual Session Held in November, 1874, Catskill, New York, 1874: 6, 8, 9.

8. *Coeymans Herald*, December 31, 1874.

9. *Coeymans Herald*, January 14, 1875.

10. Proceedings of the Board of Supervisors of Greene County at Their Annual Session Held in November, 1875, Catskill, New York, 1875: 10, 11, 13.

11. *Recorder*, March 21, 1913.

12. Town of New Baltimore, Minutes, October 17, 1899, November 25, 1899, October 4, 1901.

13. Proceedings of the Board of Supervisors of Greene County for the Year 1906, Catskill, New York, 1907: 61–64.

14. *Laws of the State of New York, Passed at the One Hundred and Thirty-First Session of the Legislature, Volume II, Chapter 330* (Albany, New York: James B. Lyon Company, 1908): 902–904.

15. *Recorder*, May 10, 1912.

16. Town of New Baltimore, Minutes, March 29, 1911.

17. Proceedings of the Board of Supervisors of Greene County for the Year 1912 (Catskill, New York, 1913): 106–107.

18. *Recorder*, June 7, 1912.

19. *Recorder*, July 5, 1912.

20. State of New York, Report of the State Commissioner of Highways for the Year Ending December 31, 1918 (Albany, New York: James B. Lyon Company, 1919).

21. *Coxsackie Union-News*, November 28, 1952.

22. *Coxsackie Union-News*, January 28, 1955.

23. *Greene County News*, October 14, 1971.

Index